D0302044

Criminal Behaviour:
A Psychological Approach to Explanation and Prevention

Clive R. Hollin

WITHDRAWN

Psychology Press
a member of the Taylor & Francis group

First published 1992

http://www.psypress.co.uk

Reprinted 1995, 1997 and 2000

Psychology Press Ltd, a member of the Taylor & Francis Group
27 Church Road
Hove
East Sussex
BN3 2FA

© Clive R. Hollin 1992

All rights reserved. No part of this book may be reprinted or
reproduced or utilized in any form or by any electronic,
mechanical, or other means, now known or hereafter
invented, including photocopying and recording, or in any
information storage or retrieval system, without permission in
writing from the publishers.

British Library Cataloguing in Publication Data

A catalogue record for this book is available from the British Library

ISBN 1-85000-951-1 (hbk)
ISBN 1-85000-955-4 (pbk)

ISSN: 1368-9207 (Contemporary Psychology Series)

Library of Congress Cataloguing in Publication Data are available on request

Cover design Leigh Hurlock
Typeset by Graphicraft Ltd, Hong Kong
Printed in Great Britain by
Antony Rowe Ltd, Chippenham, Wiltshire

Contents

For my Dad

List of Tables and Figures

Series Editor's Preface

Clive Hollin begins this book with the observation that crime surrounds us constantly — both in reality and in fantasy. Given that we generally regard crime as something both morally wrong and personally threatening, is it not surprising that so many people spend so much time reading about it and watching programmes and films about it? Last evening on television there were two series about crime, a report on psychiatric services in prisons and a full length film with a murder theme. Unless the programme makers and schedulers have got it very wrong, we are obsessed with crime.

In reality, as well as in fiction, crime is of enormous and increasing significance, as Clive Hollin makes clear in his second chapter. Coincidentally, as I was reading that chapter I happened to notice in *The Guardian* a report that recorded crime had more than doubled in England during the 1980s, and in some of the shire counties had increased by well over 150 per cent during the 'Thatcher years' of law and order.

Given that criminal behaviour is so widespread and such a pervasive cultural theme, it is no surprise that it has occupied the attention of many psychologists and other social scientists. Clive Hollin is pre-eminent among British psychologists who have made it their job to study crime and criminals in a scientific and objective manner. He has written two previous and very successful books on this topic — *Psychology and Crime* in 1989, and *Cognitive-Behavioural Interventions with Young Offenders* in 1990 — but in neither of these did he focus mainly on criminal behaviour and people who actually commit crimes. It was fortunate for me that Dr. Hollin was considering writing a book which looked mainly at psychological explanations of criminal behaviour and on psychological aspects of crime prevention still dealing mainly with the offender, rather than the physical environment or society as a whole. When I asked him to contribute to the Contemporary Psychology series, we had no problem agreeing an overall approach and draft contents.

Clive Hollin's book puts theoretical explanations of criminal behaviour at centre stage, and he marshals an impressive range of evidence relevant to each of the major perspectives he reviews. In this way he can show the significance of each piece of research that he selects to developing a deeper understanding of why people commit crimes. He does not shy away from the next and obvious step, namely to ask how these explanations may be applied to reduce criminal behaviour.

Clive Hollin is a naturally talented writer, as I am sure you will agree when you begin to read this book. This talent, combined with careful use of case histories and an absorbing topic, has resulted in a book that is scholarly, comprehensive and readable. The student beginning to investigate the psychology of criminal behaviour will find all he or she needs to get off to an excellent start in the pages that follow.

Raymond Cochrane
Birmingham
December 1991

Acknowledgments

In the customary roll call of supporting players, I would like to record my thanks to Eugene Ostapiuk, Director of Glenthorne Youth Treatment Centre, who offers me professional support of the highest calibre. To Ray Cochrane at the University of Birmingham for encouraging me to write this particular book. Thanks also to Tracey Swaffer who helped compile the reference list; and to Rita Granner who typed the references, perhaps the worst task of all. On the academic front I continue to be inspired by the work of what I think of as the 'Canadian School', Robert Ross, Paul Gendreau, Don Andrews, and their colleagues. On the personal front I suspect my partner and my children have habituated to my periods of moaning about the pains of writing, not an ounce of sympathy between them, but they know they're important.

Chapter 1

Criminal Behaviour: What Is It?

This book is about criminal behaviour, something that surrounds us constantly: we watch it on the television, hear about it on the radio, and read about it in our newspapers. Chances are that you know someone who has been the victim of a crime, or you may well have been a victim of a crime; you might even have committed one or more criminal behaviours. Criminal behaviour is part of our daily life, something with which we are all familiar, but pause for a moment to consider exactly what we mean by *criminal behaviour*. How can we arrive at a definition of those common words?

One straightforward way to solve the definitional problem is to look to the law: criminal behaviour can be defined as an act that violates criminal law and may therefore be followed by criminal proceedings and attract the appropriate punishment. (As will become clear in the next chapter, most criminal behaviour remains undetected but that should not be taken as meaning that undetected acts are not criminal behaviours. Those who break the law do not necessarily have to be caught to be considered as criminals; it is enough that they commit the act forbidden in law.)

The immediate impact of this definition is that the criminal law requires that an *act* takes place: this is termed *actus reus* (guilty act). I can think all I want about committing a criminal act and in so doing will not have done anything illegal; however as soon as I begin to translate my thoughts into actions then there is *actus reus*. In law, *actus reus* can be either an act against another person (e.g., assault), or against property (e.g., burglary), or not acting when legally required to do so (e.g., a medical doctor not acting to save a person's life).

While there must be *actus reus*, this in itself is not sufficient for an act to constitute a criminal behaviour. For an act to be criminal, it must be carried out with criminal intent: this intent is termed *mens rea* (guilty mind). Thus, for an act to be a criminal act, there must be both *actus reus* and *mens rea*. However, there are a number of ways in which the act can be committed but the absence of intent means that the act is not deemed to be a crime. For instance, the person committing the criminal act may be below the age of criminal responsibility and therefore cannot be said to have acted with criminal intent: as there is no *mens rea* the act cannot be a criminal act. Of course, the age at which a child assumes responsibility for their actions is somewhat arbitrary. The age of criminal responsibility varies from country to country: for example, in Scotland the minimum age of criminal responsibility is 8 years, in England and Wales it is 10 years, in France 13 years, and in Sweden 15 years.

Another way in which the act can be committed but not be judged as criminal is when the perpetrator is unaware that they have broken the law. For example, in cases of unlawful sexual intercourse the defence has been offered that the adult was unaware that the victim (even a 'willing victim') was under age. In such cases it is for the court to decide, taking the facts of the case into account, whether the defence stands.

Yet another example of the absence of *mens rea* is to be found in those cases where the individual's state of mind negates their responsibility for their actions. The person may have an impairment of mind so as not to know right from wrong; that is, they are of low intelligence. Alternatively, at the time of committing the act the person was suffering from a defect of mind so as not to know right from wrong; that is, a mental disturbance, such as schizophrenia or depression, impaired their ability to know the nature of their behaviour (see Chapter 6 for a discussion of both possibilities).

To complicate matters further, however, there are occasions when a crime is committed without specific intent but is nevertheless judged to be a crime. A drunken driver who injures or kills another person may not have had criminal intent, but is judged to have acted in an unreasonable and negligent manner. The law takes the position that a reasonable person would not elect to drive a vehicle when drunk and hence unable to drive in a safe manner. On the other hand, there may be instances where there is clear intent and action but no crime. If someone breaks into my house and attacks me, I might use force to defend myself and my family. In attacking the intruder it is my intention to inflict physical harm and my actions give vent to my intentions. The act of self-defence excuses the criminal act and it is unlikely that a court would find me guilty of an offence if I had used reasonable force. The catch lies in the term *reasonable*: what is reasonable force? In December 1984, Bernard Goetz shot four would-be muggers on a subway train in New York City. Two of them were shot in the back. As might be guessed from the popularity of films such as the *Death Wish* series, there was not inconsiderable public support for a plea of self-defence.

Thus there are a number of occasions when the court must decide whether there is *actus reus* and *mens rea*. In other instances there are crimes of *strict liability* as with, for example, health and safety regulations where there is a legal duty to ensure that certain commitments are met. For example, it is not an excuse to claim to be unaware that fire-doors are locked or barred. Those responsible must ensure that the doors are maintained in accordance with the law.

To return to the issue of definition, with exceptions of the type noted above, we can accept that criminal behaviour is that which is forbidden by the law of the land. Thus criminal law, it could be argued, identifies those behaviours which society will not tolerate. Such a definition immediately forces a distinction between *criminal* behaviour, as defined in law, and behaviours that are *morally* offensive but not enshrined in law. The distinction and overlap between law and morality is an important one and begins to introduce some of the complexities — not least that of whose morality and interests the law protects — underlying a 'simple' legal definition of criminal behaviour. What is the nature of the relationship between morality and criminal law?

Morality and Criminal Law

In essence there is a straightforward distinction to make: criminal behaviour is an act specifically forbidden by criminal law; antisocial or morally offensive behaviour is not criminal behaviour. For example, I find hunting animals for sport a highly repugnant form of behaviour, and I can muster a range of moral arguments to support my case. Conversely, those in favour of blood sports can advance arguments to support their position. Until there are criminal laws to forbid hunting animals, those who wish to do so can continue to kill foxes, deer, hares, and other animals without fear of penalty. Thus, while some people such as myself hold the opinion that hunting animals is morally wrong and a form of antisocial behaviour, it is not criminal behaviour.

I also hold the view, along with many other people, that a sexual relationship between an adult and a child is not in the child's best interests and is morally wrong. There are other people who profess the belief that a sexual relationship between an adult and a child is natural, normal, teaches the child about sex and so is beneficial to the child's development. However, unlike blood sports, sexual relationships between adults and children are expressly forbidden by law; an adult who has a sexual relationship with a child is therefore committing an act which many judge to be morally wrong and which is also criminal behaviour.

I incline to the view, as do others, that some soft drugs are probably less dangerous than alcohol and tobacco; I do not therefore consider that their use is antisocial nor am I morally offended by their use. However, regardless of my moral position, the possession and use of soft drugs is illegal and therefore by definition such actions constitute criminal behaviour.

Thus we see three contrasting examples of the relationship between morality and criminal behaviour: 1) where an act (e.g., blood sports) gives moral offence to some people but as no legislation exists it is not criminal behaviour; 2) where an act gives moral offence to some people (e.g., sexual relationships between an adult and a child) and legislation dictates that this is criminal behaviour; 3) where an act (e.g., using some soft drugs) causes some people no great moral panic yet laws are in force that make such an act a criminal behaviour. Why do these contrary positions exist?

Consensus Accounts

A consensus account of criminal behaviour is based on the view that the criminal law within a given society is a reflection of that society's mutually agreed mores and associated codes of conduct. Thus criminal behaviour is to be understood as behaviour that the majority of people in a society find unacceptable and wish to outlaw. It is undoubtedly true that some acts are seen as violations of some natural moral or human law: these acts are termed *mala in se crimes*, behaviours that are literally 'bad in themselves'. *Mala in se crimes* include acts against the person, such as inflicting injury as in the crimes of assault, murder, and rape; acts of acquisition of property, such as burglary and theft; and acts of destruction against property such as arson or malicious damage. These acts are judged to be abhorrent in many different societies and cultures and are forbidden, to a greater or lesser degree, in the laws of those societies. For these types of criminal acts there is agreement — as with the earlier example of sexual relationships between an adult and a child — between a general sense of what is morally right and what is forbidden in criminal law. In other words, for *mala in se crimes*, the criminal law probably does represent the consensus.

Another type of crime, referred to as *statutory crime* (or *mala prohibitum*), is not so much dependent on a natural law of right and wrong, but on current beliefs and opinions within society at any given period in history. This type of criminal behaviour can therefore pass into and out of extant criminal law. Sutherland and Cressey (1960) note how in past times acts such as printing a book, having gold in one's house, and driving with reins have all been forbidden by criminal law. More recently, for example, in the United States of America it was perfectly legal to own and sell marijuana until federal law was changed in 1937. In Great Britain changes have been made to criminalize the sale of solvents to people of certain ages, and there has been clarification of the law to make rape within marriage a punishable act. On the other side of the coin, in recent times in Great Britain we have seen the *decriminalization* of various acts such as abortion and homosexual behaviour between consenting adults. In other instances criminal law is evolving in response to 'high-tech crimes' such as computer fraud, computer 'hacking', and video piracy.

Unlike *mala in se crimes*, statutory offences can pass in and out of law to accommodate changes in morality and public opinion. However, if *mala in se crimes* do represent a consensus opinion, is the same true of statutory crimes?

There are some apparent contradictions within a consensus approach with some statutory crimes. The topic of sexual pornography provides a good example. If such pornography is morally offensive to the majority, then why are 'men's magazines' freely available and why do daily newspapers carry pictures of semi-nude women? Conversely, if sexual pornography is morally acceptable to the majority — as perhaps the contents of some newspapers, and the sales of magazines and videotapes might suggest — then why have regulatory laws about sexual pornography that must surely express the views of the minority? If sexual pornography is acceptable to the majority, why should it not be freely available? It could be convincingly argued, for example, that the laws forbidding the showing of certain films or programmes reflects not the views of the majority, but the moral codes and beliefs of those individuals who claim to know what is 'right' for the rest of us.

In the same vein (but from a very different moral stance), to return to one of my previous examples, it is probably the case that the majority of people wish to outlaw blood sports, yet the necessary legislation is being withheld to suit the interests of a minority. It is almost certainly true, however, that the majority would not wish to see soft drugs legalized and my own thoughts on this topic probably do not reflect the consensus. Yet I maintain that there is a contradiction: if marijuana and other 'soft' drugs are illegal, then why can we buy harmful drugs like tobacco and alcohol?

Finally, to extend the argument to *mala in se crimes*, we might ask if killing other people is illegal, then why do the perpetrators of large-scale industrial 'accidents' that pollute the environment and cause widespread death and destruction not face murder charges? A strong case could be made that even with the most heinous acts there is a mismatch between the consensus, that is the majority view of what is morally acceptable, and the criminal law.

In summary, if we accept a consensus approach to criminal behaviour, the purpose and function of criminal law is to protect the individual's person and their property. Further, as Walker (1965) suggests, criminal laws also serve the wider interests of society and the defence of the realm. The criminal law therefore ensures the continuing stability of the society of which we all are members and within which we must live together. Those who step outside the law, those who transgress the consensual boundaries, face the retribution as laid down in law. It is generally maintained that the punishment should fit the consensual view of the seriousness of the type of crime. As explored later in this book, however, there are not only considerable disagreements over what constitutes an appropriate punishment, but a heated debate about whether punishment is a suitable response to criminal behaviour (see Chapters 7 and 8). As will also be discussed in great detail in later chapters, the acceptance of a consensual approach has had a great influence on attempts to explain criminal behaviour. It is inherent in a consensual approach that criminals are, by definition, those who behave differently to the non-criminal majority. The search for the cause of that difference has dominated psychological research into criminal behaviour.

If a consensual approach views society as an integrated functioning unit, in which the majority are working for the greater good, then the exact opposite is the case when we move to a second view of criminal behaviour — the conflict approach.

Conflict Approach

Directly opposed to a consensus approach to understanding criminal behaviour, a conflict approach views society as a collection of diverse and competing groups. According to a conflict analysis, these societal groups are not cooperating in harmony for the greater good, but are locked in a bitter struggle as witnessed throughout history in conflicts, for example, between employers and workers, between those of different races, and between religious and political factions. According to some commentators, the basis of this disharmony and hence the cause of the conflict is not a difference in morality between groups, but the unequal distribution of wealth and power within society. If we follow this line of thinking, then the purpose of the criminal law assumes a very different meaning from that of reflecting the consensus and protecting the majority. Those with political, economic, and legal power — *power* can be defined in this context as the ability to control and determine the behaviour of other people — are able to assert their will in order to protect and advance their own interests. In other words, the powerful minority within society is able to formulate and enact the law in order to consolidate and strengthen their own position and to weaken those who challenge their authority. Thus society divides into two camps — those with authority and those who obey — locked in struggle and conflict.

The immediate impact of this way of considering crime is to broaden the scope of analysis to include not only the behaviour of the individual law-breaker, but also the process by which judgments and definitions about what is criminal behaviour are made. The classic quotation in this context is taken from the book *Criminality and the Legal Order* by Austin Turk published in 1969:

> Criminality is not a biological, psychological, or even behavioral phenomenon, but a social status defined by the way an individual is perceived, evaluated, and treated by legal authorities (p. 25).

Quinney (1970) wrote of the *social reality* of crime in which he crystallized a number of fundamental statements within a conflict perspective. Like Turk, Quinney argued that there is human behaviour, but the nomination of *criminal* behaviour is a creation of those with the power to formulate and enact such definitions. Further, Quinney suggests, public opinion and attitudes are heavily influenced by the social messages that permeate our everyday lives. As those with power control the media, so such individuals are in a position to advance their own definitions of crime, encouraging the public to come to agree with these definitions. In other words, the conceptions and definitions of crime held by those with power become disseminated throughout society as the social reality of crime.

There are a number of ways of finding support for the position that criminal behaviour is behaviour that threatens the interests of a powerful ruling minority. Thus we might look to the comparative lightness of the sentences given to those who perpetrate grand financial frauds worth millions of pounds; the token penalties given for acts of large-scale environmental pollution which damage the land, inflict death, and threaten the health and welfare of generations yet to be born; and the long prison sentences handed out for crimes of acquisition as opposed to the leniency often seen for life-threatening actions such as drunken driving. Further, it does seem that there are disproportionate numbers of convicted offenders in those segments of society — the poor, the disadvantaged, the minority groups — that have the least power. A conflict view of crime would, of course, explain this as reflecting the behaviour of those in power who have formulated criminal law to criminalize the powerless and protect the powerful.

Critical criminology

Emerging from the work of conflict theorists such as Turk and Quinney, a new criminology began to emerge in the early 1970s. While, as with any significant idea or theory, this new view of crime was the product of a history of writing and debate, the emergence of critical criminology is generally said to have begun in 1973 with the publication of the book *The New Criminology: For a Social Theory of Deviance* by Ian Taylor, Paul Walton and Jock Young, three British criminologists. This new or critical criminology pushed the conflict theories still further by seeking to suggest a framework by which to understand the distribution and structure of power within society. This framework was Marxist analysis.

The application of Marxist analysis to crime was not in itself a new idea, but by building on the notion of conflict, critical criminology sought to specify the basis of the relationships between crime, the criminal, the victim and the state. As might be anticipated by those familiar with Marxist ideas, crime and the nature of its control are understood through the dictates of a capitalist system. Within a capitalistic state the justice system is portrayed as loaded in favour of the upper classes and biased against the lower classes. Although each class commits deviant acts, the type of act and its treatment by the justice system — and hence its definition as 'criminal' — are the products of a capitalist society. Thus the frustrated, powerless poor commit acts, defined as crimes, within their limited scope: these are 'blue collar' crimes such as theft, burglary and violence. The middle classes carry out acts, also criminal but attracting less severe penalties, such as tax evasion and theft from employers. The powerful upper classes are able to endorse acts such as profiteering, exploitation and denial of human rights, which are not accorded the status of crime or, if so, attract light penalties. In this way the law serves to further the interests of those who benefit from a capitalist system.

This application of Marxist theory and the new criminology sparked an explosion of radical writings, with fierce criticism and debate centred around the apparent lack of sensitivity to individual differences and the belief that the solution to crime lies in the overthrow of capitalism (e.g., Klockars, 1980; Platt, 1985; Scull, 1977; Spitzer, 1975). While critical criminology had an undoubted impact on thinking about crime, and continues to offer a means of analysis, there is a general sense in criminology that its time has passed. Indeed, Rafter (1990) suggests that: 'Critical criminology faltered for reasons that are now fairly clear' (p. 381). These reasons, Rafter continues, are that it suffered as trends, both in society generally and in academic criminology specifically, became more conservative; and because of its failure to tackle the issue of how power is created within society. While those who espouse Marxist views will doubtless provide responses to these points, it is undoubtedly true that in mainstream criminology there are expressions of movement away from pure Marxist critiques (e.g., Heidensohn, 1989). Nevertheless, as will be discussed presently, critical criminology did have a powerful effect on the emerging 'social construction' school of thought. However, before moving to that topic, it is necessary to step back once more to the 1960s to discuss a tradition that developed alongside the emerging conflict approach — labelling theory.

Labelling Theory

One of the distinguishing features of a conflict view of crime is that, unlike consensual accounts, the focus is on the interaction between the person and their environment rather than just the person. The critical criminologists clearly formulated a powerful view of the nature of this interaction, but this is not the only interactionist view. The roots of another approach with this interactionist tradition can be found in the work of Franklin Tannenbaum (1938). Tannenbaum advanced the view that conflict over acts such as petty vandalism and truancy can be understood not in political or economic terms, but in terms of a divergence of values between groups within society. Thus while petty delinquency can be understood by the actors (those who carry out the behaviours) as a normal part of their everyday life, to the observers (other members of society) such behaviour is seen as a nuisance, an evil, or a crime. This conflict in values becomes the driving force behind the observers' responses to the actors' behaviour.

Tannenbaum's ideas were further developed by Edwin Lemert (1951, 1967) who made the distinction between *primary* and *secondary* deviance. Primary deviance is understood in terms of acts that, while breaking a law, provoke little social reaction in terms of strong penalties. This might be seen, for example, in an individual who at some stage in their life carries out acts such as under age drinking, petty theft, and joy-riding. These may be acts that are either undetected or tolerated and so do not excite any great controversy. However, if detected and not tolerated then social penalties may follow and, if the acts persist, they may be met with stronger and stronger sanctions. Lemert suggests that an uncertain and complex change can then take place; the individual begins to reorganize his or her view of themself in relation to the world, adopting the identity suggested by society's views of their conduct. In this way the person who experiments with drugs turns into a 'drug addict', the aggressive adolescent becomes a 'young thug', the pilferer becomes a 'hardened thief'. As society confers these roles, Lemert suggests that this produces the phenomenon of *deviance amplification*. The individual, in taking on the role prescribed by society, becomes more and more alienated from 'straight' society; they search for other outsiders and form 'deviant' subcultures or groups on the edge of mainstream society. Thus the very process by which society responds to what it judges to be deviant is an integral part of the creation of deviant groups. Once formed, such deviant groups perpetuate their own existence by confirming, both to their members and the rest of society, the reality of the deviance.

Erikson (1962) describes three stages in the process of deviance amplification that moves an individual from primary to secondary deviance. The first is a formal confrontation between the person and representatives from his or her society; this confrontation may take the form of a criminal trial or, in another arena for example, a psychiatric case conference. The second stage is the delivery of a judgment of the person; in a trial this takes the form of a verdict, in the case conference a diagnosis is pronounced. Finally, in the third stage, an act of 'social placement' occurs, assigning the individual a role that redefines his or her position in society; after the judgment the person become a criminal, after the diagnosis a 'mental patient'. Once assigned, Erikson argues, the stigma attached to such a role is difficult, but not impossible, to shake off as society has in place well-defined structures for ensuring that punishments endure and rewards are withheld from those it deems to be outsiders.

Where do social rules come from? As with conflict views, the power to create social rules is seen by labelling theorists as residing with select members of society. Unlike the conflict approach, however, it is not political and economic advantage that is seen as driving such powerful individuals; rather it is the wish to impose their values on society. Howard Becker (1963) calls such individuals *moral entrepreneurs*. It is not difficult to think of such individuals. In the area of censorship, for example, there are several figures who, having skilfully assembled the necessary support, have engineered positions that allow them to dictate in large part what the rest of society can read and watch either at home or at the cinema.

The contribution of Howard Becker went a great deal further; his 1963 book, *Outsiders: Studies in the Sociology of Deviance*, brought together much of what had gone before in attempts to reconcile the dynamic interplay between the person and society's reaction to their actions. Becker argued that deviants — including lawbreakers as well as other groups such as drug users, heavy drinkers, and the mentally distressed — are created by society. This act of creation, however, is not to be understood in the usual, deterministic style of describing the social conditions such as poverty or the failure of the educational system that create crime. Becker is more subtle in arguing that it is to the creation of the social rules that we should look for an explanation of deviance; it is the application of these rules and the *labelling* of rule breakers as deviants that creates deviance. Thus, in contrast to a consensus view, a criminal act is defined not by the quality of the act but by the application of rules that defines that act as a crime and labels its perpetrator as a criminal. As Becker writes, in one of the great sociological quotes: 'The deviant is one to whom that label has successfully been applied; deviant behaviour is behaviour that people so label' (p. 9).

This way of thinking about crime has a number of consequences. Heidensohn (1989) neatly summarizes these in terms of the questions they ask about crime. If, as with a consensus view, crime is objectively agreed between members of society, then the questions become centred on the individual — who becomes an offender? What psychological and sociological conditions are likely to produce criminal actions? An interactionalist perspective adopts a more subjective approach, asking not so much about the offender but about reactions to the offender: what circumstances led the person to be set apart? What processes were enacted to cast an individual into a criminal role? How does society respond once the label is conferred? What impact does the label have on the person? Thus the question about the individual offender becomes not what makes him or her different to the consensus, but how does he or she react both psychologically and socially to the change in role? Yet further, we see that there are practical issues; while consensus views lead to a focus on the individual offender to reduce the probability of future crime, interactionist formulations lead us to examine the very nature of social policies for managing those who break social rules as enshrined in criminal law.

Contemporary Views

In considering contemporary views of crime, it is informative to examine trends in the criminological literature. It is clear from a number of recent publications that following the interactionist tradition of both critical criminology and labelling theory, along with shifting trends in other areas of sociology, *constructionalism* has emerged as a dominant mode of thought. As Rafter (1990) states, constructionalism is an approach that 'analyzes the processes by which social information is produced, disseminated, "verified" and "disconfirmed"' (p. 376). Thus, as with other interactionist approaches, constructionalism is more concerned with the processes that produce (and control) offenders than with the offenders themselves. Invariably this turns to an analysis of the social position — in terms of, say, class, gender and race — of those in positions of power.

One of the main investigative methods used by researchers working in this way is termed *discourse analysis*. This method of investigation provides a means by which to analyze all aspects of communication. As Worrell (1990) notes, discourse refers not only to the content of communication, but also to 'its author (who says it?), its authority (on what grounds?), its audience (to whom?), its object (about whom?), its objective (in order to achieve what?)' (p. 8). Worrell provides an example of the use of discourse analysis to show how the identity of women who offend is socially constructed by those with 'professional expertise'. Based on interviews and case studies, Worrell attempts to unravel, or *deconstruct*, the discourse of medical, judicial, and welfare professionals concerned with women who offend. These pronouncements are set alongside the accounts of the women in order to illuminate their perception of events, and to point to the clash between the accounts of the women and the professionals. Similar accounts have been provided by Taylor (1984) and Foster (1990) of offenders' views of themselves and their activities. Worrell argues that a number of threads run consistently through the discourse of the various professional groups. This consistency, of course, is the very essence of the social and legal system that constructs and maintains the 'reality' of offending women. Thus, for example, magistrates lay claim to funds of 'common sense' upon which they can draw in order to guide their judgments about women who come before them. Psychiatrists, on the other hand, make medical and moral judgments about the women, thereby constructing female lawbreakers as mentally ill or socially needy and so making the women targets for magisterial common sense. It is readily apparent that constructionalism calls for a far-reaching examination of the attitudes, prejudices, assumptions and stereotypes that underlie all of our judgments of the behaviour of other people. As Rafter (1990) states, such an examination should not reject empiricism and should strive to be objective in its methods in order to clarify our understanding of the world, while recognizing that science is not value-free.

Philosophy, Theory, and Research

The above discussion of the way in which we understand crime, our grand philosophy of crime, is not an empty academic exercise. A philosophy of crime provides a framework within which theories of criminal behaviour are developed. Aggleton (1987) provides a helpful discussion of the nature of deviance and theories of deviance. Thus, if we follow a consensual approach, then we must ask what is it about some individuals that makes them behave differently to those who obey the law: if we follow a conflict view then we must look to the distribution of economic power to account for crime; if we follow a labelling or a constructionalist perspective then we must study the interaction between the individuals who break the law and those who deliver judgment. In other words, our philosophy of crime gives us the focus for our theory and suggests the type of research we need to carry out in order to test our theory.

There are, of course, many different theories that can be nested within a given philosophy of crime. For example, within a consensus approach we might look to biological explanations of what makes people different, or to psychological explanations, or to social explanations. Each approach will have its own characteristics and research methods, and the popularity of different philosophies and theories will wax and wane as time passes and knowledge grows. It is interesting in this light to consider the results of a survey by Ellis and Hoffman (1990) looking at the current popularity of different philosophies and theories. Ellis and Hoffman sent a questionnaire to a sample of delegates attending an American Society of Criminology convention, most of whom were teachers and researchers in sociology and criminal justice. The most popular philosophies of crime among these groups were interactionism, behaviourism, Marxist and conflict views, and positivism. The most popular specific theories were control theory, social learning theory, differential association, and biosocial theory. Many of these theories will be discussed later, but the general outcome of the survey merits comment. My own reaction to the predominance of social learning theory was one of astonishment, if only because, as Ellis and Hoffman note, 'many contemporary delinquency and criminology texts give little attention to this theory' (p. 55). As will become clear as this text unfolds, however, social learning theory is one of the major contemporary psychological theories, and its application to criminal behaviour provides a coherent account of crime.

It is clearly beyond the scope of this book to cover every theory of crime that has ever been advanced, or, indeed, to include the many varieties of psychological theory (see Hollin, 1989). My aim here is to offer a contemporary *psychological* account of the explanation and prevention of criminal behaviour.

This means that some psychological theories, such as psychoanalytic theory, are not included. This is not because such theories are to be discarded, but because they are not the theories that are attracting current research and so informing today's social policies. However, before beginning with this task, I think it is important to set philosophy, theory, and research into context by considering briefly the 'real-life' aspects of criminal behaviour: how much crime is there and what impact does it have on its victims?

Chapter 2

Criminal Behaviour: How Much of It?

In order to understand criminal behaviour, and thereby develop informed theories and social policies, we need to have as clear a picture as possible of the extent and nature of criminal behaviour within our society. How many people commit crimes? What types of criminal behaviour are most often carried out? What changes might there be in patterns of criminal behaviour as time passes? What are the effects of different social policies on rates of criminal behaviour? Yet further, we need to have an appreciation of everyday experiences of crime. What happens to people when they are victims of a crime? What effects does the experience of victimization have on people? In order to answer these and other questions it is evident that we need to have a reliable means by which to measure the number of crimes committed in society.

This need to measure the amount of crime is not newly felt. In England in the late 1700s the practice began of keeping figures, based on court convictions and the numbers held in prison, in order to monitor the moral health of the country. This custom of gathering official figures has lasted over the centuries, although now the figures are based on 'crimes known to the police' rather than court statistics. These official figures are published annually, for England and Wales, by the Home Office in the *Criminal Statistics*; the *Uniform Crime Reports*, collected by the FBI, are similarly published annually in the USA. One of the temptations easily succumbed to when faced with a collection of figures such as those presented in *Criminal Statistics* is to take them at face value and, on this basis, to make pronouncements about crime. As Bottomley and Pease (1986) document, the inevitable trend, year by year, decade by decade, is that the number of crimes recorded in the official statistics rises. Then, as sure as night follows day, each new set of figures is greeted with a wave of 'shock horror' headlines in the popular press, rhetoric of various hues from the political parties, and promises, sometimes fulfilled, of new initiatives in the 'battle against crime'.

Enticing as it might be to yield to the figures so neatly and readily packaged in the official publications, however, we must ask about the reliability of these figures. Just how accurate a picture do the official figures offer of the true extent of criminal behaviour?

Recognition of Criminal Behaviour

It is an obvious, but often overlooked, point that before a crime can be reported to the police someone has to recognize that a crime has taken place. Thus, for example, what is legally criminal violence may be perceived by onlookers as bullying rather assault and so not reported to the police. In this same light, Bottomley and Pease (1986) give the example of the violence in the sporting arena. Many physical contact sports often spill over into acts of violence in which punches are thrown, kicks aimed, and blood spilt; indeed, professional and amateur sportsmen and sportswomen have had their careers ended and their lives dramatically changed for the worse by injuries deliberately inflicted on the field of play. The number of convictions for criminal behaviour against these 'sporting perpetrators' is so few as to be negligible. Clearly criminal violence has taken place, but the perception of those involved — victim, aggressor and spectator — is that the violence is somehow legitimized by the context in which it occurs. Indeed, as Bottomley and Pease note:

> This tendency to draw the boundaries of crime much more narrowly than the criminal law permits is not restricted to the playground, the pub and the sports field. In the study of occupational crime, it can be seen that much fraud and theft are seen as perks of a job rather than crime, and that this is a perception shared with those who are their victims and employers, who seem content to live with a degree of loss which does not get out of hand (p. 20).

Of course, it is also the case that many crimes simply go unnoticed. For example, who knows how many false tax returns are made each year? Yet further, the criminal act may not have a 'victim', acts of vandalism against public property such as telephone boxes do not have a ready victim to report the crime to the police.

The failure to perceive an act as a criminal act therefore gives us our first tinge of doubt about the official figures. We can move on from this to ask whether when an act is perceived and recognized as a criminal act it is always reported to the police?

Reporting of Crime

If you witness a crime or, indeed, are the victim of a crime, will you report it to the police? A number of studies have investigated this question and their findings suggest that a substantial proportion of crimes are not reported to the police. An obvious example of this failure to report is in the case of 'willing victim'. There are a number of types of act — drug transactions, some sexual behaviour, some financial dealings — in which it is in the best interests of both 'offender' and 'victim' that their actions are not brought to the attention of the police. However, it is also the case that many 'legitimate' victims choose not to report the offence to the police.

Table 2.1: Reasons for not reporting a crime to the police (after Mayhew et al., 1989)

Reason	Most Often	Least Often
Too trivial/no loss	Theft from motor vehicle (60)	Robbery (16)
Police could do nothing	Robbery (31)	Common assault (8)
Police not interested	Robbery (23)	Wounding (3)
Fear/dislike police	Robbery (5)	*Several* (0)
Police inappropriate/dealt with self	Theft in a dwelling (47)	Theft from motor vehicle (4)
Reported to other authorities	Personal theft (19)	*Several* (0)
Fear reprisals	Wounding (5)	*Several* (0)
Inconvenient	Robbery (5)	Vandalism (<1)

Notes:
1) Figure in parentheses is the percentage of respondents who had experienced a particular offence giving that reason for not reporting;
2) the term *several* indicates that more than one type of offence shared the same percentage of least often responses;
3) definitions of the offences are given by Mayhew *et al*. (1989).

Since 1983 three British surveys of people's experience of crime have been reported (Hough and Mayhew, 1983, 1985; Mayhew, Elliott and Dowds, 1989). One of the topics investigated in these surveys is the willingness of victims to report crime to the police. If we look at the most recent of these surveys (although the pattern is broadly similar in all three) then the most common reason for not reporting a crime with oneself as a victim is was that it was 'too trivial; no loss or damage'. As might be expected, however, the type of crime has a role to play in people's decision-making about whether to report the offence to the police. In 60 per cent of cases of theft from a motor vehicle and 57 per cent of cases of vandalism, the police were not notified on the basis of the triviality of the crime; however, in only 16 per cent of cases of robbery and 18 per cent of cases of theft in a dwelling was the crime thought to be too trivial to report. (Theft in a dwelling is a theft carried out by someone legitimately inside a person's home, such as party guests, builders, and service engineers.) The figures shown in Table 2.1 give the full range of reasons offered for not reporting a crime to the police, together with the types of crime for which these reasons were most and least often offered.

It is immediately evident from the information in Table 2.1 that the patterns of reporting will have the consequence that the police recording is biased according to the crimes that people choose to report. In other words, there is what might be thought of as a public 'filter' between criminal behaviour and the police. This filter appears to operate in the main on the public's judgments of triviality, thereby influencing what they decide to bring to the police's attention. However, it is highly unlikely that this filter operates equally across the society — both in terms of the people doing the reporting and who and what they report. There might be a greater willingness to report crimes committed by certain members of society — selected on the basis, say, of age or race, or certain groups within society might be more willing to report crimes to the police. On the latter point, Hough and Mayhew (1985) note: 'People from non-manual households were slightly more inclined to report property crimes than others. Older people, the well-educated and those with favourable attitudes to the police were more likely to report' (p. 25). Overall, the net effect of this personal element is to add a further layer of selectivity to the public filter. Such a filter has both advantages and disadvantages. It has the disadvantage of creating a *dark figure* of unreported crime, thereby creating difficulties in using the official figures as reliable estimates of the true extent of crime; it has the practical advantage of not swamping the police with trivial crimes and so wasting expensive public resources.

When considering the reporting of offences, a note of caution must be added when it comes to violent offences against the person. While people are selective in what they report to the police, they are presumably also selective in what they will tell researchers. It might be easy to tell a researcher that one's house has been burgled, but it is a quite different matter to say that you have been sexually victimized. It may well be, therefore, that *both* the surveys and the official figures seriously underrepresent the rates of some types of crime. It is, of course, entirely understandable that a victim of, say, a sexual crime does not want to talk about the offence to anyone; the victims may find it too painful to recount the experience, or they may fear a reprisal from the attacker if the crime becomes public knowledge. Similarly, parents of children who have been sexually victimized may wish not to make the details public.

Thus there are many reasons why a victim or a witness may decide not to report a crime to the police. The next issue to be addressed is whether, once a member of the public contacts the police to report a crime, that crime will be recorded by the police and so appear in the official statistics.

Police Recording

It is fair to say at the outset that the police are burdened with a less than enviable task in attempting to record reported crime. It would be entirely unreasonable to expect any system to manage perfectly with the sheer volume of information with which the police have to contend. We can assume therefore that there will be some human error in misrecording crimes reported to the police; the magnitude and effect of this misrecording is, of course, unknown. As well as human error, however, there is also the possibility that, like the victims discussed above, the police themselves might act as a filter, exercising discretion over their recording of reported crimes. As is clear from any number of studies, the police do exercise considerable control over the crimes they record (Bottomley and Pease, 1986; Hood and Sparks, 1970). This exercise of discretion and selection should not necessarily be seen in a poor light; as Hough and Mayhew (1985) note, the police may judge with justification that a reported crime is an error, or that there is a lack of evidence to support the reported offence. In other instances the police may decide that a caution is appropriate; this is duly administered and the crime is not recorded in the official statistics. Yet further, the police may be selective in administering cautions; evidence for this is seen, for example, in the fluctuations in cautioning rates in different parts of the country (Laycock and Tarling, 1985). Alternatively, the decision to caution might operate according to the type of crime, or even to the disadvantage of certain types of offender as defined by, say, race, age, or social class.

In other instances the appearance of a police officer at the scene of the crime might resolve matters there and then, meaning that the crime does not need to be recorded and so fails to appear in the official figures. Arguments in public houses and family disputes are typical examples of the type of situation in which an incident can be quickly resolved by the appearance of a police officer. Another way in which a crime can be 'lost' is when the police record an offence but at a later date the injured party asks for the crime to be dropped. In such a situation the incident is written off as 'no crime' and once again fails to be recorded for the official figures. It is likely that substantial numbers of crimes are 'lost' in this way; for example, Sparks *et al.* (1977) in a survey of three areas of London, found that 'no crime' cases accounted for between 18 and 28 per cent of all initially recorded crimes. The time span between the criminal event and its reporting to the police is yet another factor that can influence the decision of the police in terms of recording the crime. Crimes seen as 'too stale' to merit investigation and thereby wasting valuable resources may also fail to be recorded (Farrington and Bennett, 1981).

While crimes can be lost at the stage of police recording, it is also the case that 'extra' police activity can cause a rise in recorded figures. If, for example, there is a police crackdown on certain crimes, such as drug offences or violent crimes, then it follows that the recorded figures will show a rise in that particular crime. This does not mean, of course, that the absolute number of such crimes has risen; rather that the recorded figure is getting closer to the real figure — which has probably remained fairly stable throughout. Further, if it is the case that police practice varies from region to region, then some remarkable variations in crime rate can appear. Farrington and Dowds (1985) have shown how the methods used to record crime by the police in Nottinghamshire gave that county the appearance of the most crime-ridden in the country.

The British Crime Surveys have attempted to quantify the extent to which reported crimes fail to be recorded by the police. This is done by asking victims of crime whether they reported the crime to the police, then calculating from this the estimated number of crimes reported across the whole population. This estimate can then be compared with the offences recorded by the police as documented in the official figures, in turn producing an estimate of 'percentage recorded of reported'. An examination of the latest British Crime Survey reveals that for some crimes there is a good match between reporting and recording. For example, 91 per cent of reported car thefts were recorded, and 65 per cent of reported household burglaries were recorded. For other crimes the percentage was not so high; only 36 per cent of reported theft from the person were recorded, while only 38 per cent of reported robberies were recorded. This pattern is a common one in all three British Crime Surveys and — in an account that draws together many of the points already made here — has been discussed by Hough and Mayhew (1985):

One likely reason for the shortfall is that the police do not accept victims' accounts of the incidents: they may — quite rightly — think that a report of an account is mistaken or disingenuous, or may feel that there is simply insufficient evidence to say that a crime has been committed. Some incidents *will* have been recorded, of course, but in different crime categories — where, for example, it is indisputable that criminal damage has been committed, but less clear that a burglary has been attempted. Some incidents may have been regarded as too trivial to warrant formal police action — particularly if the complainants indicated they wanted the matter dropped or were unlikely to give evidence, or if the incident had already been satisfactorily resolved (p. 13).

In summary we can seen that the public are selective in the crimes they report to the police, and that the police are selective in which reported crimes they record. An awareness of these two filtration systems leads us to pause for even longer in considering the accuracy of the official figures as estimates of the true level of crime. It is clear that there are substantial numbers of unreported and unrecorded crimes — the *dark figure* — but we cannot know from official figures the extent of this unknown crime. In attempting to shed some light on the dark figure, researchers have moved away from officialdom and towards the other two main parties involved in crime — the offenders and the victims.

Offender Surveys

In offender surveys the most frequently used methodology is to select a sample on the basis of age, geographical location, or criminal record, and then to ask members of the sample whether they have committed any crimes, either detected or undetected. The information from the sample can be gathered by either interview or questionnaire. There are a substantial number of self-report studies in the literature (e.g., Belson, 1975; West, 1967); two studies have been selected here to illustrate this type of research.

Groth, Longo and McFadin (1982) carried out a self-report study with a group of 137 men who were convicted for sexual offences against both women and children. With confidentiality assured, the sex offenders answered a series of questions about their history of committing sexual offences. One question asked 'How many sexual assaults have you attempted or committed for which you were *never* apprehended or caught?'. The men admitted to an average of about five undetected sexual offences, with in some cases men saying they had carried out up to 250 undetected sexual assaults.

Furnham and Thompson (1991) reported a quite different self-report study with a group of 100 undergraduate students at the University of London, none of whom had a criminal record. The students were asked to complete a fifty-item Self-Reported Delinquency Questionnaire, based on the

Table 2.2: The most and least common delinquent acts in a non-delinquent sample (from Furnham and Thompson, 1991)

Most Common	Percentage Reporting[a]
I drank alcohol under the age of 16	88
I have trespassed on private property	76
I viewed an X-rated film while under age	74
I have travelled deliberately without the correct ticket or fare	72
I have taken an illegal drug	50
Least Common	
I have stolen from a large store or supermarket	1
I have planned to break into someone's flat with the intention to steal valuables	1
I have stolen a bicycle	2
I have stolen a motorbike or car, and have not returned it	2
I have stolen something out of a car	4
I have stolen a car or motorbike, but returned it after use	4
I have broken into a small store	4

Note:
a n = 100

questionnaires used in previous self-report studies (Gibson, 1967; Shapland, Rushton and Campbell, 1975). With a maximum score of fifty, Furnham and Thompson found that the undergraduates self-reported a mean of 12.46 offences, with the males reporting significantly more delinquent acts than the females. The five most commonly self-reported delinquent acts are shown in Table 2.2.

The general finding that consistently emerges from the self-report studies is that, for both serious offences and petty delinquency, the official figures underestimate the true extent of crime. While it is a dangerous game to attempt to estimate numbers, one might hazard a guess that the official figures represent about one-quarter of all crimes committed. Needless to say, this overall estimate will vary greatly for different types of crime.

The findings of the offender studies are informative on a number of levels. They give some impression of the true extent of criminal activity of offenders; they can provide important information on crimes such as rape where victims are unwilling to report; and the general level of petty delin- quency — even among undergraduates at the University of London! — casts doubt over the view that some types of criminal behaviour are in any way unusual or abnormal. However, once again we must ask questions about the accuracy of the data produced by the self-report studies — do respondents in self-report studies always tell the whole truth? The undergraduate students in Furnham and Thompson's study, age range 18 to 25 years, might not mind admitting to having drunk alcohol under the age of 16. Whether they would feel the same way about admitting to undetected sexual or violent offences they might have committed (about which they were not asked) is another matter. (Indeed, one could criticize some studies for concentrating on a narrow range of less serious crimes; although practically this is probably necessary in order not to offend most potential respondents from the general public.) The most frequently employed verification check, especially with convicted offender samples, is to compare self-report accounts with police records. Other verification methods include cross-checking with peer reports, testing twice over a period of time to see if reports match, and including lie questions in the questionnaire as a general check on honesty. Following an extensive review of self-report methods, Hindelang, Hirschi, and Weis (1981) concluded that there is a reasonable match between self-reported criminal behaviour and official recording. It therefore seems likely that, within limits, we can accept as reliable many of the findings from self-report studies.

Victim Surveys

While offender surveys reveal something of the behaviour of those who break the law, victim surveys have the added advantage of not only giving details about the *extent* of crime, they can also reveal something of the *effects* of crime both in terms of general fear of crime, and the impact of crime on victims. The first modern victim surveys were carried out in the United States of America in the late 1960s, with the first American national survey following in 1972. Other countries, including Australia and the Scandinavian countries, similarly began national surveys in the mid-1970s. In England a number of small-scale surveys were carried out in different parts of the country including the Midlands (Farrington and Dowds, 1985), London (Jones, MacLean and Young, 1986; Sparks, Genn and Dodd, 1977), and Merseyside (Kinsey, 1984). As noted previously, the first national British Crime Survey was published in 1983, followed by a second in 1985, and the most recent in 1989.

There are various ways of conducting victim surveys (Sparks, 1981), but *household surveys* offer one of the most widely used means of gathering information. The 1988 British Crime Survey (Mayhew *et al.*, 1989) provides a good example of this methodology. From the electoral register a sample was formed to give a representative cross-section of people from the general population aged 16 years and older living in private households. In order to produce a sample that was as representative as possible of the general population, the selection of the sample proceeded through five stages: 1) selection of parliamentary constituencies; 2) selection of wards within these constituencies; 3) selection of polling districts; 4) selection of addresses; and 5) selection of individuals for interview from the selected addresses. This selection procedure finally yielded a sample of 13,800 addresses, drawn from all parts of the country, including people from cities, towns, and villages alike. After selection of this sample, a small proportion of addresses were discovered to be empty or demolished, while at other addresses the selected occupant refused to be interviewed. Finally a total of 10,392 interviews were successfully completed, a response rate of 77.4 per cent from the addresses where interviews were possible. (The 1988 British Crime Survey also contained a 'booster sample' selected specifically to make it possible to examine victimization among ethnic minorities. However, not all crime surveys follow this practice.)

The interviewers gathered information from respondents using four questionnaires: a *main questionnaire* asking for details about attitudes to crime, and personal experience of crime either by the interviewee personally or by other members of their household; specific details about victimization, where appropriate, were then collected on a *victim form*; personal details were recorded using a *demographic questionnaire*; finally a *follow-up questionnaire* asked for views about security and crime prevention. As Mayhew *et al.* state, these questionnaires were designed to gather information on nine main topics: 1) the extent and nature of household and personal victimization; 2) the extent of verbal abuse at work; 3) fear of crime and perceptions of risk; 4) contacts with the police; 5) drinking behaviour and drunken driving; 6) attitudes to sentencing; 7) membership of and attitudes to Neighbourhood Watch schemes; 8) security behaviour in relation to burglary and auto crime; 9) household fires.

It is obvious that surveys such as this are going to produce vast amounts of data, yielding a myriad of figures and statistics. While a selection of the main findings from the 1988 survey is briefly presented here, it is recommended that the original publication be consulted. The British Crime Survey reports, written and published by members of the Home Office Research and Planning Unit, are all extremely 'user friendly' and easy to digest. (Unlike, it might be added, the *Criminal Statistics* which always leave me with a headache!)

The Extent of Crime

From the information gathered from the respondents the next step is to calculate an estimate of levels of offences across the country as a whole. Thus, for example, the numbers of offences in England and Wales are calculated by multiplying the rate per 10,000 offences, as indicated by the survey data, by factors reflecting both the numbers of households and the size of the population aged 16 and over. Given the magnitude of the information on which they are based, it is inevitable that there will be some sampling error in the final estimates. However, it is possible statistically to produce a range of likely sampling error and, within that, a 'best estimate' can be calculated that attempts to allow for likely sources of error. The figures quoted below from the 1988 British Crime Survey are best estimates.

The immediate point to note is that the 1988 survey estimates that in that year there were 13 million crimes against individuals and their personal property. While this is undoubtedly a large figure, it is accounted for, in the main, by relatively trivial offences against property. Incidents involving motor vehicles — theft of the vehicle, theft from the vehicle, and vandalism of the vehicle — accounted for approximately one-third of the incidents uncovered by the survey. Burglary, on the other hand, accounted for less than 9 per cent of the survey crimes. Similarly, violent offences, incorporating wounding, robbery, and sexual offences (but see below regarding sex offences), totalled only 6 per cent of survey crimes. On the basis of these figures it is difficult to resist the conclusion that, particularly for more serious crimes, victimization is not a common experience. Surveys in other parts of the world have arrived at broadly similar conclusions and Sparks (1981) has observed that: 'Criminal victimization is an extremely rare event . . . crimes of violence are extremely uncommon' (p. 17). Indeed, on the basis of the figures from the first British Crime Survey, Hough and Mayhew (1983) estimated that the 'statistically average' person over the age of 16 years can anticipate being burgled once every forty years and being robbed once every 500 years.

Crime is not a random event, however. While some people do not experience crime — Sparks (1981) estimates that about 90 per cent of survey respondents do not experience criminal victimization — other people are the victims of two, three, four, or even more offences in the time covered by the survey. In order to reflect this variation within the population it is important to make the distinction between the *incidence* of victimization and the *prevalence* of victimization. The former refers to the crime rate averaged out over the whole of the population; the latter is that proportion of the population who actually experience crime. Of the two, the prevalence rates probably tell us more about the social reality of crime. We see, for example, that burglaries are most prevalent in the inner cities; cars parked on the street at night are most likely to be stolen; and that it is not the elderly but young males, who typically have assaulted other young males, who are most often the victims of assault. On the subject of risks experienced by ethic minorities, the latest British Crime Survey concluded that:

> Both Afro-Caribbeans and Asians tend to be more at risk than whites for many types of crime. This is largely explained by social and demographic factors, particularly the area in which they live. However, taking account of this, ethnic minority risks still tend to be higher, with Asians particularly at greater risk of vandalism and robbery/theft from the person (p. 50).

While this survey was not designed to investigate the extent of racially motivated crime, reading the quotation cited above in conjunction with the findings of researchers such as Billig (1978) and Foster (1990), makes it not unlikely that a substantial proportion of offences against ethnic minorities were racially motivated.

Moving on from the quantity of estimated numbers of crime, one of the advantages of repeated victim surveys is that it is possible to look at changes over time in the estimated numbers of offences. Yet further, these changes according to victim surveys can be compared to changes over the same period of time in police recording of crime. Table 2.3 shows the changes for a number of crimes in both sets of figures — survey estimates and police recording — emerging from comparisons of the 1981 and 1987 figures.

It can be seen from Table 2.3 that in most instances there is a substantial discrepancy between the changes recorded by the crime surveys and by the police. This discrepancy can be seen as one of the products of the victim and police 'filters' discussed previously in relation both to the reporting and recording of crime. In addition, there is the added complication that reporting and recording practices will themselves change over time. Nonetheless, the

Table 2.3: A comparison of changes in self-reported and police recorded crime
(after Mayhew et al., 1989)

| Crime | Per Cent Change 1981–7 | |
	Police	British Crime Surveys
Burglary	38	59
Theft from motor vehicle	17	36
Robbery	62	9
Vandalism	52	9
Wounding	40	12
Wounding and Robbery	44	11

most important point to take from Table 2.3 is that crime is rising; the small crumb of comfort is that it appears that the greatest increase is for relatively trivial property crimes.

Fear of Crime

Any crime is costly in financial terms; there is the victim's loss to consider, along with the costs to society in terms of insurance, police, and so on. However, financial consequences are only a part of the impact of crime; the actual experience of victimization can have profound effects on its victims, while a more widespread appreciation of the likelihood of becoming a victim of crime can make people fearful that they too will become victims. The personal effects of victimization are discussed in the next section, in this section the focus is on fear of crime.

Public fear of crime has been examined by many crime surveys. In the British Crime Surveys in particular, the first two reports provided detailed information on fear of crime (see also Maxfield, 1988). Before looking at these findings, however, it is perhaps worth noting how difficult it is to define what is meant by 'fear of crime'. The actual emotion of fear is something that we most closely associate with a specific threat to our person. While the soft tread of a burglar in the middle of the night would cause most people to experience fear, it seems unlikely that the majority of people are generally fearful of crime in this sense. It is also unlikely that fear of crime correlates highly with perceived risk of victimization. It is perfectly possible to acknowledge the likelihood of being victimized yet not be worried by this possibility; alternatively, there might be a low risk of victimization yet a high level of fear (see below). It is much more likely that fear of crime, in the widely used sense, refers to diffuse feelings of worry and anxiety about being vulnerable to crime and about the anticipated consequences, both personal and financial, of victimization.

The first level of information provided by the 1984 British Crime Survey reveals the numbers in the population who say they are 'very worried' about being the victim of a crime. Table 2.4 shows the numbers expressing high levels of worry, broken down according to various types of crime.

While the figures in Table 2.4 give a broad picture of the incidence of fear of crime, the prevalence rates begin to block in some of the finer details. For

Table 2.4:   Percentage feeling 'very worried' about crime (after Hough and Mayhew, 1985)

Crime	Per Cent Very Worried[a]
Burglary	23
Mugging	20
Rape	30[b]
Sexual Harassment	28[b]
Vandalism	22
Stranger Attacks	18
Stranger Insults	10

Notes:
a n = 10,913
b Women respondents only, n = 5,730

example, men express less fear than women, and for most crimes it is people aged 16–30 years that tend to be the most fearful. Further, fear varies according to the type of neighbourhood. For example, those survey respondents living in 'less well-off council estates' and in the 'poorest council estates' were the groups most worried about mugging, while those in 'agricultural areas' and living in 'affluent suburban housing' showed the lowest levels of worry about mugging.

The relationship between the risk of crime, as revealed by survey data, and fear of crime is difficult to untangle. For burglary there is some correspondence between risk and fear. In other words, in the areas where most burglaries take place, and hence risk is highest, there is the greatest degree of fear of burglary. (Although the risk of being burgled tends to be over-estimated, especially in areas where the frequency of burglary is relatively low.) This contrasts with fear of 'street crime' — robbery, assault, theft from the person — in which the group that feels most unsafe, the elderly (particularly elderly women), are by far the least likely victims of such crimes. On the other hand, the most common victims of street crimes, men aged 16 to 30 years, express little fear of this type of attack. However, as with burglary, in all groups there is an exaggerated estimation of risk of being a victim of street crime.

When people are fearful of some event they usually take steps to try to avoid it happening; it is evident from the British Crime Surveys that fear of crime has a definite impact on bahaviour. Essentially people curtail their activities in order not to put themselves at risk. In its most extreme form, this curtailment can take the form of a self-imposed curfew: 10 per cent of those questioned in the 1984 British Crime Survey said that because of fear of crime they never went out of doors after dark for leisure purposes. Less dramatically, many people took precautions, such as avoiding certain streets or areas or going with a companion, if they went outdoors after dark. Other ways in which people curtailed their activities because of fear of crime was to avoid occasions such as football matches, and not to go to local entertainments such as pubs and the cinema. We can see from these 'precautions' why fear is sustained even in low risk groups. There is a well-documented principle in learning theory, termed *negative reinforcement*, in which the continual avoidance of a feared event or situation serves to maintain that fear.

Effects of Victimization

For the person who experiences victimization, the criminal intrusion into their lives can have a number of effects. Most obviously there is the financial loss and the practical inconvenience; writing as one whose car has had its windows smashed and radio, tapes, and other personal belongings stolen on two separate occasions, I can testify to both the financial loss and the inconvenience! The personal impact of these crimes took a number of forms: my initial emotional reaction on the nights of both incidents was anger about the damage to my brand-new car and the loss of the tapes from my collection, followed the next morning by intense irritation at the inconvenience of calling out people to repair the broken windows, then having to pay for the radio to be replaced, then later still having to fill in insurance forms. After the second incident, only a matter of months after the first, I decided to take preventative action and have a car alarm fitted. This seems to have been effective, in that my car remains intact, although given the cost it might have been cheaper to leave the car door open so that people can help themselves without having to break the windows! Of course, the immediate emotional impact of this type of minor crime soon dies away with no long-term effects (except, to my annoyance, I am still not exactly sure which tapes went missing).

As indicated by the 1984 British Crime Survey, the sequence described above is a common one for most victims of minor crime: anger or distress in the short-term that quickly dissipates, perhaps precipitating some preventative action to minimize future risks. For more serious crimes, however, it is clear that the effects on the victims can be much more profound. Thus crimes that threaten one's safety and security, such as burglary and personal attacks, can have highly destabilizing effects both in the short-term and the long-term. This is exemplified most starkly by the research findings that have looked at the sequelae to sexual attacks on women.

Resick and Markaway (1991) have summarized the psychological reactions to sexual assault in terms of the cognitive, emotional, and behavioural reactions following the offence. Women who have been sexually victimized overwhelmingly report feelings of confusion, fear and worry immediately after the assault, together with physical reactions such as shaking and trembling. Such reactions continue to be felt in the hours after the crime, together with an increase in feelings of depression, exhaustion and restlessness. Resick and Markaway note that a number of studies of victims of sexual assault have shown a typical pattern in the weeks after the assault: during the first week the distress remains at a high level, subsides a little during the second week, only to increase to a peak level in the third week. In addition to the symptoms of distress already noted, during the weeks after the assault the woman may experience lowered self-esteem, problems with social adjustment and difficulties with sexual dysfunction.

After these weeks of intense distress, Resick and Markaway suggest that most victims begin to show some positive readjustment two or three months after the attack — although their levels of fear, anxiety and personal difficulties still remain at a high level. Indeed, as Resick and Markaway note:

Other studies concerned with the long-term effects of sexual assault have found clinically significant problems with fear, social adjustment, depression, and sexual dysfunction in women who had experienced a sexual assault an average of six years ago (p. 262).

Other long-term consequences of sexual assault that may be experienced by some victims are severe curtailment of social activities, an increase in signs of mental disturbance such as paranoia and even suicide. If this is taken in conjunction with work that suggests that sexual assault in childhood, for both males and females, can have profound effects in adulthood (Jehu, 1988, 1991), then it is clear that sexual assault can have serious very long-term effects. A suggestion made by Resick and Markaway, Jehu and other writers, is that the effects of sexual assault can best be understood in terms of the formal diagnostic category of Post-Traumatic Stress Disorder (APA, 1987). It is hoped that the product of this research and enhanced understanding of the effects of sexual attack will enable even more effective counselling and support services to be developed for victims.

Victim Surveys: Strengths and Limitations

As is clear from even this brief discussion, victim surveys can have a number of strengths; they reveal something about the types of crime that fail to appear in the official statistics, they allow comparisons with official crime levels, they offer information on victim decision-making about reporting, and repeated victim surveys can say something about changes in patterns of crime. Crime surveys can also lead to an appreciation of everyday fear of crime and reactions to petty offences, while helping us to appreciate the suffering of victims of serious personal attack. For all these and other reasons, it is evident that victim surveys contribute greatly to our understanding of criminal behaviour. However, as there are disadvantages in accepting official statistics as a 'true' reflection of crime in society, so the same is true of an uncritical acceptance of the findings of victim surveys. In this sense, the findings of victim surveys should be treated rather like an alternative set of criminal statistics.

The limitations of the victim surveys cluster around three main areas: the types of crime they record, the reliability of the information they generate, and the quality of the information they gather.

Types of Crime

As victim surveys are, by definition, about victims they do not take account of 'victimless crimes'. Thus victim surveys say nothing about organizational crimes, such as fraud or violations of safety law; they do not include vandalism to public property or shoplifting; nor do they record crimes such as commercial burglary. Similarly, 'white collar crimes', such as tax evasion, are not represented in the victim surveys. Further, 'consensual crimes' such as drug dealing and some sexual offences are highly unlikely to appear in victim surveys. In addition, as the sampling is typically of people over the age of 16 years, crimes against children are not represented in many surveys.

Reliability of Information

In addition to the difficulties of sampling an accurate cross-section of the population, there are also difficulties specifically associated with the intricacies of the task facing participants in the survey. When people are asked to recall their experience of crime, there are a number of factors that might influence their reply. Mayhew *et al.* (1989) list six such factors. They suggest that:

> The respondent may: simply forget a relevant incident (or be ignorant of it); remember an incident, but think it happened before the reference period; remember an earlier incident as happening within the reference period; remember a relevant incident but not be prepared to mention it; fail to realise that an incident meets the terms of the question; or even make an offence up (p. 5).

In addition, other factors such as the type of interview (personal or telephone), interviewer characteristics (age, race, sex), and the interviewee's level of educational attainment can influence the amount and quality of the information gathered.

While there is much that could be said following from all of these considerations, perhaps one of the most important points to make concerns those instances where the victim remembers an offence but is unwilling to disclose any information about it. This reticence has led to the suggestion that victim surveys may tell us something about 'street crime' but say little about hidden crimes, such as domestic crime and sexual offences, that have a lasting impact on the victim (e.g., Stanko, 1988). If we follow this point about levels of domestic violence, then perhaps we must also ask questions about the interpretation of some of the findings of victim surveys. This particularly applies to survey findings on fear of crime that suggest that 'low risk' groups are disproportionately fearful of victimization. However, if fear in low risk groups in related to risk of domestic violence (not well recorded by crime surveys) rather than to street violence (seemingly well recorded) then fear of crime in 'low risk' groups may become entirely more realistic. 'Low risk' for street crime does not mean low risk for all crime; it would be a mistake to assume that for everyone home is a safe haven from criminal attack.

In total, therefore, we can learn much from victim surveys, and it may well be that they played a role in the emergence of greater concern in criminology for the role of the victim — the so-called 'victim movement' (e.g., Maguire and Pointing, 1988). Balanced against this, however, any reading and interpretation of the findings of victim surveys must be both critical and realistic. The need now is for the development of methodologies that systematically allow information to be gathered about the types of crime not included

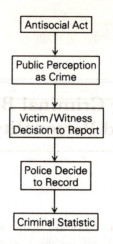

Figure 2.1. From real world acts to criminal statistics.

in the victim surveys. An accurate understanding of crime and its effects on victims will not emanate from one type of survey alone; multiple methodologies are required to appreciate the full complexity of crime.

Summary

On the basis of what has been covered in this chapter, what can we say about the extent of criminal behaviour in our society? Figure 2.1 illustrates the sequence and flow of information about criminal behaviour that influences what eventually surfaces as 'official crime'.

It is clear from Figure 2.1 that a dynamic social system is in operation that constructs our conception and even our understanding of criminal behaviour. It is important to note that many theories of criminal behaviour have been tested only on samples — perhaps not always random samples — of those offenders whose crimes are officially recognized. Whether or not these 'official criminals' differ in any way from unapprehended offenders is a moot point which will be touched on in a later chapter.

Chapter 3

Explaining Criminal Behaviour:
Biology and Personality

As suggested in Chapter 1, there are many ways to understand crime. Any recent criminology textbook will include a vast range of theories that draw on concepts from sociology, politics, psychology and economics (Hagan, 1987; Siegal, 1986). While some of these theories will be considered in due course, the immediate concern here is with those theories that specifically focus on the individual offender. Again, as I have discussed elsewhere (Hollin, 1989), a range of theories of this type have been applied in attempts to explain criminal behaviour. As might be expected, the main theories that take this particular emphasis on the individual are those that principally concern themselves with understanding human actions — biology and psychology. In this chapter and the next we will consider the application of biological and psychological theories and concepts to attempt to explain criminal behaviour.

It is, of course, impossible to cover in detail every theory and the research evidence it has generated. I have decided therefore to select what seems to me to be the dominant contemporary themes in an individual approach to explaining criminal behaviour: these are *biological theories, personality theories, learning theories, rational choice theories* and *developmental theories.*

Biological Theories

The term biological is used here in the sense of the individual's physiological functioning. A biologically based explanation of criminal behaviour would therefore seek to describe the physiological factors inherent in both the acquisition and maintenance of criminal behaviour. In its most simple form a theory of crime based upon biological factors would suggest that criminal behaviour is a product of heredity; in other words, that criminals are born not made. This view provides us with a convenient starting point to trace the development of biological research and thinking on the topic of criminal behaviour.

Genetic Transmission

In discussions of genetic transmission and criminal behaviour it is customary to begin by pointing to the absurdities of some of Lombroso's early writings and so, either implicitly or explicitly, dismiss the need to consider biological influences on behaviour. Cesare Lombroso (1835–1909), an Italian physician and 'criminal anthropologist', put forward the proposition that criminals were the product of a genetic configuration unlike that found in the normal, non-criminal population. His research led him to the view that the signs of a criminal genetic constitution were to be found in the atavistic anomalies — physical characteristics such as enormous jaws, high cheek-bones, handle-shaped ears, solitary lines on the palms of the hands, insensitivity to pain, and, best of all, a craving for orgies — that clearly marked the criminal as a throwback to more primitive times when people were savages. Plainly, such a genetic constitution must come about through heredity, either directly by being related to a family of criminals, or indirectly from association with a 'degenerate' family marked by a history of insanity, physical disease or addiction. In his later work Lombroso changed his views somewhat, suggesting that as well as genetic forces, it is necessary to consider psychological factors such as human greed and environmental conditions such as educational provision when seeking to understand criminal behaviour. Indeed, this nomination of biological, psychological, and social factors as playing an interactive role in the aetiology of criminal behaviour has led to Lombroso being called 'the father of modern criminology' (Schafer, 1976).

It is easy to criticize Lombroso's research with the benefit of eighty years of hindsight. For example, he did not use non-criminal control groups, and it is likely that he sampled highly unusual populations containing large numbers of people with mental disturbance and chromosomal abnormalities. Further, Lombroso's central thesis, that criminal behaviour can be explained in genetic terms, we now know to be fatally flawed on at least two counts. First, it is not the case that complex aggregates of behaviour can be accounted for in terms of a specific gene or combination of genes. As Rowe (1990) notes 'No responsible geneticist would argue that a specific gene exists for crime, as specific genes may be identified for Huntington's disease or eye color' (p. 122). Indeed, to quote Plomin (1990):

> Genes are chemical structures that can only code for amino acid sequences. These amino acid sequences interact with all of what we are and can thus indirectly affect endpoints as complex as behavior, but there is no gene for a particular behavior (p. 20).

Second, criminal behaviour is a socially defined legal label rather than a behavioural act that can be properly defined and measured. To complicate matters still further, few human behaviours have the quality of fixed action patterns that inheritance determines in other animals such as birds, fish, and other mammals.

Clearly then a Lombrosian view of the role of genetic inheritance in criminal behaviour is incorrect. Does it then follow, as some critics would suggest, that there is no place for a genetic contribution in attempts to explain criminal behaviour? The answer to this is that if that genetic contribution is thought of in Lombrosian terms of a single 'defective' or *pathological gene*, then genetic research has no contribution to make. However, another way of understanding the contribution of heredity is in terms of *normal polygenetic variation*. In this sense behaviour is not the result of a 'bad' gene but the end-product of a chain of events beginning with some variations of a normal genetic constitution. If the contribution of heredity to behaviour is understood in this latter sense then perhaps there is a role for a genetic factor in seeking to formulate an explanation of criminal behaviour.

Of course, the field of behavioural genetics has advanced enormously since the time of Lombroso and now focuses on highly complex polygenetic-environmental explanations to formulate models of the development of behaviour. In other words, the contemporary view is that what each of us inherits is a biological system that may provide an orientation or tendency to respond in a certain way to our environment. As Rowe (1990) notes, 'The human nervous system is clearly the organ of behavior, and its structure is organized by genetic inheritance' (p. 123). Thus, if our cognitive and learning abilities are dependent upon the functioning of our nervous system — particularly the central nervous system which includes brain functioning — and if the organization of the nervous system is at least in part genetically determined, then clearly genetic inheritance has a role to play in explaining behaviour. However, it cannot be over-emphasized that this role is not seen as a direct causal role, as in a Lombrosian conceptualization of faulty genetic inheritance, but rather more in terms of normal genetic variability that sets the potential for future behaviour.

If inheritance is thought of in this way, then it follows that in order for any genetic potential to be realized some environmental 'trigger' is needed. These environmental events and stimuli that play an interactive role with biological factors can be any event, beginning at the instant of conception, external to the individual. Such external events take the form of both the physical and social aspects of the environment. Further, the unfolding of biological and psychological development throughout the life-span adds another factor to the explanatory equation. Thus any behaviour must be understood by reference to a number of factors — biological, psychological and environmental — with the additional understanding that *none* of these are fixed. All three aspects of an individual's functioning can change, through both natural and artificial means, and therefore it would be quite wrong to think of genetic factors as somehow irrevocably predetermining all future behaviour.

If we take this contemporary view of the place of genetic inheritance in understanding behaviour, then how can we discover the role, if any, of genetic factors in criminal behaviour? There are two main questions to be answered. First, does genetic inheritance have any role to play in explaining criminal behaviour?; second, if there is a genetic influence, then how does it function? There are three main methods used by researchers to attempt to answer the first question and estimate the extent of the contribution of genetic factors: these are the *family study*, the *twin study*, and the *adoption study*.

Family Studies

Studies of families are of benefit to researchers in that they provide an opportunity to see whether behaviour is consistent through generations that share both genetic and environmental influences. It is a long-standing finding in criminological research that criminal behaviour runs in families. In a typical study, Osborn and West (1979) found that about 40 per cent of the sons of criminal fathers had a criminal record themselves, compared to a figure of 13 per cent among the sons of non-criminal fathers. There are many, many similar findings in the research literature as described by, for example, Hurwitz and Christiansen (1983), West (1982), Farrington *et al.* (1986) and Rutter and Giller (1983). However, it is precisely because families share both inheritance and environment that family studies do not allow researchers to disentangle the relative contributions of genetic and environmental factors in the genesis of the criminal behaviour. The finding that crime runs in families may reflect the influence of either (or both) genetic and environmental influences. In order to gauge the relative effects of environment and inheritance, a method is required that enables researchers to control or hold constant one side of the equation in order to enable the other side to be examined in detail. Twin studies and adoption studies arguably provide the means by which this control can be achieved.

Twin Studies

The basis of twin studies — a type of study to be found in many areas of psychological research — lies in the difference between two types of twins. Monozygotic (MZ) twins develop from the splitting of a single egg at the time of conception: such twins share 100 per cent of their genes, meaning that they are identical twins. Dizygotic (DZ) twins, on the other hand, develop from the fertilization of two eggs and are therefore no more alike than ordinary siblings, sharing on average 50 per cent of their genes. If it is assumed that members of a twin pair, be they MZ or DZ twins, share on average the same environment, then any major differences in the behaviour of the members of a pair of twins must be due to genetic variation. As MZ twins have identical genes then there should be a greater resemblance or *concordance* in the behaviour of each member of the pair than in DZ twins who are not genetically identical.

The first twin study of criminal behaviour was published by the German physician Johannes Lange in 1929. In the years that followed up to 1941 a number of twin studies were carried out with the general conclusion that MZ twins showed a much higher degree of concordance (about 75 per cent) than DZ twins (about 24 per cent) for criminal behaviour (see Hollin, 1989). At face value these early studies provide support for a genetic component in criminal behaviour. There are a number of reservations about these studies, however: the sample sizes are small, only four pairs in two studies; the sample selection is open to question; and there are reservations about the methods used to determine zygocity. To elaborate on the latter point, it is not necessarily a simple matter for researchers to determine if a twin pair is MZ or DZ: the early studies made judgments mainly on the basis of physical appearance which may have introduced some error in to their findings. (Although, as Eysenck, 1973, notes, we cannot assume the direction of the error; a wrong classification of a twin pair is as likely to decrease as to increase concordance rates.) Nonetheless, more recent twin studies have been able to take advantage of technological advances such as blood typing and serum protein analysis to make correct classifications of twin pairs. In addition, modern-day researchers are also able to utilize highly sophisticated statistical modelling techniques in order to account for the effects of more and more of the range of influences on behaviour, thereby making more informed estimates of the relative contribution of genetic and environmental factors.

In a study typical of those using a more sophisticated design, Rowe and Osgood (1984) examined the relative influences on delinquency of three factors: genetic variation, i.e., type of twin pair; shared environmental influences that affect both twins, e.g., a broken or intact home; and environmental influences specific to the individual, e.g., type of peer group. Their behavioural genetic analysis led Rowe and Osgood to estimate that the genetic factor accounted for over 60 per cent of the relationship between the three factors; the shared environmental influences accounted for about 20 per cent of the three-way relationship; and the individual environmental influences also accounted for 20 per cent of the relationship. Rowe and Osgood concluded that genetic factors play a significant role in accounting for delinquent behaviour. This broad conclusion is also drawn in several reviews of the contemporary literature. For example, Hollin (1989) noted that five studies reported between 1961 and 1977 showed a mean concordance of 48 per cent for MZ twins, compared to 20 per cent for DZ twins; DiLalla and Gottesman (1990) suggest very similar figures from the studies included in their review (51 per cent versus 22 per cent). As DiLalla and Gottesman (1991) remark, 'Although no one study is conclusive, the convergence between studies using different methods is striking' (p. 126).

As many writers on this topic note, however, it would be highly unwise to interpret the findings from twin studies as anything other than striking in the general trend that they show. There are a number of issues that remain unresolved with respect to twin studies of criminality. Fishbein (1990) lists five potential sources of error: 1) MZ twins being selected more frequently thereby giving disproportionate sample sizes when compared to DZ twins; 2) the selection of MZ twins may be biased towards those pairs that show similar behaviours; 3) MZ twins may in reality share more similar environments than DZ twins and it is this, rather than genetic influences, that contributes to the larger concordance rates; 4) the possibility of misclassification of twin pairs (as discussed above); and 5) measurement errors inherent in the research procedures followed. The last of these potential sources of error can emanate from a number of sources. The measure of criminal behaviour may be important, especially in light of the point made earlier about criminal behaviour being legally defined. Thus, as discussed in the last chapter, researchers can use either the official statistics or they can rely on self-report data; criminal behaviour can be defined according to legal constraints or as loosely as 'antisocial' behaviour; the measure might be of criminal behaviour generally or for specific, defined acts. Any or all of these considerations, together with the age of the study population (adult or juvenile), can have a potential effect on the outcome of a given study. For example, Cloninger and Gottesman (1987) reported different estimates of heredity for property crimes and crimes against the person.

While twin studies are clearly important, they are obviously not without limitations. An alternative research strategy is to study children separated from their biological parents and raised in another family. The study of adopted children offers a means to achieve this type of research, and a number of investigations have been carried out specifically looking at criminal behaviour in individuals raised in an adoptive family.

Adoption Studies

The procedure in adoption research involves identifying the parents of adopted children and then making a comparison between the criminal behaviour of the natural parents and their adopted offspring. The logic behind this is, of course, that if the children's behaviour is more similar to their biological parents than to their adoptive parents then a strong case for inheritance emerges. If, on the other hand, the adopted children's behaviour is closer to that of their adoptive parents, then a strong environmental influence is favoured.

In one of the first adoption studies to investigate criminal behaviour, Crowe (1974) selected a sample of adopted children whose biological mothers had a criminal record and a matched sample of adopted children whose mothers did not have a criminal record. In the group of adopted children whose mothers had a criminal record, almost 50 per cent of the adoptees had a criminal record by the age of 18 years; in the control group the rate was only 5 per cent. This finding adds support to arguments for a genetic component to criminal behaviour. However, one of the assumptions inherent in reaching this conclusion is that the placement of children for adoption is not selective. In other words, that the quality of upbringing is the same for those children from both criminal and non-criminal backgrounds. To control for any effects of placements being made on a selective basis, as seems entirely likely in practice, it is necessary to include in the research design some measure of the criminal behaviour of the adoptive parents as well as of the biological parents.

A number of studies have included a measure of criminal behaviour for both natural and adoptive parents in their design. These studies all reach the same general conclusion: while 'criminal' genetic and environmental factors are both important individually in seeking to explain criminal behaviour, it is when they are combined that they exert the greatest influence. For example, Mednick, Gabrielli, and Hutchings (1983) investigated the prevalence of criminal records among male adoptees set against the criminal history of both their natural and adoptive parents. As shown in Table 3.1, there is a clear effect of both environment and inheritance on criminal behaviour. While even with the

Table 3.1:   Percentage of male adoptees with criminal records according to parental criminality (after Mednick et al., 1983)

Adoptive Parents	Biological Parents	
	Criminal	Non-Criminal
Criminal	24.5% (n = 143)	14.7% (n = 204)
Non-Criminal	20.0% (n = 1,226)	13.5% (n = 2,492)

most favourable conditions — non-criminal biological *and* adoptive parents — there is a base rate of 13.5 per cent of adoptees with criminal records, the highest rate of 24.5 per cent is to be found when *both* genetic and environmental factors are conducive to the development of criminal behaviour.

As with twin studies, adoption studies are not without their shortcomings. As noted already, there may be a selection effect due to non-random allocation of adoptees according to the characteristics of the biological parents. In addition, there are problems with small sample size in some studies, there is the perennial problem of measurement of criminal behaviour, and there is the need to ensure that children are adopted at birth so as not to 'contaminate' environmental effects. Nonetheless, the force of the adoption studies is to add to the evidence for a hereditable component to criminal behaviour.

Indeed, the overall conclusion to be drawn from the family, twin, and adoption studies is that heritable factors appear to increase the likelihood of criminal behaviour. That is not to say that heredity predetermines a life of crime; nor that criminal behaviour will not be apparent in the absence of any hereditable influence. The point is made, however, that with the 'right' genetic and environmental antecedents, there is a heightened risk of criminal behaviour.

If it is accepted, bearing in mind the limitations on research noted above, that there can be a heritable element in criminal behaviour, then the question that next arises is how does that genetic element function? Simply, heredity functions by the passage, from parents to children, of genetic material. This genetic material contains the 'blueprint' for our physical features, our biological system, and at least some behavioural responses. The genetic blueprint is properly termed the *genotype*; the observable manifestation of the genotype, such as eye colour or the suckle reflex in babies, is termed the *phenotype*. One route by which researchers seek to measure the unfolding of a genotype is through the functioning of the nervous system. The immediate difficulty here, of course, is that while it is possible to measure a phenotype and its biological correlates, there are other influences as well as the genotype on nervous system functioning. These 'extra' influences, all environmental in origin, include physical insult and injury, biochemical exposures as with drug-taking or through toxic pollution, diet, and disease and illness. Thus it cannot be assumed that observed physiological functioning is directly related to heredity unless environmental influences have been accounted for in full. Further, when considering the evidence on biological correlates of criminal behaviour, it is important to place a firm emphasis on the term *correlates*. A correlation is not a cause; therefore while there may be various biological factors associated with criminal behaviour, pending further confirmatory evidence these correlates cannot be elevated to causal status in any explanation of behaviour.

Research in this area faces a number of difficulties. There are various technical problems associated with the reliable measurement of physiological functioning, but there are also difficulties with research design. As well as the problems of obtaining matched offender and non-offender groups, there may well be differences *within* offender populations. Thus, for example, comparisons between studies of juvenile and adult offenders may be misleading, while the findings from research conducted with psychopathic offenders may not be easily extrapolated to other offender groups. These factors should be held in mind while considering the research findings in this relatively new field of study.

Biological Correlates of Criminal Behaviour

The human biological system is infinitely complex and any attempt to compartmentalize it for the sake of convenience is bound to have a Procrustean flavour. However, for present purposes I have concentrated on three areas of human physiology: these are the *central nervous system*, the *autonomic nervous system*, and *hormonal physiology*.

Central Nervous System

The central nervous system (CNS) comprises the brain and the spinal cord. Therefore studies of the CNS are concerned with brain activity both in terms of brain function and the transmission of information through the CNS. In the last decade there has been a tremendous growth in research in brain-behaviour relationships, a little of which has touched on the topic of criminal behaviour (Miller, 1988).

Electroencephalogram recording
One of the traditional ways to assess brain functioning — and thereby detect the likelihood of conditions such as epilepsy — is through the use of electroencephalogram (EEG) recording of cortical activity. The interest in the study of electroencephalograms in connection with criminal behaviour stems from two sources. The first source is the view that EEG abnormalities in criminal populations is a characteristic of cortical immaturity; as Venables and Raine (1987) point out, however, there is little empirical support for this contention. The second lies in a long-standing hypothesis about the relationship between abnormal EEG, epilepsy, and violent behaviour (Gunn and Bonn, 1971).

A typical research strategy in this field of enquiry is to make EEG recordings using matched criminal and non-criminal groups, then compare the patterns of the two groups. While this sounds straightforward it is in practice more complex: the EEG recording can be affected by technical factors, such as the type and positioning of the electrodes, while subject factors, such as previous cortical insult, will show on the EEG but may well have nothing to do with the main dependent variable of criminal behaviour. While there are a number of studies of EEG functioning in criminal groups, the findings should be read with these points in mind.

A number of early studies suggested a relationship between abnormal EEG patterns and extreme crimes such as murder by the insane (e.g., Hill and Pond, 1952). However, to reinforce the points made above, it is difficult in such studies to disentangle the relative contributions of psychiatric disturbance and criminality, as well as any other factors such as socio-economic status, to the abnormal neurological recordings. The pattern that emerges from more recent research is somewhat equivocal. Some studies have suggested links between EEG abnormalities and violent behaviour (Krynicki, 1978), while other studies have not found such a relationship (Moyer, 1976). Studies conducted with delinquents have similarly proved indecisive; Loomis, Bohnert, and Huncke (1967) and Lewis *et al.* (1982) both reported that approximately one-quarter of their samples of delinquents showed EEG abnormalities. However, as Hsu *et al.* (1985) point out, in the absence of baseline information on EEG abnormalities in non-delinquent adolescents it is difficult to make much sense of such findings. Accordingly, Hsu *et al.* designed and conducted a study to attempt to rectify several of the sampling and methodological shortcomings of previous studies. While conceding that more research is needed to be absolutely conclusive, and that those juvenile offenders with EEG abnormalities merit further study, Hsu *et al.* concluded their thorough investigation with the statement that there is 'no compelling reason to believe that epilepsy and abnormal EEGs are major determinants of juvenile delinquency' (p. 315).

Neurotransmitters
Simply, it is well established that the CNS is characterized by chemical neurotransmission as a fundamental way of transmission of information through the system. As Green (1991a) notes, by 1970 neurophysiological research had identified six chemical neurotransmitters: these are *noradrenaline, dopamine, serotonin, acetylcholine, gamma-amino butyic acid*, and *glutamate*. However, since 1970 there has been a veritable explosion in the rate of identification of neurotransmitters, as Green once again comments: 'Added to this list by now are anywhere between 20 and 30 possible neurotransmitters discovered over the last two decades, whose precise role in brain function has not yet been identified' (p. 158). Given that much basic research remains to be completed in the identification and functioning of neurotransmitters, it follows that not a great deal of sophisticated research has been carried out with offender populations. In the main, the research that has been conducted has concentrated on aggressive and violent offenders, focusing on one or two of the neurotransmitters (mainly serotonin and noradrenaline). To give a flavour of the research in this field, there follows a brief discussion of the possible relationships between serotonin and violent behaviour.

From the findings of both animal and human studies, it seems highly likely that the neurotransmitter serotonin acts to inhibit behavioural responses to provocative, emotional events and thereby plays a role in the regulation of aggressive and violent acts. Given this, it might be predicted that violent people would have lower levels of serotonin and hence are disadvantaged in controlling aggression once provoked. A number of research studies have indeed suggested that this hypothesis is accurate; compared with non-aggressive control groups, lower levels of serotonin have been found in violent individuals (e.g., Linnoila *et al.*, 1983; Virkkunen *et al.*, 1989). Thus, as Fishbein (1990) notes, 'A decrease in serotonic activity may produce disinhibition in both brain mechanisms and behavior and result in increased aggressiveness' (p. 47). As Fishbein goes on to discuss, however, there are a number of obstacles that stand in the way of an unreserved acceptance of this position. As in other areas of research there are difficulties in defining the behaviour in question — for example, do all studies use similar definitions of 'violence'? — and of ascribing individuals reliably to control groups. In addition, the concentration on serotonic activity in isolation from other biological systems tells only part of the story, how large a part it is impossible to say. Another complicating factor, perhaps particularly in the field of criminal behaviour, is that neurotransmitters are significantly affected by high levels of alcohol and drug use (Fishbein and Pease, 1990). Thus, the possibility must be admitted that variations in biological functioning between offender and non-offender groups may, in part at least, be a reflection of drug use rather than an abiding characteristic of criminal groups *per se*.

Laterality

One of the features of mammalian physiology is that we are bilaterally symmetrical — that is, our bodies divide into two mirror-images. This symmetry includes the forebrain which is formed by *two* cerebral hemispheres — the left and right cortical hemispheres — joined by a bundle of fibres called the *corpus callosum* that allows the passage of information from one hemisphere to the other. In the majority of people there is a lateral preference for one of the two hemispheres; some people are predominately right-sided, others predominately left-sided. One obvious way in which this lateral preference is manifest is in hand and foot preferences. A body of research has investigated the relationship between lateral preference and a range of types of behaviour, including antisocial and criminal behaviour.

A string of studies carried out in the years leading to the end of the 1970s suggested an association between a left-side preference (hand and foot) and delinquency (see Porac and Coren, 1981). However, more recent research on offender samples has failed to show this association (Feehan *et al.*, 1990; Hare and Forth, 1985). There are a number of possible explanations for this discrepancy. The more recent studies may have used improved measures of lateral preference; there may have been changes in the way society reacts to left-handedness, so that it is no longer 'wrong' to be left-handed; or there many be differences in the populations sampled in the different studies. This latter point is made clear by Buikhuisen *et al.* (1988) who found a very high association between laterality and delinquency, however as they note:

> More than half our sample consisted namely of youngsters with either a schizophrenic parent, a psychopathic father, or a character-disordered mother. The remaining subjects were part of a matched control group of youngsters with parents who had never had a psychiatric hospitalization. Everything considered this was anything but a random sample of youngsters (p. 130).

Buikhuisen *et al.* conducted further analysis on their data and suggested that the finding of an association between laterality and criminal behaviour might be robust, but that the possibility of a sampling effect could not be ruled out completely.

As hinted above, even if it were established that there was a link between laterality and criminal behaviour, this does not establish a neurological basis for offending. For many years right-handedness was seen as correct and proper, left-handedness as incorrect and abnormal. Indeed, many children were taught to be right-handed despite being naturally left-handed. This social pressure may well have created other social difficulties which, in turn, may have had an adverse effect on later development. This situation is particularly understandable in terms of labelling theory: early in life, because of their handedness, a child is labelled as 'odd' by parents, teachers, and peers; in turn, this label affects the child's self-image, their schooling and the quality of their environment. Thus it is not the handedness that causes the offending, rather the train of events triggered by a social reaction to handedness.

Another explanation lies in the hypothesized association between hemisphere dominance and cognitive and personality factors. Left-handed people may be right hemisphere dominant — although this is not an invariable rule. As language abilities are, for most people, located in the left hemisphere then left-handed people (assuming they are right hemisphere dominant) may be less verbally able. Verbal ability, in turn, is thought to be related to the development of self-control, especially of heightened emotional arousal; self-control may well be a factor in the commission of criminal behaviour. (Although it should be noted that not all authorities agree with this view. Feehan *et al.* (1990) state firmly that, in their view, there is no convincing evidence that lateral preference is related to cognitive abilities. However, Feehan *et al.* do raise the possibility that it is not left preference but mixed-handedness that is related to delinquency. They suggest that by classifying mixed-handedness as left preference previous research may have confused the issue.) Yet further, the admixture between biological and psychological factors may be a determinant of personality. Buikhuisen *et al.* (1988) and Miller (1988) have developed hypotheses along these lines, and the particular contribution of Hans Eysenck will be explored later in this chapter. Thus theorists are beginning to suggest a complex path of events stemming from hemisphere dominance, to localization of cortical function stressing the role of verbal ability, to psychological constructs such as self-control and personality and their role in offending. While conceptually neat, the empirical evidence in support of such a path of events remains to be gathered.

'Soft' signs of CNS functioning

There are numerous ways in which both researchers and practitioners can gather information about CNS functioning without actual physiological measurement of the CNS itself — the findings from such methods are often referred to as 'soft' signs of functioning. From a range of studies a little can be said about such soft signs in relation to criminal behaviour.

The controversial notion of *minimal brain disorder* (MBD), sometimes termed *minimal brain dysfunction*, has been around for a long time. Briefly, MBD refers to a syndrome, most often associated with children and adolescents, not specifiable in terms of a specific, exact neurological condition, but evinced by a loose ensemble of behavioural, cognitive, neurological, and other medical variables including psychophysiological response patterns. Given the broad range of indicators and the vagueness of the diagnostic indicators, it may well be that MBD, if it exists, is really a cluster of similar but independent syndromes (Rutter, 1982). More recently, as Campbell and Werry (1986) note, the trend has been to move away from the use of the term MBD, and to favour the term *attention deficit disorder* (ADD). ADD can be diagnosed either without the presence of hyperactivity (ADD), or with the presence of hyperactivity (ADD-H). The key components of ADD-H are developmentally inappropriate degrees of inattention, impulsiveness and, of course, hyperactivity. These behavioural and cognitive factors are assumed, in part at least, to be a function of some level of minimal brain disorder.

There has been a considerable amount of research into the relationship between ADD and delinquency. For example, a large scale study by Zager *et al.* (1989) investigated the incidence of both ADD and ADD-H in a sample of almost 2,000 court adjudicated adolescents referred for clinical assessment. The assessment took the form of a battery of physical, psychiatric, educational, psychological and social evaluations. The percentages within the sample assessed as ADD and ADD-H were 46 per cent and 9 per cent respectively. As might be expected, the ADD and ADD-H groups showed greater evidence of a range of developmental disorders, but there was no significant difference in the average number of offences committed by those young people assessed as with or without ADD and ADD-H. However, the sample in this study was selective in the sense that they were both court-adjudicated and referred for clinical assessment. These factors probably account for the difference with Loeber's (1988) conclusion, based on an overview of a number of studies, that a constellation of factors analogous to ADD and ADD-H is associated with an accelerated rate of offending in young (mainly male) people.

A recent study by Farrington, Loeber, and Van Kammen (1990) has shed further light on this topic. They analyzed the data from a longitudinal study of young males, repeatedly tested at various ages from 8 to 21 years. The advantage of such research is that it allows the long-term outcomes of child and adolescent variables to be assessed. The variables measured in this study included those indicative of ADD and ADD-H; measures of conduct problems such as misbehaviour at school and at home; and both official and self-report measures of offending. The data analysis showed that, as might be expected, measures of both attentional difficulties and of conduct problems showed a significant relationship with offending. (Attentional disorders and conduct problems can, of course, be found in the same person, but they can also occur independently of each other indicating that they should be seen as different disorders.) However, while there was some overlap in their impact on offending, Farrington *et al.* note that the type of impact of the attention deficit and conduct problems was different. The attention deficit problems were related to cognitive handicaps and low IQ, and these young men tended to come from homes with both criminal parents and a large family size. Offenders with this type of personal and family profile showed an offence pattern of a criminal conviction at a young age, progressing to chronic offending in later life. On the other hand, those young males with conduct problems were most strongly characterized as coming from homes with poor and inadequate parenting, so that there was a low level of parent-child socialization. The offence pattern for this group of young men was different to the early chronic offending seen with attentional disorders; conduct problems were most strongly associated with self-report of (mainly minor) delinquent acts in late childhood and adolescence and later adult offending and recidivism. These different pathways to the same outcome of adult offending led Farrington *et al.* to the conclusion that attentional and conduct problems 'could be part of different causal chains or different developmental sequences leading to offending' (p. 77).

The complexity of the research hints at the problems of understanding the relationships between ADD and criminal behaviour. It is clear that some relationship exists — although the research has been conducted on males rather than females and this places obvious limitations on its generalizability — but how that relationship comes about is uncertain. The attentional disorders *may* be the result of an unspecified brain dysfunction — perhaps via genetic factors or caused by insult through, say, the effects of toxicity — but the attention disorder (or brain dysfunction) is not an explanation in and of itself. The findings of researchers such as Farrington *et al.* show that social factors such as parenting and early arrest and conviction are also precursors to continual offending.

Another cluster of 'soft' signs of CNS dysfunction is found in the research which has looked at psychometric test performance in offender samples. The most frequently used psychometric tests are neuropsychological tests, intended to offer indications of brain damage or dysfunction, and intelligence tests. A number of investigations of the neuropsychological functioning of offender samples using such test batteries have been reported. However, before looking at the findings of some such studies, it is important to note at the outset that not all offenders will show any marked deviation from the norm on these tests. Indeed, some studies fail to find any systematic relationship between test performance and offending (e.g., Tarter *et al.*, 1983).

In a study typical of those that do report an association between test performance and criminal behaviour, Yeudall, Fromm-Auch, and Davies

(1982) found that some (but not all) of the delinquents in their sample showed neuropsychological difficulties compared to non-delinquent controls. There was no difference on any of the tests between the violent and non-violent delinquents. For those delinquents in the Yeudall *et al.* study who did show evidence of neuropsychological problems, the specific pattern of difficulty suggested by the test results was for frontal brain dysfunction, particularly in the non-dominant hemisphere. This pattern of dysfunction was, in turn, interpreted as indicating that the delinquents may experience difficulty in planning their actions, perceiving the consequences of their behaviour, and hence in adjusting their behaviour in light of its impact on other people and themselves. This view accords neatly with the literature on problem-solving abilities in offenders (see Chapter 4), and is suggestive of the way in which some theorists see the relationship between neuropsychological functioning and behaviour. That is, the level of a given individual's neuropsychological functioning plays a role in their cognitive development, such as the development of self-control over their emotions and behaviour, and hence in their ability to learn from and cope with their environment, perhaps particularly in terms of their social environment.

Moving to IQ tests, the nature of the relationship between IQ and criminal behaviour is one of the longest running sagas in criminology (which says nothing about the conceptual problems with the concept of intelligence and its testing — see Radford and Hollin, 1991). Suffice to say that the debate has gone through a number of stages. There are the early findings of researchers such as Goring (1913) who saw a strong relationship between 'defective intelligence' and criminal behaviour; the essentially similar findings in the 1930s, 1940s and 1950s that suggested that delinquents typically show lower IQ scores than non-delinquents (Glueck and Glueck, 1934, 1950; Merrill, 1947); a period during the 1960s when many methodological doubts were rightly raised such as whether IQ tests measure intelligence or social disadvantage (Caplan, 1965); to contemporary opinion that favours a relationship between low IQ and criminal behaviour even when factors such as sampling variations and family background have been allowed for (Wilson and Herrnstein, 1985). Recent findings by Lipsitt *et al.* (1990) are of interest because of the design used in this study. Lipsitt *et al.* conducted a longitudinal study in which over 56,000 pregnancies, enrolled between 1959 and 1966, were followed until the children were 7 years of age. From this very large population, used in a number of studies of child development, a cohort of 3,164 people were identified who had at the time of Lipsitt *et al.*'s study reached 18 years of age. From this selected cohort, court records revealed that there were 431 convicted juvenile offenders. By looking back at the test scores gathered during the cohort's childhood, Lipsitt *et al.* could compare the scores of those children who became convicted delinquents and those for whom there was no court record. The findings showed that the disadvantage in intellectual performance in the delinquent sample, found for males but not for females, was not present at 8 months of age, but was evident at 4 years of age and was maintained at 7 years of age. While it is interesting that IQ differences between male delinquents and controls were found in this type of study, the cause of the difference remains unclear; nor is it certain why the difference was not found for female delinquents. While there are these imponderables, what is altogether more certain is that the IQ and criminal behaviour debate has many miles left to run.

However, to return to CNS functioning, interest in IQ testing has also focused on the distinction within IQ tests between scores on sub-tests of verbal ability and motor skill performance. A typical IQ test, such as the Weschler Adult Intelligence Scale (WAIS) or the Weschler Intelligence Scale for Children (WISC), yields three IQ scores — *Verbal IQ*, *Performance IQ*, and *Full Scale IQ* (Full Scale being an aggregate of the Verbal and Performance scores). A large difference in Verbal and Performance IQ, generally of the order of 8–12 IQ points and typically in the direction of a lower Verbal IQ, is often seen as an indication of brain damage or dysfunction. A number of studies have looked at Verbal versus Performance IQ in offender populations. Quay (1987b) has reviewed these studies and concludes that:

> It now seems clear that the frequently obtained eight-point discrepancy is due to the less adequate performance of delinquents on tests involving verbal skills, including word knowledge, verbally coded information, and verbal reasoning. In fact, on these sorts of tests, delinquents, especially the more aggressive, perform at levels close to one standard deviation below nondelinquents (p. 113).

In summary, there is a substantial body of research that suggests that *some* delinquents are characterized, to a greater or lesser extent, by CNS impairment or dysfunction. Another body of research has been concerned with the possibility of a relationship between autonomic nervous system (ANS) functioning and criminal behaviour and it is to that area that attention is now turned.

Autonomic Nervous System

Functioning and responsiveness

The ANS is concerned with the internal running of the body, connecting the CNS with various organs. As Green (1991b) notes, 'It is a purely motor system, with fibres innervating the smooth muscle of the digestive tract and blood systems, the musculature of the heart, and various glands (e.g., adrenal medulla, pancreas, salivary glands, etc.)' (p. 170). The ANS plays a crucial role in, for example, the regulation of breathing, heart rate, and blood flow according to the physical demands placed on the body. In the normal course of events the ANS regulates internal biological functioning in an involuntary fashion — when running for a bus we do not have to 'ask' our ANS to speed up blood flow to increase our chances of success in catching the bus. In studies of psychophysiology researchers are generally concerned with various measures of ANS activity such as *heart rate* and the *skin conductance response*. The distinction is usually made between resting levels of the ANS, termed *tonic arousal*, and active levels, termed *phasic arousal*.

In terms of the relationship between ANS functioning and criminal behaviour, a large proportion of empirical studies have been with psychopathic offenders and these are discussed in Chapter 6. With respect to other criminal populations, the central focus of much research has been the responsiveness of the ANS. Slow responsiveness as measured in terms of tonic arousal suggests that the individual will only respond to strong stimuli; slow responsiveness as measured via phasic arousal suggests that the individual will show only minimal responding to stimuli. Slow responsiveness is thought to be linked with poor learning, particularly in terms of aversion learning, that is, learning which situations to avoid because they produce harmful outcomes. The available evidence, which is summarized in several reviews (Trasler, 1987; Venables, 1987; Venables and Raine, 1987), leans towards the conclusion that slow responsiveness is a feature of ANS activity in offender groups.

The pathway from slow ANS responsiveness to criminal behaviour is not understood. As will be seen presently, Eysenck offers an explanation in terms of personality, while Raine, Venables, and Williams (1990) suggest that the pathway might be cognitively mediated via attention to external events. Specifically, Raine *et al.* argue that slow responsiveness is associated with a deficit in the allocation of attentional resources to the environment: 'Such a deficit may explain some early social and cognitive impairments in antisocial individuals, such as poor school work, antisocial school behaviour, and difficulties in sustaining training courses and jobs' (p. 936). Although, to complicate matters, Raine *et al.* note that when a task is motivating and involves active rather than passive attention, then offenders can show enhanced levels of attention.

Another of the functions of the ANS is the regulation of hormonal activity which leads us to the final topic in this section.

Hormonal Physiology

A body of research has accumulated investigating the possibility of a relationship between hormonal activity and criminal behaviour. There are a number of strands to this research, including areas such as hormones and the menstrual cycle (Harry and Blacer, 1987). To illustrate the principles involved, however, I have selected for discussion here the research on the sex hormones, particularly *testosterone*.

The gonadal hormones, in particular the androgens (the main one of which is testosterone), play a central role in sexual differentiation and behaviour; specifically, they masculinize any individual exposed to them as evinced, for example, by the effects on male development during puberty of the surge in testosterone levels. The thinking behind the possibility of a relationship between androgens and criminal behaviour is based on a number of assumptions: as delinquency and aggressiveness tend to become most pronounced during puberty then it may be that individual differences in hormonal activity are involved; as the androgens are sex hormones, so it might be the case that they have some relationship with sexual offending; assuming that males are more violent than females, then factors such as androgen levels may play a part in the commission of violent behaviour.

The assumption relating sex, hormonal activity, age and criminal behaviour remains largely untested. While a number of authorities have remarked on the association between age-related changes in hormonal activity and the rise in delinquency, and elegant theoretical models have been advanced (e.g., Ellis and Coontz, 1990), the intricate research necessary to substantiate such a relationship has not as yet been conducted. With respect to the assumption regarding sex offences, an interesting pattern emerges from the empirical studies. Following a discussion of the relevant studies, Thiessen (1990) makes the point that: 'Such evidence suggests that normal levels of blood testosterone at full sexual maturity are associated with the probable use of extreme violence in committing rape, but certainly cannot be considered instrumental in causing rape' (p. 154). This then brings us to the third assumption, that the androgens are involved in aggressive and violent behaviour. The research investigating the relationship between testosterone and violent behaviour suggests that for both adolescents and adults there may be a relationship between testosterone level and violence (e.g., Ehrenkranz, Bliss and Sheard, 1974; Olweus, 1987). However, it is important to note that the relationship is not invariable; high testosterone levels have been found in men with no history of criminal violence (Kreutz and Rose, 1972). Thus while hormonal factors may play some role in the aetiology of violent behaviour, there must clearly be other causative factors involved.

Summary

The research on biological correlates of criminal behaviour leads to a number of conclusions. It appears that there may be a heritable component to adult criminal behaviour, although this is by no means certain (Walters and White, 1989). How exactly such a genetic factor works is unclear. *If* there is a genetic influence, the next question to be asked is what is inherited? One suggestion is that genes produce differences in nervous system functioning that, in turn, influence the individual's capacity to learn from the environment (e.g., Rowe, 1990). The complexities of researching nervous system function are daunting in themselves, to study nervous system functioning in relation to a behaviour as problematic to define and measure as criminal behaviour is daunting in the extreme. This complexity is perhaps evident from the brief discussion of the generally mixed findings of studies of nervous system functioning and criminal behaviour. One of the problems faced by such research is the sheer magnitude of the task; while CNS, ANS, and hormonal systems can conveniently be set apart here for the purposes of discussion, in reality they form an integrated system in which changes in one part can profoundly affect another. Ellis's (1987) view of androgens affecting CNS arousal, the probability of brain dysfunction, and causing a right-hemisphere shift in neocortical functioning shows the way researchers are beginning to develop more and more complex models of the role of biological factors in criminal behaviour. However, there is also the issue of causality: are the biological factors a *cause* of behaviour, criminal or otherwise? Of course, there is no right or wrong answer to this question. Ellis (1987) expresses one view with the assumption that

> the physical-chemical functioning of the brain is directly responsible
> for all behavior ... the physical-chemical functioning of the brain
> is assumed to be the result of the interaction of genetic and environ-
> mental factors, not simply the result of environmental factors (p. 511).

As previously discussed in Chapter 1, such a determinist view stands in direct opposition to theories based on free will and rational choice as the cause of criminal behaviour. This issue is returned to in Chapter 4.

Before following more directly in the next chapter Rowe's lead on the concept of *learning* as the next link in the chain to explaining criminal behaviour, I wish to focus on one particular theory of criminal behaviour that directly builds on much of what has already been discussed in this chapter. This theory which seeks to integrate genetics, nervous system functioning, and the psychological concept of *personality* was developed and refined by Hans Eysenck.

Crime and Personality

Eysenck's theory of criminal behaviour is an attempt to combine biological, social and individual factors to understand the development of criminal behaviour. Eysenck's book *Crime and Personality* that first articulated his theory was published in 1964, with second and third editions published in 1970 and in 1977; Eysenck himself has offered periodic summaries of his views (Eysenck, 1984, 1987; Eysenck and Gudjonsson, 1989), as have other writers on psychology and crime (Bartol, 1980; Feldman, 1977; Hollin, 1989).

The basis of Eysenck's theory is the proposition that the child's socialization occurs through the process of conditioning via the association of antisocial behaviour with unpleasant punishment. The child learns by association — following the principles of classical conditioning first discovered by Pavlov — that antisocial behaviour brings about punishment, say from parents or teachers. This process of learning by association leads to the development of a fear response that controls the child's instincts or impulses to act in an antisocial manner. In everyday language, the child develops a conscience that prevents their behaving in an antisocial way. Now, not all people condition to their environment with the same ease; some people condition easily, others condition poorly. An individual's degree of conditionability, Eysenck argues, is in large part genetically determined via the inherited characteristics of his or her nervous system.

In terms of CNS functioning, some individuals will be cortically *under*-aroused which has two consequences. First, underarousal is linked with poor conditionability; second, such individuals will seek to act in ways that will stimulate their optimal level of arousal. Eysenck uses the term *extrovert* to describe the personality of such individuals. At the other end of the continuum there are individuals with high levels of cortical *over*arousal, termed *introverts*, who condition easily and seek to behave in ways that minimize arousal levels.

Thus at one extreme of this dimension of personality, generally termed *Extroversion* (E), there is the sensation-seeking, sociable, lively, carefree extrovert; while at the other extreme there is the reserved, quiet introvert.

In terms of the functioning of the ANS, some individuals are characterized by a highly labile system that causes strong reactions to any unpleasant or painful stimulus. As with extroversion-introversion this has two consequences: first, the exceedingly strong reactions interfere with the process of conditioning; second, the individual's behaviour is marked by high levels of anxiety, depression and other emotional reactions. At the other end of the continuum are individuals with a stable ANS; such people condition well and do not display overly strong emotional reactions. Eysenck terms this personality dimension *Neuroticism* (N).

At a later date in the development of his theory Eysenck introduced a third personality dimension termed *Psychoticism* (P), which has continued to be developed and revised (Eysenck, Eysenck and Barrett, 1985). The biological mechanisms underlying psychoticism are not fully articulated and, indeed, the suggestion has been made that *psychopathy* might be a better term (Eysenck and Eysenck, 1972). Individuals scoring high on this dimension are characterized by aggressive, cold, and impersonal behaviour.

The important point to make is that P, E and N are separate dimensions of personality, as Eysenck and Gudjonsson (1989) note, 'In all three personality dimensions we are dealing with a continuum, with a majority of people at neither extreme, but rather in the middle' (p. 44). This situation is illustrated in Figure 3.1 for the E and N personality dimensions.

Now, if E and N are related to conditionability then it would be predicted that stable-introverts (Low N–Low E) will condition best; stable-extroverts (Low N–High E) and neurotic-introverts (High N–Low E) will be at some intermediate point; and neurotic-extroverts will condition least well (High N–High E). If conditionability is related to the development of control over antisocial behaviour and hence effective socialization, then it follows that offender groups should be characterized by the personality types associated with low conditionability and socialization — High N and High E. In addition, High P is also seen as a predictor of criminal behaviour although, as Furnham and Thompson (1991) state, 'it seems almost tautological to say that psychoticism is linked to criminality because the measurement of the former includes items that look very much like the latter' (p. 586).

As P, E and N are easily measured using simple pen and paper tests, Eysenck's theory immediately becomes one of the most testable in the history of criminology. There has been a multitude of studies conducted to test Eysenck's theory, many published in the 1970s, and there are a number of summaries available (Bartol, 1980; Eysenck, 1987; Feldman, 1977; Powell, 1977). The broad position is one of unanimous support for the prediction that offenders will score high on P; the majority of studies find higher N scores in offender samples; but the evidence for E is mixed, with some studies finding higher E scores in offender samples, others no difference between offenders and non-offenders, and a small number of studies finding *lower* E scores in offender groups.

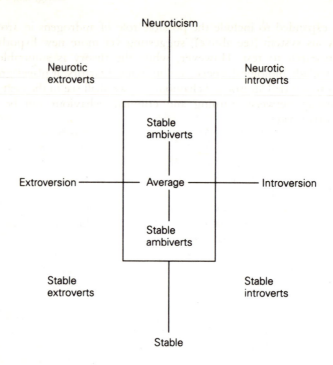

Figure 3.1. The personality dimensions of extraversion and neurorticism.

The problem with many studies, however, is that they have examined the personality traits in isolation from each other — Eysenck's theory suggested that *combinations* of personality traits would predict delinquency. In this light strong support for Eysenck's theory comes from studies that have looked for clusters of personality dimensions in offender and non-offender populations (see Hollin, 1989, for a summary). One such study was reported by McGurk and McDougall (1981), which used a cluster analysis to look at the P, E and N scores of samples of delinquents and non-delinquents. The analysis showed four personality clusters in each sample, with Low E–High N and High E–Low N types in both samples. The clusters predicted to be related to criminal behaviour, however — High E–High N and High P–High E–High N — were found only in the delinquent sample; a Low E–Low N group, predicted by the theory to be highly socialized, was found only in the non-delinquent group.

Eysenck's theory continues to generate both comment and empirical investigation, some favourable, others not. The criticisms include the particular view of personality inherent in the theory and, as Trasler (1987) points out, some of the basic assumptions relating to conditionability and its physiological correlates remain to be proved. Its positivistic, deterministic stance would also lead many commentators to distance themselves from theories of this type. Nonetheless, as evinced by Eysenck and Gudjonsson (1989), the theory continues to develop and several theoretical gaps have been filled. Indeed, the theory has expanded to include the possible role of androgens in arousability of the nervous system (see above), suggesting yet more new hypotheses for empirical research to test. However, while the theory is admirable for its attempt to include biological, social, and individual factors, it places great store on learning to control antisocial behaviour. As we shall see in the next chapter, the relationship between learning and criminal behaviour can be conceptualized in other ways.

Chapter 4

Explaining Criminal Behaviour: Learning, Cognition and Age

There are many, many attempts, offered by people from all walks of life, to explain why we are what we are. One of the earliest beliefs was that our actions are governed by mystical forces, by gods and demons who could inhabit our earthly bodies and mould our thoughts, words and deeds. Another ancient belief, found in the writings of the Greek teacher Hippocrates, is that it is biological forces that determine our personality and behaviour. While differing in emphasis, these time honoured beliefs in the forces of the spiritual and biological worlds have one important similarity — they locate the cause of behaviour *inside* the person. The emphasis on an inner world — be it biological, mental or spiritual — in seeking to explain our behaviour is also found in some philosophical and psychological theories. The ideas of Sigmund Freud are undoubtedly the most widely known and influential of such more contemporary theorists. The essence of Freud's position is that our outward, observable behaviour is the product of tension and conflict between inner forces. These inner forces, thought by Freud to be psychological in nature but biological in origin, were conceived of as part of an intricate psychodynamic system, active at both conscious and unconscious levels. While Freud followed a mentalistic path, other more recent theorists have taken a biological road. Again dating from the turn of the century, the thesis was developed by a number of eminent scientists, including Sir Francis Galton (1822–1911), that genetic forces govern the level of our mental abilities such as intelligence and hence directly influence our behaviour. Lombroso's views on criminal behaviour, discussed in the previous chapter, fall into a similar camp. Thus the search for an understanding of the causes of behaviour has a long history steeped in the tradition of looking inside the person to explain his or her outward and observable behaviour. The beginnings of a new and different way of explaining behaviour took place around the turn of this century, in the laboratories of the Russian physiologist Ivan Pavlov (1849–1936). The basis of this new approach lay in the phenomenon of classical conditioning or learning by association.

Learning by Association

Pavlov's research, for which he was awarded a Nobel prize, was concerned with the digestive system in canines, and it was while engaged in this work that Pavlov made what was to prove to be a momentous observation. He noticed that dogs who were accustomed to the laboratory salivated not only at the sight or smell of food, as would be expected of all dogs, but also to cues related to the presence of food such as the sound of the food pails. Hungry dogs salivate naturally to the sight or smell of food but why should these dogs salivate to the noise of clanking pails? The answer, as of course Pavlov discovered in his famous experiments, is to be found in the process of learning by association. Certain stimuli such as sights or sounds can become associated over time with a naturally occurring reflex response, such as salivation; as a result these environmental stimuli become able to elicit the reflex response. Thus the laboratory dogs had learned an association between a certain sound and the arrival of food, so that the sound itself was able to elicit the salivation even if no food was forthcoming. In other words, the salivation had become *conditional* on certain environmental events. This process of learning by association is called *classical conditioning.*

While the discovery of classical conditioning was important in itself, its conceptual basis had a fundamental impact on the future of psychological theorizing. Pavlov's work heralded the notion that behaviour could be explained not by recourse to mysterious inner forces, but by the interaction between the person (or animal) and the outside world. Thus, rather than seeing behaviour as the product of some biological or psychological force *inside* the person, an alternative understanding of the world could be formulated in which the emphasis was on events *external* to the person. This concept was to revolutionize the discipline of psychology as researchers turned directly to the study of behaviour, now treating behaviour as a phenomenon in its own right, rather than simply the by-product of some biological or psychodynamic force. The founding father of this new behavioural approach to psychology was the American psychologist John B. Watson (1878–1958), whose 1913 paper 'Psychology as the Behaviourist Views It', caught the mood of the times in an American university system ill at ease with the unscientific European mentalistic tradition.

Simply, Watson argued that humans, like other animals, are born with various innate stimulus–response reflexes such as the grasp reflex and the eyeblink reflex. Building on these primary reflexes through the process of classical conditioning, Watson argued, we learn more and more complex chains of behaviour. The role of psychology therefore was to formulate an understanding of such learning, thereby discovering the laws by which behaviour could be predicted and nurtured. With the benefit now of almost eighty years of research and debate we know that the acquisition and development of behaviour is almost certainly too complex to be reduced to chains of association originating with innate reflexes. In one sense, however, that hardly matters; it is the line of thought invoked by Watson and the following eighty years of research and debate which is important (which is not to say that classical conditioning can be dismissed — far from it as Rescorla (1988) shows — rather that other theories are needed to account for the richness of learning). Pavlov and Watson, rather like Freud, had set into motion a new way of thinking about the world, a way that looked not so much at the person but rather on the effect of the environment on the individual. The ripples of any new approach are bound to touch many different fields, and this was true for the notion of learning by association and theories of criminal behaviour.

Differential Association

The foundations for differential association were first laid by Sutherland (1939), and there have been various refinements since (e.g., Sutherland and Cressey, 1974). Sutherland begins his theory of criminal behaviour from the standpoint that crime itself is socially defined; there are within society some individuals who hold the power to define what behaviour will be tolerated and what will be deemed unacceptable or criminal. Thus the concept of crime, for Sutherland, cannot be divorced from sociological and political forces. However, Sutherland does not stop there — he asks the crucial question, why do some people obey the law while others do not? Or, in the terminology of differential association, why do some individuals hold definitions of acceptable behaviour different to and at odds with those defined by the law makers?

The answer that Sutherland favoured involved understanding each individual's personal learning experiences. In parallel with the learning theory of the time, Sutherland suggested that learning took place through the processes of *association* — association with other people favourably disposed towards crime. It is important to note that Sutherland is not suggesting that the association has to be with criminals, rather with people who might either encourage or fail to censure criminal acts. Sutherland set out a number of postulates, some of which are given below, that encapsulate his approach.

1 Criminal behaviour is learned.
2 The learning is through association with other people.
3 The main part of the learning takes place within close personal groups.
4 The learning includes techniques to carry out certain crimes and also specific attitudes and motives conducive towards committing crime.
5 The learning experiences — differential associations — will vary in frequency and importance for each individual.
6 The process of learning criminal behaviour is no different from the learning of any other behaviour.

Sutherland's theory is remarkable in the way that it anticipates much of what was to follow in both psychology and criminology. The theory is clearly sociological in its portrayal of powerful social forces defining the nature of crime. With its focus on the individual, however, it is also psychological in orientation. The proposition that crucial learning takes place through associations within intimate social groups and relationships is now to be found in contemporary social learning theory and in social structure theories in criminology. That each individual's learning experiences are unique has become a central tenet of learning theory over the past few decades. That the content of learning includes both skills and cognitions is exactly in line with contemporary learning theory, while cognition, particularly the notion of rational choice, has become one of the hot topics in criminology in the last few years. Finally, Sutherland's view that criminal behaviour is acquired behaviour and hence no different to any other behaviour stands in direct contrast to theories that portray criminal behaviour as evidence of some underlying psychopathology. Such a non-pathological view of criminal behaviour is very much in harmony with the views of many contemporary criminologists and psychologists.

While, to my way of thinking, Sutherland set the agenda for the following generations of researchers and theorists, his theory leaves many questions to be answered. How exactly does learning take place?; what is the nature of the social conditions that are conducive towards learning criminal skills and attitudes?; what is the relationship between attitudes and skills? At the time he was writing, Sutherland did not have the theoretical or empirical base from which he could begin to answer these and other questions. However, with the benefits of decades of research some progress has been made.

If we move on from Watson's behaviourism to the next significant theoretical step we encounter the individual destined to become the most influential figure in the history of psychology. (This judgment of eminence is not mere personal whimsy — see Korn, Davis and Davis, 1991.) Between 1930 and 1935 this young researcher at Harvard University developed the basic concepts for a new way of analyzing and understanding behaviour. This new approach was called *behaviour analysis* and its proponent was the American psychologist B.F. Skinner (1904–1990).

Behaviour Analysis: Learning by Consequences

As Kazdin (1979) notes, one of the great errors made in many textbooks is to dismiss the principles of behaviour analysis as simplistic and mechanistic. While the foundations of behaviour analysis may be understandable, the philosophical and theoretical issues are complex and taxing. It is not my aim to discuss here these theoretical issues in depth, however. Any readers who wish to grapple with the complexities of behaviourism should attempt the recent books by Catania and Harnad (1988), Hayes (1989), Lee (1988), Modgil and Modgil (1987), Rachlin (1991) and Zuriff (1985).

The basis for Skinner's contribution can be traced to a line of research — perhaps most often associated with the American psychologist Edward Thorndike (1874–1949) — concerned with the relationship between the outcome a behaviour produces and the probability of that same behaviour recurring in the future. Skinner's quest was to understand this relationship between behaviour and its consequences. As was the fashion in psychology research in the 1920s and 1930s, Skinner's early studies were conducted with animals such as rats, pigeons and squirrels. In a typical study the animal would be placed in a closed box — now known as a Skinner Box — and its behaviour closely observed and recorded. The use of a closed environment such as a box allows the researcher to control events and so see precisely their effect on behaviour.

When placed in a Skinner Box the animal, say a rat, will explore its new environment; the Skinner Box contains a bar and when the rat approaches the bar the researcher arranges for food to be delivered into a tray inside the box. After eating, the rat will return to the bar and explore further, eventually placing its front paws on the bar. With a click, the bar drops down and food is automatically delivered into the tray. Very quickly the rat learns that through its behaviour, the bar press, it can operate on its environment to produce various consequences (food in this example, although many other consequences are possible, such as drink, access to other rats, and so forth). This type of behaviour, that which operates on the environment to produce specific consequences, Skinner called *operant* behaviour and hence this type of learning, *operant learning*. The relationship between behaviour and its consequences is called a *contingency*, and Skinner formulated the principles of two important types of contingency which he termed *reinforcement* and *punishment*.

Reinforcement

A reinforcement contingency is defined as a situation in which the consequences of a behaviour *increase* the likelihood of that behaviour occurring in the future. There are two types of reinforcement contingency — positive reinforcement and negative reinforcement. *Positive* reinforcement takes place when behaviour is either maintained or increased by producing consequences which the person (or animal) finds rewarding. *Negative* reinforcement, on the other hand, is when the behaviour produces the consequence of avoiding or escaping from an aversive situation. It is important to note that there is no law about what is and is not reinforcing. It is easy to assume that the same things, such as money or praise, are rewarding for everyone. This is not the case; for example, some people, perhaps particularly adolescents, find praise far from rewarding (Brophy, 1981). Alternatively, what might be seen by most people as unrewarding or even aversive, such as verbal or physical abuse, can in extreme situations act as a reward for some people and so reinforce their behaviour.

Punishment

The term 'punishment' as used in behaviour analysis has a different meaning to that found in everyday usage. A punishment contingency is one in which the consequences of a behaviour are related to a *decrease* in the frequency of that behaviour. As with reinforcement there are two types of punishment, sometimes termed positive and negative punishment, which can be used to change behaviour. With positive punishment the behaviour decreases because it produces an outcome that the person finds aversive. Negative punishment, on the other hand, is when the behaviour has the consequence of a loss of something the person finds rewarding. It is important to emphasize that in the sense used by behaviour analysts the term punishment refers to a particular relationship between behaviour and its consequences; it does not mean physical pain or highly distressing events.

Three-term contingency

Having considered behaviour and its consequences there is one more factor to include to complete this brief introduction to behaviour analysis. Behaviour, in the main, does not happen at random, typically environmental events signal to us that if we act in a certain way, then on that occasion our behaviour is likely to be reinforced or punished. The relationship between setting or antecedent events, the behaviour and the consequences is called a *three-term contingency*, giving rise to the much used A:B:C analysis — *A*ntecedent: *B*ehaviour: *C*onsequence. The goal in conducting a behavioural analysis is, through an A:B:C formulation, to understand the *function* of a behaviour in terms of its reinforcement and punishment contingencies for the individual concerned. Hence an A:B:C analysis is properly referred to a *functional analysis*. While it is historically true that the principles of behaviour analysis were formulated in studies with animals, often referred to as the *experimental* analysis of behaviour, the task of *applied* behaviour analysis is to use these principles to understand human behaviour in the real world.

Differential Reinforcement Theory

The elucidation of the principles of operant learning were applied to criminal behaviour as an extension of differential association theory in that they offered a means to account for the way in which behaviour could be both acquired and maintained. Jeffery (1965) suggested that criminal behaviour is operant behaviour; that is, within the context of the associations that an individual experiences, criminal behaviour is acquired and maintained by the reinforcing consequences it produces for the offender. Further, criminal behaviour will take place when the setting events signal that it is likely to produce the rewarding outcome the person desires. Thus, in order to understand why a person commits a crime, it is necessary to understand that individual's learning history and the rewarding consequences of the criminal behaviour. One needs, therefore, to understand not only the person, but also the nature of the environment in which they live.

In most instances of acquisitive crime — burglary, embezzlement, theft — the rewards are financial and material gain. Such rewards can be positively rewarding in themselves, or negatively rewarding in that they allow the person to avoid the aversive situation of having no money. However, as well as material rewards, criminal behaviour can produce social rewards, a theme that will be returned to in Chapter 5.

Jeffery also made the point that criminal behaviour can produce aversive consequences — being arrested, loss of liberty, disruption of family relationships — that might have a punishing (in the operant sense of the word) effect on behaviour. Overall, it is the balance of previous reinforcement and punishment in a person's life that determines the likelihood of criminal behaviour when the opportunity presents itself. In keeping with operant principles, each person will have their own unique learning history. The following case study illustrates the use of applied behaviour analysis with an individual who had attempted multiple murder.

A Behavioural Analysis of Attempted Multiple Murder

This case study is taken from a longer paper by Gresswell and Hollin (in press). I am grateful to Mark Gresswell for agreeing that I could reproduce some of the details here.

DB is a man who had formulated a plan to kill twenty people. He had attacked two victims by the time he was caught by the police; fortunately both victims survived the attacks and DB pleaded guilty to two counts of attempted murder. Psychiatrically diagnosed as having a psychopathic disorder, he is at present detained for treatment at a maximum security hospital without limit of time. From painstaking interviews with DB, his family and his former GP, together with careful collation of information from police and medical files, we were able to construct the following sequence of events. It is, however, important to note at the outset that, while every effort has been made to check and double-check the accuracy of the facts, the formulation is our systematic interpretation of events. We do not claim that this is absolutely correct or the only way to proceed; what we do claim is that our analysis makes sense of a morass of information to allow us both to understand what happened and to begin to generate targets for rehabilitation. That is as much as any practitioner, regardless of their profession or theoretical persuasion, can hope to achieve.

DB's childhood and adolescence were marked by an unhappy relationship with his immediate family, by the development of cystic acne as he grew older, and difficulties in forming relationships with his peers. DB reports that he coped with these stresses by constructing fantasies in which his parents loved him, he took revenge on those who mocked his appearance by disfiguring them, and a miracle cure for his acne suddenly appeared. To make these fantasies seem more real and powerful, he secretly spied on people to gain knowledge about them, while also making journeys to the wasteland where he imagined making his attacks. Despite the relief afforded by these fantasies, DB made several suicide attempts during this period in his life.

These details can be summarized in an A:B:C format as follows:

    A: Family functioning, rejected and tormented at school
    B: Fantasies, suicide
    C: Social isolation

Key Learning: *He is different to other people; fantasy offers an escape and makes him feel good.*

At the age of 19 DB left his job as a printer because of the tormenting from his workmates to begin work in a shop. This new job gave him training in sales techniques which was important for two reasons: it gave him the skills to interact effectively with other people; and if he was rejected it was the 'salesman' not the 'real DB' that was being rejected. He enjoyed the new job and became a successful sales assistant, recalling that customers and staff were friendly towards him; however the problem was that it was the 'salesman' not the 'real DB' that was popular. He began to invent an imaginary social life, involving friends, activities and holidays, so that his colleagues would think him successful in his private life as well as at work. This strategy was successful, despite DB's fears of being caught out and one further suicide attempt, and his career as a salesperson progressed satisfactorily as he moved to a larger store and developed his sales skills still further. However, in order to enjoy the use of his sales techniques, he devised a game that he called 'musical coat hangers' in which he would toy with customers by having them try on as many clothes as possible.

A: *Sequence as above, change of employment, sales training*
B: *Success at new job, lying to colleagues*
C: *Customers and staff are friendly, private social isolation*

Key Learning: *He can manipulate other people's behaviour; he can appear normal by lying; he is vulnerable to discovery.*

After a period of stability, the next major event took place when DB was 29 and he was told by his plastic surgeon that no more could be done to relieve his acne scarring. He felt that all his hopes had been quashed and he no longer had the rationalization of waiting for a cure before forming real close relationships. Shortly after being given the medical news, his mother died of cancer and his relationship with his father deteriorated still further, with the result that he moved away from home to live on his own in a council flat. Living alone his sense of isolation increased and he reports being more anxious and lonely, being preoccupied with thoughts of death and the after-life, and intense feelings of hostility towards those people who are successful in life. As in his earlier life when faced with stressful situations, he began to construct fantasies of revenge, specifically thoughts of a massacre at work. To enhance the power of his fantasy — in exactly the same way that he had visited the wasteland as an adolescent — he started taking a knife into work. This was discovered by the occupational health nurse, whom he was seeing for his anxiety, who asked him not to do this and he left the weapon at home. His GP finally referred him to the local lay counselling service.

A: *Sequences as above, medical news, mother's death*
B: *Leaves home, increasing personal difficulties, revenge fantasy, enactment of elements of fantasy*
C: *Increased social isolation, involvement of counselling services*

Key Learning: *Real life enactment of elements of fantasies offers a sense of power and satisfaction as well as relief from personal problems*

After a time DB's anxieties increased to the point where his fantasies offered little relief; in desperation he took his knife to his GP's and told him of his massacre fantasy. The GP persuaded him to leave the knife and made an unsuccessful referral for psychiatric assessment. DB then made threats to his counsellor but it was not until he returned to the GP's the following week claiming to have taken an overdose that he was admitted to the local psychiatric hospital. After a stay lasting one month he was discharged and returned to work after a further six weeks' sick leave. It was during this time on sick leave that Michael Ryan perpetrated the Hungerford massacre.

The Hungerford massacre was important for DB in two ways: it reassured him that there were other men like him, that he was not alone in his anger against society; but it made him feel inferior to men who were prepared to act out their feelings. He made a decision to 'beat' Ryan's total of twenty killings.

From late summer he began to prowl his local area at night, seeking to identify two types of potential victim: the first were successful, rich, good looking people on whom he could take revenge for his own social failings; the second were people whom he thought would make interesting companions in the after-life. He found the prowling to be exciting now that he had a firm purpose, and he added to this by peering through open curtains and stealing and reading mail. This secret observation of other people and learning their personal details can be seen as a re-emergence of the strategies he used during childhood. The observation eventually turned to action: he began vandalizing property, damaging cars, and throwing stones at courting couples. Once he was stopped in his car by the police, the thrill of this was intensified by having a knife in the car. Eventually even these adventures began to pale so that by late spring the lighter nights began to make his nocturnal outings seem more trouble than they were worth. Something else was going to have to happen.

In late spring a woman was attacked near DB's home and he was interviewed by the police in their door-to-door enquiries; while this attack was not carried out by DB (someone else has subsequently been convicted) it proved to be the final push to action. On a Friday night he purchased a crowbar to use as a weapon and went out prowling; on the Saturday he again went out prowling and committed minor acts of vandalism at the home of his GP and another house in the same street. On the Sunday night he returned to the house in the GP's street that he had damaged the night before and, using a rehearsed plan of pretending to be a motorist whose car had broken down, gained access to the house. Once inside he attacked the elderly female householder with a wooden dowelling club, intending to render her unconscious before killing her. However, he had underestimated the amount of force needed to subdue her and he fled when his club broke.

DB reported that while his attempt had failed he felt that his plan had gone well; he had seen the fear in his victim's eyes and now she would be like him, never to know peace of mind.

The next night DB went to a local park armed with a knife, intending to slash a victim's face so that they, like him, would know what it was like to be disfigured for life. Despite a wait of several hours, no suitable victim presented themselves; and next night the same pattern was repeated. Frustrated, he returned, on that second night, to the town to select a victim from the people he had previously spied on. Selecting a house he pulled his car up out of sight on the drive leading to the house waiting for his intended victims to return home. When the houseowners arrived, the man spotted DB and left his wife in the car to approach and challenge DB. DB stabbed him in the chest, then got back into his own car and drove away. The second victim and his wife were able to alert the police and DB was arrested before he was able to get back home.

This then enables a final formulation to be made of the final, tragic stages in the total sequence.

A: Sequences as above, Hungerford and other attack
B: Decides to turn fantasy into action, excitement of prowling, escalation with petty acts of vandalism, final acts of extreme violence
C: Victim's fear reinforces violent actions; caught by police.

Now in a secure hospital, it is doubtful that DB will be released back into the community for many years to come.

Social Learning Theory

As the early psychological research matured and began to move away from controlled animal studies and into the real world two major issues emerged. First, the complexity of most people's lives makes it impossible to discover every event in their learning history. Second, people differ from animals in a number of important ways — principally in our cognitive abilities, in our highly evolved use of verbal language, and in our social environment — which necessitates adjustments in the principles derived from animal studies. A number of points follow from these two difficulties. The first is that the completeness of a functional analysis will always be limited; the second is that applied behaviour analysis depends on the skill and ability of the analyst, it cannot be reduced to rigid, mechanical formulas; third, our understanding of the place of 'human' factors in behaviour analysis is constantly changing as research progresses (e.g., Lowe, 1983).

The 'Problem' of Private Events

In seeking to establish a scientific basis for the then emerging discipline of psychology, Watson favoured the view that because the private world inside the skin is impossible to study scientifically it should not be of concern to the psychologist. One of the unfortunate legacies of Watson's behaviourism that persists to the present day is the criticism that behaviourism denies the existence of, or at best ignores, 'private' events such as thoughts and feelings. Contemporary behaviourism does not, of course, take this view; indeed, as Skinner (1974) states, 'A science of behaviour must consider the place of private stimuli. . . . The question, then is this: What is inside the skin and how do we know about it? The answer is, I believe, the heart of radical behaviourism' (pp. 211–12). In part answer to his own question, Skinner (1986) has suggested the place of private events in a sequence as follows: 'In a given episode the environment acts upon the organism, something happens inside, the organism then acts upon the environment, and certain consequences follow' (p. 716).

The key issue which arises, and which is the essence of the 'problem', is whether what happens inside the skin should be considered as behaviour, and hence be part of behaviour analysis, or whether private events should be accorded a different, perhaps mentalistic or spiritualistic, status and so fall outside the realms of behaviour analysis. The view of applied behaviour analysis is that private events are behaviours and so can be understood within the terms of behaviour analysis. That is, private events are seen as being established by a particular environment, and they are maintained and modified by environmental consequences.

Do private events cause — i.e., reinforce or punish — behaviour? Again Skinner is clear: 'Private events . . . may be called causes, but not initiating causes' (see Catania and Harnad, 1988, p. 486). The initiation of all behaviour, including private behaviour, is to be found in the environment — most often our social world. Once initiated, however, one behaviour can lead to another and so on; thus triggered by environmental cues, private behaviour such as thoughts and emotions can be the first step towards overt, observable behaviour.

The practical difficulty in settling the philosophical conundrum posed by private events lies in gaining access to those events inside the skin. By definition, private events are not observable and so we must rely on self-report to find out about them. The problems here are concerned with the accuracy and reliability of self-reported information. Self-report can be unreliable for a number of reasons: the person may want to withhold the truth; or the very act of self-observation can change the nature and functioning of the private event; or some private events may in part occur outside awareness, such as when dreaming, and so are not amenable to self-observation. It may be that as scientific technology progresses these problems will be overcome, but at present we must work within these limitations. One theory that seeks to develop further behavioural theory, principally in its treatment of private events, was elaborated by the American psychologist Albert Bandura — this theory is social learning theory.

Social learning theory is in part an extension of operant principles, but with modifications in the role and status of cognitions with respect to the acquisition and initiation of behaviour (Bandura, 1977, 1986). In operant theory behaviour is acquired through reinforcement and punishment; social learning theory extends the process of acquisition to include learning by imitation. Through observation of the behaviour of other people, termed *models*, we learn at a cognitive level actions that we may later try for ourselves in order to gain some rewarding outcome. In operant theory behaviour is initiated and reinforced by the environment; however Bandura prefers the use of the term 'motivation' to reinforcement to explain the initiation of behaviour. Motivation can take three forms: *external reinforcement*, as in operant learning; *vicarious reinforcement*, gained from observing other people; and *self-reinforcement*, as in a sense of pride or achievement in what we do. The introduction of motivation as a cause of behaviour, as well as the introduction of internal as well as external reinforcement, marks a clear divergence from operant behaviourism. While social learning theory retains some overlap with applied behaviour analysis, there are areas where the two theories are clearly at odds.

Social Learning Theory and Criminal Behaviour

The ideas and concepts from social learning theory have been applied to the study of criminal behaviour by both psychologists (e.g., Nietzel, 1979) and criminologists and sociologists (e.g., Krohn, Massey and Skinner, 1987). Ronald Akers, based at the Department of Sociology at the University of Florida, is perhaps most closely identified with attempts within mainstream criminology to develop a theory of crime based on elements from differential association theory, reinforcement theory, and social learning theory (Akers, 1985).

From the perspective of social learning theory, the acquisition of criminal behaviour — in terms of both attitudes and skills as proposed by differential association theory — is accounted for either through direct reinforcement, as in operant terms, or via modelling and imitation. The models for behaviour, including criminal behaviour, are to be found in the social environment: in the behaviour of friends and family, in the prevalent subculture, and in sources of cultural symbols such as television, magazines, and books. Criminal behaviour is similarly maintained by a social environment that provides a range of rewards for successful criminal acts; these include tangible, financial rewards, and social rewards such as peer group status. In addition there may be personal rewards such as a sense of pride and increased self-esteem in successfully stealing a car or avoiding detection for a burglary.

In keeping with Sutherland's original theory, Akers also turns to the definitions or meanings of the criminal behaviour for the offender. These definitions may be positive, so that criminal behaviour is seen as desirable or permissible; for example, car thieves may argue that it is desirable to steal cars to experience the joy of driving. Alternatively, definitions may be neutralizing, so that they negate the impact of what are considered to be intolerable behaviours; for example, tax dodgers may agree that it is wrong to steal, but neutralize their wrongdoing by arguing that in their case the sums involved are very small, or that as there is no 'real' victim then no harm is done. These definitions, which clearly involve sophisticated cognitive processes, set the meaning of the criminal behaviour for the individual concerned; as such they constitute a highly personalized aspect of the individual's criminality.

Social learning theory is perhaps the most psychologically complete mainstream theory in criminology, as Akers (1990) notes:

> The full behavioral formula in social learning theory includes both positive and negative punishment and positive and negative reinforcement. It also includes schedules of reinforcement, imitation, associations, normative definitions (attitudes and rationalizations), discriminative stimuli, and other variables in both criminal and conforming behavior (p. 660).

More recent research following a social learning approach has focused on two aspects of delinquent functioning — social cognition and social skills (Hollin, 1990a; Ross and Fabiano, 1985). Social cognition is discussed below; social skills are covered in Chapter 5.

Cognition and Crime

Social Cognition

Ross and Fabiano (1985) make the distinction between *im*personal cognition and *inter*personal cognition. The former deals with our knowledge of the physical world; the latter is concerned with our attitudes and beliefs about other people, their behaviour, and our own behaviour in relation to other people. A number of types and styles of social cognition have been associated with criminal behaviour and these are briefly described below.

Empathy

The ability to see things from the other person's point of view, to show empathy, is an important part of social cognition. A number of studies, although not all, have suggested that offenders do not score highly on measures of empathy (e.g., Kaplan and Arbuthnot, 1985). The lack of unanimity in the research findings may be due to a number of variables such as differences in empathy according to the offender's age and sex, and with the type of offence.

Locus of control

The term locus of control refers to the degree to which an individual perceives their behaviour to be under their own *internal* control, or under the control of *external* forces such as luck or people in positions of authority. Some studies have shown that offenders tend to see themselves as being externally controlled; that is, they see their behaviour as being caused and maintained by forces outside their own personal control (Beck and Ollendick, 1976). Again the findings are not unanimous which may be due to variations between studies such as type of offence; for example, violent young offenders have been shown to display greater external control than non-violent young offenders (Hollin and Wheeler, 1982).

Moral reasoning

Moral reasoning is a part of social cognition that has been particularly associated with criminal behaviour in young people. Specifically, delinquency is thought to be associated with a delay in the development and maturation of moral reasoning. When the opportunity arises, the person has not developed the cognitive ability to control and resist the temptation to offend. While there is some research evidence in support of this position (Nelson, Smith and Dodd, 1990), it is probable that the strength of the relationship varies in accord with other factors; for example, a study carried out by Thornton and Reid (1982) showed that young offenders who had committed offences without financial gain (assault, murder, sex offences) showed more mature moral judgment than another group of young offenders who had committed crimes of acquisition (burglary, robbery, theft, fraud).

Self-control and impulsivity

A lack of self-control is often linked to impulsive behaviour, sometimes described as the failure to stop and think between impulse and action. Some studies have shown that delinquents are characterized by high levels of impulsivity (e.g., Rotenberg and Nachshon, 1979); although, probably for the reasons already noted above, not all studies have found this link between low self-control and delinquency.

Social problem solving

Our social world continually sets us problems with regard to our relationship with other people. In order to negotiate successfully interpersonal problems we need to have the ability to weigh up the situation, generate possible courses of action, consider the various outcomes that might follow, and plan how to achieve our desired outcomes. A number of studies have shown that compared to non-delinquents, offenders use a more limited range of alternatives to solve interpersonal problems, and rely more on verbal and physical aggression (e.g., Slaby and Guerra, 1988). This appears to hold true for both male and female offenders. (This particular aspect of social cognition is also discussed in Chapter 5.)

Rational Choice

As Akers (1990) forcefully argues, it is debatable whether rational choice constitutes a unique theoretical approach to criminal behaviour. However, the concept of rational choice does serve at least two important functions: first, it heralds the re-emergence of a classical philosophy of crime; second, it marks a clear distinction between behavioural (i.e., differential association, differential reinforcement, and social learning theory) and cognitive theories of crime.

Most psychological and some sociological research into criminal behaviour is 'dispositional' in orientation; that is, it seeks to account for the individual, social, cultural, and legal variables that will interact at a given time in a given place to dispose the person towards an act of criminal behaviour. Such a dispositional account necessarily involves a multitude of factors such as biology, cognition and emotion, and action on the person side of the interaction, and an array of environmental factors, such as family, education, peer group, and the legal system on the other side of a highly complex interaction. During the 1970s there was a growing disenchantment among some theorists with this dispositional approach to understanding crime. A new approach began to emerge with its roots in the view that our actions are motivated by self-interest; rather than attempting to generate sophisticated models — based on research findings from biology, psychology, and sociology — to explain the acquisition and maintenance of criminal behaviour, the emphasis shifts to the economic concept of *expected utility*. A quote I have used previously (Hollin, 1989), simply because it illustrates this approach with such clarity, comes from a paper by Van Den Haag (1982):

> I do not see any relevant difference between dentistry and prostitution or car theft, except that the latter do not require a license....The frequency of rape, or of mugging, is essentially determined by the

expected comparative net advantage, just as is the rate of dentistry and burglary. The comparative net advantage consists in the satisfaction (produced by the money or by the violative act itself) expected from the crime, less the expected cost of achieving it, compared to the net satisfaction expected from other activities in which the offender has the opportunity to engage. Cost in the main equals the expected penalty divided by the risk of suffering it (pp. 1026–7).

In order for a crime to take place, according to this theoretical view, two events must coincide; there must first be the opportunity for the offence to take place, then the person must decide that the potential gains outweigh the potential losses and therefore choose to act in order to take advantage of the opportunity. The decision to offend is seen as an act of rational decision-making, in which the offender takes into account such factors as the likelihood of detection and the ease of success. A body of research evidence has amassed that shows that crime rates do appear to be related to increased opportunity, and that, in some cases at least, offenders do make rational choices when confronted with the opportunity to offend (Cornish and Clarke, 1986). Take, for example, the crime of burglary: there is a strong argument that the increase in burglaries over the past few years can be accounted for in terms of increased opportunity. As more family members go out to work, so houses are empty for longer periods of time. Recognizing this opportunity, the offender will decide to burgle an empty house, specifically choosing a home that displays signs such as not having a dog, no burglar alarm, and easy access to the rear of the property to avoid detection.

The issue at the heart of the division between the dispositional and rational decision-making theorists centres on the role and functioning of cognition. There is a long-standing tradition in this debate that battle lines are drawn between, on one side, the *determinists*, and on the other, proponents of *free will*. In keeping with the former position, one way of conceptualizing cognition is suggested by Ross and Fabiano (1985): 'Social cognitive skills are *learned* skills: their acquisition is very strongly influenced by environmental factors' (p. 143). Thus, if we follow the standpoint advocated by Ross and Fabiano, then we see that offenders are disposed to think in certain ways. Thus, we might account for the burglar's actions by saying that, given certain circumstances, personal and environmental factors had culminated to dispose him or her to engage in cognitions that led to the decision to commit the burglary. The process of decision-making may have been entirely rational, but the disposition to reach the final decision was determined by individual and environmental factors. Thus Roshier (1989) suggests that: '*Determinism*, in the more general positivist sense, means that crime is seen as *behaviour* that is *caused* by biological, psychological or social factors, depending on the academic origins of the criminologist concerned' (p. 21). (Personally I prefer the term *disposition* to *cause*. I doubt whether many empirical researchers would be happy to say that they had discovered a specific cause of criminal behaviour; they may be more likely to say they had identified some factor associated with crime and hence likely to dispose some individuals towards criminal activity.)

Standing opposed to dispositional theories is the view that we are free to act as we will and, of course, most of our actions are rational: 'The goal of our rationality is personal satisfaction; rational self-interest is the key motivational characteristic that governs our relationship with crime and conformity' (Roshier, 1989, pp. 14–15). This particular view is, as discussed in Chapter 1, espoused by adherents of classical criminology. The criminal is simply a person who rationally decides, of his or her own free will, to take advantage for personal gain of an opportunity to commit an act forbidden by law. In this sense we all stand equal before the law; we have all got the same choice to make in yielding to the temptation to err.

Which view is correct? The debate about free will versus determinism is centuries old and is unlikely to be resolved in the near future; for oneself it is a question of reading the evidence and attempting to reach a personal preference. Both sides present a coherent argument, neither side have the command of empirical data to support their position; indeed it is difficult to see where the supporting data comes from. Both sides of the debate have their problems, principally that neither can demonstrate the existence of their central tenet. Despite many hundreds, probably thousands, of studies we remain without a real understanding of the dynamics that produces a disposition to criminal behaviour. On the other hand, proponents of classical criminology are apparently untroubled by questions of aetiology:

> If human action expresses motives and purposes, a question that arises is where the motives for *criminal* action come from. . . . The classical answer is simply that they are there; they are taken as given. They are part of a conception of human rationality which . . . is one of the starting assumptions of classical criminology (Roshier, 1989, p. 72).

For the future it seems likely that both sides will continue to refine and develop their arguments, perhaps one day merging into a grand theory of human action. Until then research and argument continue in both camps. In the classical field there is movement towards a postclassical perspective which seeks to incorporate social, political, and economic factors into that particular understanding of crime. On the dispositional side, there are the developments in biology and psychology outlined in this and other texts, as well, of course, as in sociology and criminology. One particular development, with a strong psychological component, lies in the developmental studies of age and crime.

Age and Crime

One of the problems faced by researchers in many fields is to devise a methodology that will enable them to chart the unfolding of a given behaviour. A snapshot of an individual's functioning and circumstances at a given time and in a given place can be informative, but how much better if we could watch from the beginning the whole movie of an individual's life. Snapshot research, which represents the bulk of research in the social sciences, is generally called *cross-sectional* research; life-span research, of which there is comparatively little, is usually called *longitudinal* research. It is not difficult to see why cross-sectional research dominates the literature; a thorough, prospective longitudinal study demands that a number of people — usually hundreds, and termed a *cohort* — are followed and repeatedly tested and interviewed from childhood to adulthood. This demands great continuity among the researchers engaged in the study, not to mention extensive long-term funding for such an undertaking. Despite the practical difficulties, there are a number of longitudinal studies — across a range of fields such as temperament and personality, schizophrenia, and drug use (Robins and Rutter, 1990) — with the twin aims of investigating whether behaviour is stable from early to later life, and to search for childhood predictors of adverse outcomes in adolescence and adulthood.

There are strong arguments for such a longitudinal approach to the study of criminal behaviour (Farrington, Ohlin and Wilson, 1986) and, indeed, several longitudinal studies have been reported. The findings of these studies will be briefly discussed here, focusing first on what they tell us about patterns of juvenile offending, then moving to the identification of early predictors of adult offending.

Juvenile Crime

What types of offences do young people commit? How many young people commit criminal offences? The distinction can be made between *status* offences and *index* (or *notifiable*) offences. Status offences are those acts which apply only to young people and not to adults — acts such as truancy, drinking alcohol, and driving a motor vehicle under age. Index offences, on the other hand, are serious offences — such as murder, rape and sexual assault, burglary, arson, robbery — which are criminal acts regardless of the age of the perpetrator. Young people do commit both status and index offences but, to turn to the second question, how many young people commit offences?

If we consider both status and index offences, then the research estimates very high — figures in excess of 80 per cent of the population are not uncommon — rates of offending among adolescents. Indeed, Farrington (1987) suggests that if unrecorded offences were included alongside the official figures, this would 'undoubtedly push these figures close to 100 per cent' (p. 34). What percentage of these juvenile offences are status offences as opposed to serious index offences? Farrington (1987) states that in both England and the United States about 30 per cent of criminals apprehended for serious crimes are juveniles. As this figure is based on official records it can, of course, only include those offences known to the authorities. It is possible therefore that more adolescents are committing serious offences than this figure suggests. How many more is a matter for conjecture, but it is highly unlikely that the number of serious offences even begins to approach the high levels of status offences.

While statistics of this type tell us something about rates of delinquency, they do not tell the whole story. As with crime statistics generally (see Chapter 2) it is important to distinguish *prevalence* and *incidence*. Thus, in the specific area of juvenile crime, prevalence rates refer to the number of young people committing offences, while incidence rates are the number of offences committed per young offender. The force of this distinction is seen in the findings of the studies looking at the relationship between age and offending. It is well established that for the adolescent population delinquency rates consistently increase from about 8 years of age, reach a peak at about 16–17 years of age, then rapidly decline into the late teens and early twenties (e.g., Farrington, 1986). However, is this relationship between age and crime due to increasing prevalence, i.e., more young people committing crimes; or is it due to a rise in incidence, i.e., the young people who commit crimes committing more offences as they grow older? It is difficult for researchers to disentangle absolutely prevalence and incidence rates, but there seems to be agreement that the rise in rates of offending with age reflects a rise in prevalence not incidence. Thus, from their longitudinal study carried out in the United States, Wolfgang, Thornberry, and Figlio (1987) reach the conclusion that the peak in rates of offending at 16–17 years of age is due 'almost entirely to an increase in the number of active offenders and not to an increase in their annual "productivity"' (p. 44).

Can we conclude from this that the general message from research on age and offending is that if young people are left alone they will 'grow out' of delinquency? While it is tempting to think so, this is highly unlikely to be true for all offenders. While most of the offences committed by adolescents are relatively trivial in nature, the longitudinal studies have identified a number of factors associated with long-term offending.

Predictors of Long-Term Offending

One of the benefits of longitudinal research is that once the data are collected they enable the investigators to look back and try to identify any early factors that differentiated those who do and do not display a given behaviour. With regard to criminal behaviour, the Cambridge Study in Delinquent Development is the most widely cited longitudinal study conducted in Great Britain. This study began in 1961 with a cohort of 411 young males, aged 8–9 years, and is currently in progress with 94 per cent of the sample still alive as they reach the age of 32 years. The study has involved repeated testing and interviewing of not only the males in the cohort, but also their parents, peers, and schoolteachers; in addition, the researchers have had access to official records. This methodology has allowed a vast range of data to be collected on the individual members of the cohort, parental child-rearing practices, economic factors, school behaviour, and so on. The main results of the Cambridge Study have been published in four books and over sixty journal articles, with summaries made available by West (1982) and Farrington and West (1990). Obviously only the briefest overview is possible here. It should also be noted at the outset that as the cohort used in this study consisted entirely of males, its findings are therefore restricted to male patterns of behaviour.

Looking first at offending, approximately 20 per cent of the cohort in the Cambridge Study were convicted as juveniles, with about 33 per cent convicted up to the age of 25 years. Self-reported delinquency proved to be a reasonable match with official convictions; that is, the males who were convicted also self-reported the greatest intensity of delinquent acts. Thus it proved possible at each stage of the study to compare the worst offenders with the remainder of the cohort.

With regard to childhood experiences — childhood being defined as up to their tenth birthday (the age of criminal responsibility in England and Wales) — there were marked effects, described by Farrington and West (1990):

> The future juvenile delinquents were more likely to have been rated troublesome and dishonest in their primary schools. They tended to come from the poorer families, to come from the larger-sized families, to be living in poor houses with neglected interiors, to be supported by social agencies, and to be physically neglected by their parents. However, they did not tend to come from low socio-economic status families (as measured by occupational prestige) or to have working mothers. The delinquents were more likely to have criminal parents and delinquent older siblings (p. 118).

Thus for the juvenile-delinquents-to-be there emerges a picture of a childhood characterized by broken homes and harsh parenting, of early behaviour seen as troublesome — impulsive, hyperactive, attention deficient, daring, unpopular with peers — by authority figures, and poor attainment on intelligence and educational tests. In addition, those young males committing their first serious offence at an early age, and those adolescents who accumulate more than six criminal convictions, are at greatest risk of progressing to an adult criminal career (Farrington, 1983).

Moving to the age of 18 years, the offenders in the cohort had taken to a life-style characterized by heavy drinking, sexual promiscuity, drug use, and minor crimes involving motor vehicles or group violence and vandalism. In terms of frequency of criminal behaviour, the offenders committed more offences while unemployed rather than while in employment. Interestingly, the types of crime committed while unemployed were for financial reward — theft, burglary, fraud — not crimes against the persons. This accords with the previously expressed view of *negative* reinforcement of criminal behaviour; that is, the crime is committed to avoid the aversive position of having no money. The formation of close relationships in early adulthood was found to be related to a *decrease* in offending. Specifically, those offenders who married showed a decrease in offending — with the proviso that their partner was not a convicted offender.

The most recent data in the Cambridge Study were collected when the cohort had reached 32 years of age. Farrington and West (1990) paint a bleak

Table 4.1:   Early factors associated with juvenile offending (after West, 1982)

'Troublesome' at primary school
Low family income
Large family size
Criminal parent
Harsh child-rearing
Lower quartile of IQ

picture of the life of those men who had continued to offend and be convicted as adults:

> *Convicted* men differed significantly from unconvicted ones at age 32 in most respects of their lives: in having less home ownership, more residential mobility, more divorce or separation from their wives, more conflict with their wives or cohabitees, more separation from their children, more unemployment, lower take-home pay, more evenings out, more fights, more heavy smoking, more drunk driving, more heavy drinking, more drug-taking, more theft from work, and more other types of offences. . . . While convicted and unconvicted men were significantly different in many respects, it should not be concluded that all convicted men were more deviant than all unconvicted men. The two groups overlapped significantly (p. 126).

'Social failure', to use Farrington's (1990) expression, does not it seems irredeemably lead to conviction, but it does massively increase the risk of criminal behaviour. Nor should it be thought that a disadvantaged background inevitably leads to crime. Farrington and West (1990) note the phenomenon of 'good boys from bad backgrounds'. Such males, for whom all the signs indicated a criminal career, appeared to be characterized by shyness during adolescence, and as adults by social withdrawal and isolation, spending most of their leisure time at home. However, while not following a life of crime, these particular unconvicted males were experiencing interpersonal problems with their parents or partners.

In summary, the findings of the Cambridge Survey strongly suggest that a range of adverse features, summarized in Table 4.1, are associated with social difficulties and the onset of antisocial behaviour, later sanctioned as criminal behaviour, in young people. The intensity and severity of such disadvantage appears to be predictive of chronic offending in later life.

It would be wrong to conclude that the stage has been reached when it is possible to construct a longitudinal model of a criminal career. As Greenberg (1991) demonstrates, there are as yet too many unanswered questions to begin to be so bold as to assume to predict human behaviour. However, if the daunting research agenda mapped out by Tonry, Ohlin, and Farrington (1991) can be completed then answers to at least some of the uncertainties might be forthcoming. For the present, while the findings of the longitudinal surveys are important in describing the conditions associated with the onset of criminal behaviour, they also demand an explanation of *how* they cause delinquent behaviour. In other words, we need a grand theory to explain the process by which the interaction between the young person and his or her environmental circumstances culminate in criminal behaviour. The theories described earlier in this chapter perhaps offer a light at the end of the tunnel — which might be an oncoming train! — but much remains to be done.

Chapter 5

Explaining Criminal Behaviour: Social Factors

This chapter picks up where the last one ended — looking at the individual in interaction with his or her *social* world. Before considering the role of families and peers in the development of criminal behaviour, we begin by continuing with the theme of social behaviour, focusing specifically on the topic of social skills and offending.

Social Skills and Criminal Behaviour

Humans are social creatures and the orderly functioning of our world depends in large part on our ability to communicate effectively with other people. In order to communicate we need to be able to convey information to other people about our own needs and intentions, and similarly to understand the messages being sent by other people. To facilitate this process of communication we have evolved a highly complex verbal language that involves both the written and spoken word. In addition, like many other animals, we have also developed a highly sophisticated means of communication that depends on *non*-verbal communication. Argyle (1983) discusses the many different forms of non-verbal communication — such as the use of gesture and posture, facial expression, bodily contact, and eye contact. For effective social communication, these discrete elements of non-verbal behaviour, sometimes termed *micro-skills*, blend to form more complex aggregates of social behaviour such as holding a conversation, being assertive, expressing our thoughts and feelings, and so on. These amalgams of micro-skills are often referred to as *macro-skills*. We use macro-skills to achieve the social goals we desire in life — to form friendships, to maintain intimate relationships, to succeed at work, to be a parent . . . the list is endless.

Following the original social skills model (Argyle and Kendon, 1967), the suggestion has been made that social skills consist of three related components — social perception, social cognition, and social performance (Hollin and Trower, 1988). Social perception skills are the cognitive skills that enable us to 'decode' the other person's non-verbal messages; simply, if someone smiles we might perceive them to be happy, if someone shouts we might perceive them to be angry or upset. Of course, non-verbal messages are often a great deal more complex than this, with many subtle shades of meaning, thereby demanding sophisticated social perception skills. In total, a socially perceptive person is aware of which messages to attend to, and understands the shared meaning of those messages. Social cognition, in the sense used by Argyle and Kendon, is analogous to social problem solving. Having perceived and understood the communications from other people, we must translate these perceptions into action. This process of translation or problem solving demands that the person must consider the range of options they can take in a given situation, evaluate the likely consequences of these options, and select the course of action that will produce the desired outcome. Social performance, the last part of the sequence, calls on the individual to put into action their own verbal and non-verbal skills in order to behave in, as they see it, an appropriate manner. However, as this is a social account of behaviour, so it must take into account social impact of our actions. Other people will, in turn, perceive our actions and respond accordingly; we, again in turn, perceive these social reactions to our own behaviour ... and so the sequence rolls on. The concept of social skills therefore involves a dynamic interaction between the person and his or her social world, in which the individual's thoughts and actions are continually changing to suit the demands of the situation. Thus social communication is rather like a game of tennis; two (or even four) players with a mutual understanding of the rules of the game move in harmony as one makes their shot, and the other begins to respond in order to make an effective return.

As we grow through childhood so we learn and refine our social skills; the socially skilled person can manage most social encounters without too much difficulty, as most of us do every day of our lives. Indeed, the use of many of our social skills is automatic or habitual; if we had to think and plan our way through every social situation life would be dreadfully slow. However, suppose that an individual had failed to develop appropriate social skills at any or all of the three levels discussed above. That person might be insensitive to the social cues delivered by other people, might not be able to 'think through' a social situation, might not have the performance skills necessary to communicate their needs and intentions to other people. Such problems with social skills have been seen to play a role in many of the difficulties experienced by people from all walks of life (Hollin and Trower, 1986a, b). In this large area of psychological research, some attention has been paid to the relationship between social skills and criminal behaviour. The basic proposition here is that perhaps because many persistent offenders come from impoverished social backgrounds they fail to develop fully functional social skills. This developmental failure then places the young person at a great social disadvantage, leading to subsequent social problems with peers, social adjustment problems at school and with authority, and, in later life, in intimate relationships. Such a thesis appears plausible but raises two questions: what evidence is there that offenders have social skills difficulties?; second, even if such difficulties could be demonstrated, are they related to offending? Most of the evidence has been gathered with young offenders and this is discussed first;

with respect to adult offenders, the research has in the main concentrated on sex offenders, and this is covered after the young offender research.

Young Offenders

Social perception

I know of only one study of social perception in young offenders. McCown, Johnson, and Austin (1986) investigated the ability of delinquents to recognize emotion from facial expression. They found that compared to non-delinquents, the delinquents could recognize happiness, anger, and fear equally well; but were less able to detect sadness, surprise, and disgust. While this single study is interesting, clearly this is an area in which more research is needed.

Social cognition

As noted above, the translation of perception into action demands the ability to generate feasible courses of action, consider alternatives, and make plans towards achieving the desired outcome. A number of studies have suggested that young offenders experience difficulties with this aspect of social cognition. For example, Freedman *et al.* (1978) found that young offenders gave less competent responses than non-offenders to a series of social problems, as assessed using the Adolescent Problem Inventory (API). The delinquents used a more limited range of alternatives to solve interpersonal problems, and tended to rely on the use of verbal and physical aggression as a means of resolving difficulties. Another study reported by Veneziano and Veneziano (1988) also used the API, in this instance to define three groups of delinquents: those classified as incompetent in their knowledge of social skills, those deemed to be moderately competent, and finally a competent group. It was found that these three groups differed significantly in a number of ways — in the number of behavioural difficulties they experienced, on measures of personality, and on measures of social values and morality. In general, the group with less knowledge was disadvantaged compared to their peers on the measures used in this study. Overall, as in the Freedman *et al.* study, the delinquents showed a lower knowledge of social skills than a sample of 'good citizens'. Gaffney and McFall (1981) developed the Problem Inventory for Adolescent Girls (PIAG), a self-report measure of social competence in dealing with awkward social situations. They found that delinquent girls gave less socially competent statements as to their probable actions in the various social situations. Further, it was found that delinquency was more closely related to skill deficits in interacting with adults in positions of authority rather than in interacting with peers. Ward and McFall (1986), also using the PIAG, found that female young offenders gave less competent responses to the problem situations.

Social performance

Spence (1981a) compared the social performance skills of eighteen young male offenders with eighteen non-delinquent controls matched for age, academic performance, and social background. The delinquents showed significantly less eye contact and speech, but more 'fiddling' and gross body movements — an aggregation of behaviours known to relate to poor ratings of social skill (Spence, 1981b). Indeed, on global ratings of social skill, social anxiety, and employability the delinquent group were rated less favourably than the non-delinquents.

In summary, the force of much of the research is that *some* delinquents do experience a degree of difficulty with all three components of social skills. However, with respect to this body of empirical evidence, there are two points to bear in mind. The first is that the number and range of empirical studies carried out with young offenders is not extensive. Thus any conclusions that may be drawn should, at best, be tentative in nature — especially given the artificiality of many experimental situations in which the data are gathered. The second point concerns the heterogeneity of the delinquent population. Veneziano and Veneziano (1988) suggest that their findings show that: 'Delinquents are a diverse group with respect to social skills, with a wide range of knowledge and presumably behavior' (p. 167). Indeed, the sample of delinquents taking part in the study presented by Renwick and Emler (1991) did not show any clear signs of poor social skills. Overall, it would be quite wrong to assume that all young offenders have social skills difficulties.

Social skills and offending

The suggestion has been made that some young people behave in a delinquent fashion because they lack the skills necessary for prosocial behaviour (McFall, 1976). If that is the case that we should expect to see some systematic relationship between social skills and offending. A small number of studies have tested this assumption, with rather mixed results. The studies by Hunter and Kelley (1986) and by Veneziano and Veneziano (1988) found no relationship between social competence, as assessed by the API, and offending. A study by Furnham (1984), looking at self-reported delinquency, also failed to show any relationship between social skills and offending. Similarly, Renwick and Emler (1991) could find no relationship between social skills and delinquency in a sample of young offenders. However, Ward and McFall (1986) did find that performance on the PIAG was related to self-report measures of offending, in that less competent scores were associated with higher rates of offending. In total there is only limited evidence that social skills are related to offending, so that the statement made in 1981 by Gaffney and McFall still stands as an accurate summary: 'Although the data show a relationship between a lack of competence in social situations and delinquent behavior, the research does not provide evidence that delinquency is caused by a lack of social skills' (p. 967). It is important to make the point that this does not mean that such a relationship, at least for some young offenders, does not exist. It is possible that more sensitive research might uncover some relationship for a specific sub-group of young offenders, perhaps according to a certain type of offence as discussed in the next section.

Social Skills and Sex Offenders

In a review of social skills and criminal behaviour in adult populations, Howells (1986) made the suggestion that:

> Social competence with females is generally a necessary condition for consenting sexual behaviour with an adult and it is not difficult to see that impaired social skills might make an adult partner inaccessible and that, in some cases, offenders might resort to either children (paedophilia) or coerced sexual behaviour with an adult (rape) as an alternative sexual outlet (p. 191).

The empirical evidence looking at this suggestion has provided mixed results. A number of studies have not found any difference in the social performance skills of rapists as compared to either other offenders or non-offenders (e.g., Segal and Marshall, 1985). Other studies, however, have found specific types of skill problem in rapists such as difficulties with assertion (Stermac and Quinsey, 1986), and with conversational skills (Overholser and Beck, 1986). A study by Lipton, McDonel and McFall (1987) looked at the social perception skills of rapists, in which the offenders watched videotaped sequences of a 'first date' or an 'intimate couple' then rated the content of the videotape on various dimensions. The results showed that on some sequences, particularly the 'first date' sequence, compared to offender and non-offender controls the rapists showed a low degree of sensitivity to negative and bad mood cues.

The evidence linking social skills and sex offences against children is altogether less equivocal. A number of studies have found that the social skills — in terms of both social perception and social performance — of child molesters are poorer than a range of offender and non-offender control groups (e.g., Overholser and Beck, 1986; Segal and Marshall, 1985). Thus, sex offenders against children show a much clearer picture of heterosocial inadequacy than rapists and other offenders.

While the findings of the studies concerned with social skills and criminal behaviour are interesting and informative, they do not, of course, constitute in themselves an explanation of delinquency or of sex offending. Such theories will need to encompass a great many more factors that just the individual's social skills — which is not to say that this factor might not be an important element in explaining criminal behaviour. Such a broader view of criminal behaviour will need to look beyond the individual to the world in which the individual functions.

The Cambridge Study of Delinquent Development discussed in the previous chapter clearly identified a number of environmental factors associated with the onset of criminal behaviour. The family featured strongly in these environmental factors and, indeed, family functioning and criminal behaviour has generated a considerable amount of research literature. Loeber and Stouthamer-Loeber (1986) completed a large scale review of family factors and delinquent behaviour and noted that, as discussed in Chapter 3, there is a strong association between parental criminality and criminal offspring.

However, Loeber and Stouthamer-Loeber also highlighted several factors in terms of family functioning that consistently characterized the families of delinquents: these can be summarized as *parental disharmony*, *large family size*, and a harsh, rejecting *style of parenting*. I have therefore used these three factors to structure the following discussion of family influences on the development of criminal behaviour.

The Family

Parental Disharmony

Perhaps the most dramatic manifestation of parental disharmony is when the relationship between the parents comes to an end, producing a broken home. The phenomenon of broken homes and criminal behaviour has a long research history; Slawson (1923) reported that delinquents were twice as likely as non-delinquents to come from a broken home, a finding receiving support from Burt (1925). In summarizing the research findings, McCord (1982) noted that research reported during the decades up to the late 1950s produced a number of empirical studies unanimous in their agreement that broken homes were more common among delinquents than non-delinquents (e.g., Merrill, 1947; Monahan, 1957; Shaw and McKay, 1932). The data for these studies were generally gathered from court records, court referrals, or from institutionalized young offenders. More recent research has confirmed this finding for *convicted* offenders. For example, Stratta (1970) reported that 46 per cent of a sample of 361 imprisoned young offenders came from broken homes, while, with a similar sample, Bottoms and McClintock (1973) found just over half came from homes in which the parental relationship was disrupted because of death, desertion, or separation.

Nye (1958) pointed out two related problems with the use of convicted offenders: first, the measurement of delinquency relies on official measures; second, there are sampling problems in that the courts might be selecting offenders for custody influenced by the presence of a broken home, thus inflating the broken home rate among convicted young offenders. (This notion of selection for custody on the basis of personal disadvantage may not be as punitive in intention as it appears. When there was a strong belief in the rehabilitative powers of young offender institutions to send a delinquent to custody may have been intended as a positive gesture. Whether such a gesture was misguided or not is a point for debate.)

In addition, there is also the issue of the process by which the home is broken — does a break caused by death of a parent have the same impact as a break precipitated by a parent's divorce or desertion? Yet further, from a contemporary standpoint, the concepts of 'home' and 'family' are heavily ideologically loaded. The 'traditional' home and family, one suspects, is defined in the terms laid down by white, Western society; the family will consist of a married, heterosexual couple living together under the same roof and acting as parents to their own (i.e., biological) offspring. It can rightly be argued that this is only one type of home and family and that legitimate variations can exist, for example, in terms of the marital and sexual relationship between the parents; whether one, either, or both of the parents are the biological parents to the children; and single-parent families. It is possible, however, that society may have shifted to a greater or lesser extent in its conception of what constitutes a home and family. Such a change, in turn, may have affected social and legal perceptions and reactions to family breakdown; if this is so, it might follow that the impact of a broken home on delinquency rates would be less now than, say, forty years ago.

In an attempt to overcome some of the problems set by concentrating on convicted young offenders, Nye used a self-report methodology in gathering information on delinquent activity among American high school students. In contrast with previous studies, Nye found only a slight relationship between self-reported criminal behaviour and broken homes in this non-delinquent (i.e., unconvicted) population. This pattern of results using a self-report methodology has been replicated in more recent research (e.g., Hennessy, Richards and Berk, 1978).

A number of commentators have suggested that broken homes may have different criminogenic effects on males and females (Offord, 1982). However, the pattern of the empirical evidence is mixed. Some studies suggest that broken homes have a greater impact on males (e.g., Peterson and Zill, 1986); others that the impact is greater on females than on males (e.g., Biron and LeBlanc, 1977); while others do not record any such difference (e.g., Rankin, 1983). Similarly, other variables have historically been seen as important in mediating the effect of a broken home; these include the race of the family (e.g., Monahan, 1957), and the age of the child at the time of the breakdown (e.g., Glueck and Glueck, 1950).

In an attempt to resolve some of the difficulties due to varying research methodologies and definitions of study variables, Rosen and Neilson (1982) reanalyzed the findings of fifteen studies of male delinquency published between 1932 and 1975. This reanalysis was conducted by using a standard statistical procedure to convert the findings of the studies to a common measure of the relationship between delinquency and broken homes. Their reanalysis led Rosen and Neilson to conclude that:

> Despite the variation in time, locale, sample size, nature of population, definitions of both delinquency and broken home, and in basic research design, the conclusion is clear: the strength of the relationship [between broken homes and delinquency] is very small (p. 128).

The step taken by Rosen and Neilson in attempting to apply a common statistical standard to empirical studies of the same topic but that used different measures, subject populations, and so on marks the beginnings of an important step in the development of a methodology that allows us to take a considered overview of a large body of research evidence.

The usual approach to assessing and integrating a large body of research is the narrative research review. With this narrative approach the reviewer identifies either all or a sample of studies in a given area, describes and evaluates their findings, and finally offers a synthesis and conclusion. While the narrative review is of undoubted importance, it is not without its drawbacks. These drawbacks include reviewer bias in selecting the studies for review; the tendency to 'vote count', that is providing numbers of studies for and against a specific effect without taking account of variations between studies; the qualitative rather than quantitative nature of any conclusions; and the subjective and theoretical slant inherent in the work of most reviewers. However, over the past few years a new, more rigorous method for reviewing a large body of experimental research has been developed. This new method is called *meta-analysis*. As Wells and Rankin (1991) explain,

> This strategy treats the findings of prior studies as empirical data points in a new, second-order analysis, resulting in a statistical summary of the prior studies that is more precise, quantitative, objective, and replicable than the traditional narrative review (p. 72).

It would be a mistake to believe that meta-analysis is the answer to all the shortcomings associated with the narrative review, however it certainly does represent an important advance in review techniques. As will be seen in Chapter 8, meta-analysis has been applied in the field of offender treatment, however for present purposes the meta-analysis of broken homes and delinquency reported by Wells and Rankin (1991) is of interest.

Wells and Rankin identified fifty studies on the topic of broken homes and delinquency, published between 1926 and 1988, and used the technique of meta-analysis to produce a quantitative summary of the effects found by these studies. The findings from the meta-analysis were divided by Wells and Rankin into *methodological* and *substantial* outcomes. The main methodological finding was that 'official' samples of delinquents and measures of delinquency produced inflated estimates of the size of the relationship between broken homes and delinquency. This perhaps confirms suspicions of a selection effect by broken home with respect to convicted samples of delinquents. With regard to the substantial findings, Wells and Rankin concluded that taking everything into account across all fifty studies there is a real impact of a broken home: 'The prevalence of delinquency in broken homes is 10–15 per cent higher than in intact homes' (p. 87). However, to add the fine details to this summary, the relationship is stronger for less serious status offences than for serious index offences; and the type of break has an effect in that the link with delinquency is slightly stronger when the break is caused by divorce or separation than by the death of parent. However, there is no consistent pattern of impact of broken homes according to the sex or race of the child, or according to the age of the child at the time of the breakdown; step-parents do not produce any special effect on delinquency rates; and there is no evidence of any historical shift in the magnitude of the effect, in other words the relationship between broken homes and delinquency has remained stable over time. Now, as Wells and Rankin note, their meta-analysis does not represent the final word on the topic of broken homes and delinquency. It is better to see meta-analysis as a means of producing a summary of present knowledge; this summary can then be used to generate informed questions for future research.

Family Size

Family size, as with broken homes, has had a long held association with delinquent behaviour. A string of studies over the past decades have consistently found that delinquents belong to larger families than non-delinquents (e.g., Glueck and Glueck, 1950; Hirschi, 1969; Nye, 1958; Weeks, 1940; West and Farrington, 1973). This association between family size and delinquency holds true for studies using either official or self-reported measures of delinquent behaviour. When reading these studies it is apparent that the definition of 'large' has moved with the times. In the study reported in 1950 by Glueck and Glueck the average number of children in delinquent families was 6.8 (compared to 5.9 in non-delinquent families); however, by 1973 West and Farrington were defining a large family as four or more siblings (and hence small as fewer than four siblings). Thus, as the definition of what constitutes a large family has changed considerably over the past decades, the continual association between large family size and delinquency is unlikely to be simply due to absolute numbers of children. Could the effect be due to family composition? A number of studies have found that the large family size effect on delinquency is more marked for males than for females (see Offord, 1982). Within large families the birth order of the delinquent and the sex of his or her siblings appear to play but a marginal role; however, a *delinquent* sibling seems to be of significance (West and Farrington, 1973).

Why should large families have an increased likelihood of producing a delinquent? A number of hypotheses have been formulated to explain the link: 1) family size may be related to social disadvantage and paucity of income and resources; 2) in large families each child receives less parental attention, monitoring, supervision, and control; 3) 'contagion' through association with delinquent siblings. Many of the studies noted above have attempted to control for factors such as socioeconomic class and parental supervision to see what effect this has on the association between family size and delinquency. Fischer (1984) concludes his review of family size and delinquency:

> There can be little doubt that large families are related to greater delinquency. The relationship has been noted when a number of variables, i.e., income, socioeconomic status, parental criminality, family composition, e.g., age, sex have been controlled. The higher birth rate for lower classes does not appear to be an adequate explanation for the relationship between family size and delinquency, nor do 'less close parent-child affectional ties' or less parental supervision, although all of these may have some influence. The presence of an 'infectious example' seems partially to account for the relationship (p. 532).

Thus, while the presence of a delinquent sibling is significant, giving some weight to the 'contagion' hypothesis, there is unlikely to be one clear explanation for the relationship between family size and delinquency. While family size is of importance it too must be considered within the context of the total family system and environment.

Style of Parenting

As we have seen thus far a number of family sociodemographic characteristics — a criminal parent, a broken home, large family size — have been associated with the development of delinquent behaviour. While these are important indicators of the state and circumstances of the family, they do not say anything about family functioning. Another line of research has been concerned with patterns of family interaction and delinquent behaviour. There are several reviews of this extensive body of research (e.g., Henggeler, 1989; Patterson, 1986; Rutter and Giller, 1983; Snyder and Patterson, 1987), and a brief overview is given below.

Control

At some time all parents will be faced with having to control their child's behaviour. The way in which parents manage this process of disciplining their child is known to play a role in a number of family problems, for example physical child abuse (Frude, 1989), of which delinquency is but one. Parents who discipline their children successfully are able to define the behaviour to be controlled, to watch for occurrences of that behaviour, and use effective, but not harsh or physically punitive, methods to inhibit the child's behaviour and bring it under control. The studies that have looked at parental discipline in delinquent families show that this pattern of effective parental control is not a characteristic of such families. The parental style of discipline in delinquent families is marked as lax, erratic, inconsistent, harsh, and overly punitive; as Patterson (1986) notes,

> In discipline confrontations, the parents of problem children have been shown to threaten, nag, scold, bluster, and natter, but they seldom follow through on their threats. . . . At infrequent intervals, parents explode and physically assault the child (p. 436).

The link between ineffective discipline and delinquent behaviour can follow one of two paths. With the first, termed an *enmeshed* disciplinary style, the parents are continually reprimanding their child's every move through the use of verbal threats and expressions of disapproval. Such a disciplinary style sets up coercive patterns of family interaction. When the child behaves in certain ways, other family members respond in a negative, aversive fashion; the child responds in turn in a negative way, and this continues until one side gives in. Thus a situation is reached in which family functioning is characterized by cycles of aversive interactions; the child then acts in this negative coercive manner outside the family, with for example peers and schoolteachers, setting in train further difficulties (see below). The second problematic style of discipline is termed a *lax* disciplinary style. As the name suggests, this is characterized by very low levels of parental control over the child's behaviour, hence the child does not learn to curb antisocial and delinquent actions.

Encouragement

While one of the tasks parents must accomplish is to exert discipline, the other side of the coin is to be positive in reinforcing prosocial behaviour.

As discussed at the beginning of this chapter, the development of social skills and social competence is a fundamental part of successful socialization. It is well established that parents have a crucial role to play in the child's acquisition of social skills, and that this aspect of a child's development demands both the modelling and reinforcement of appropriate behaviours (Herbert, 1986). Thus parents must provide models of skilled behaviour and when interacting with their child they should focus on the positive aspects of their child's actions, providing consistent positive feedback to the child for his or her achieving normative social goals. Thus for optimum socialization, parents will talk regularly with their children, take an interest in their activities, and behave generally in a caring and supportive manner. Of course, parents who do this are likely themselves to be reinforced by their child's words, actions and achievements. It is a consistent finding in the family functioning research literature that compared to the parents of non-delinquents, the parents of delinquents are less supportive and affectionate, spending less time with their children in shared tasks and interests. In other words, the parents fail to provide good role models and fail to reinforce the child's socially competent actions. As discussed previously, it is clear from the empirical evidence that some delinquents experience social skills difficulties — although exactly how these difficulties relate to criminal behaviour is as yet uncertain. Snyder and Patterson (1987) suggest a complex sequence of events:

> The relationship between skills deficits and antisocial behavior is reciprocal. Conduct problems during childhood interfere with the development of skills and may lead to rejection by normative socialization agents. This lack of skills reduces further socialization opportunities and fosters association with deviant peers which, in turn, promotes continued antisocial behavior (pp. 223–4).

Supervision

The administration of discipline and the giving of encouragement demand that parents are aware of their child's actions. Effective supervision means a clear setting of the boundaries about what is and is not permissible, and taking the time and trouble to make sure these boundaries are being respected. With a young child who spends most of their time at home supervision is relatively easy; as the child grows older and begins to spend more and more time away from home then supervision becomes more difficult. With children past the age of about 10 years, the parents must begin to change their style of supervision to look at indicators of their child's behaviour such as school attendance and achievement, peer group members and activities, and the use of cigarettes, drugs, and alcohol. It follows that parents who monitor effectively their child's behaviour will be better placed to detect and, assuming they have the necessary skills, do something about the wayward situation. The majority of studies have found that parents of delinquent children and adolescents have poorer monitoring skills than parents of non-delinquents. It follows that parents of delinquents are less likely to detect their child's delinquent behaviour in order to attempt to remedy matters.

Managing conflict

Any family will at times face disputes and crises that place family members under stress and in positions of conflict. The family must resolve these conflicts and reduce stress. The research conducted with families with a delinquent child strongly suggests that such families are characterized by high levels of parental conflict. It is a standard finding that families in which there are excessive arguments, conflict and unhappiness are much more likely to contain delinquent children. Further, the longitudinal studies suggest that such conflict is antecedent to the delinquent behaviour; the conflict is more likely to be a contributory factor to the development of delinquent behaviour rather than the product of having a delinquent child in the family. When it comes to problem solving, again the research consistently shows that in families with a delinquent child problems are faced with anger, blame, denial of responsibility, and less cooperative talk. In itself, this may appear relatively trivial and not uncommon; however, it must be seen in conjunction with the characteristics of family functioning already described. In other words, what we must look towards is the way in which all the family variables — parental criminality, control, encouragement, supervision, and managing conflict — interact to culminate in the child's delinquent behaviour. The development of complex, multivariate models of the relationship between family functioning and the development and maintenance of criminal behaviour relies first on the quantity and quality of basic research data, then on the building and testing of complicated models to discover the inter-relationships between the different factors. Of course, there is not as yet a tried and tested model of family functioning, although all the signs are that this goal may not be out of sight (e.g., Loeber, 1990; Patterson, 1986).

Peer Influences

As with broken homes, another consistent finding in the research literature is that adolescents with delinquent friends are significantly more likely themselves to behave in a delinquent manner (e.g., Elliott, Huizinga and Ageton, 1985; Hirschi, 1969; Jessor and Jessor, 1977; West and Farrington, 1973). Further, the predictive power of peer influence remains strong with self-report and official measures of delinquency, in longitudinal and cross-sectional research designs, with a range of offences, and when other factors such as social class or age are controlled (Henggeler, 1989). If the effect of delinquent peers is agreed, however, an explanation is not: *how* do delinquent peers influence an adolescent to turn to delinquent behaviour?

Differential association theory argues that the learning of criminal behaviour occurs within intimate personal groups. Thus, by forming close relationships with a delinquent peer group, the adolescent may learn both the skills and attitudes favourable to delinquent behaviour (see Chapter 3). Following from differential association theory, differential reinforcement theory and social learning theory suggest the means by which peers can influence behaviour. It is well established that peers, especially those the individual holds in high regard and accords a high degree of status, are potent models for future behaviour (Bandura, 1977). Brownfield (1990) found that there were two sides to adolescent status: measures of popularity among peers such as dating, drinking and smoking were associated with higher levels of self-reported delinquency, while more conventional measures of status such as popularity with teachers, responsibility at home, and good academic performance were associated with lower levels of self-reported delinquency. It is not difficult to imagine the type of model portrayed by those with high delinquent status as opposed to those with high conventional status. In addition to providing models, peer groups are a potent source of both tangible and social reinforcement. In this light, a delinquent peer group has many positive effects on behaviour; it is instrumental in the acquisition of delinquent attitudes and skills, and a rich source of reinforcement for that delinquent behaviour. Indeed, the delinquent peer group can become an institution itself in the form of a gang, with its own social organization, rules and ethics (Huff, 1990). Such social cohesion can, as Fagan (1990) notes, 'offer a wide variety of opportunities and services: status, economic opportunity, affiliation, and protection' (p. 211). Of course, not all delinquent groups reward the same type of delinquent activity. Yablonsky (1963) outlined three different types of gang: *social* gangs that form to follow some common interest such as sport or music; *delinquent* gangs that are characterized by crimes of acquisition such as burglary and theft; and *violent* gangs in which the focus is on carrying weapons and on crimes such as assault. Similarly, the social rewards and structures differ across the three types of gang. In the first two types of gang, the social and delinquent gangs, the members are able to form stable relationships with each other, and a coherent group structure is evident. However, the violent gang is characterized by conflict between members and an unstable social structure.

While membership of a delinquent peer group or gang can be a rewarding experience, the other side of the coin lies in findings that suggest that young people who deviate from the norm are *less* popular among their conforming peers. Children who are persistent absentees from school have few school friends and tend to be unpopular among their broad peer group (Reid, 1984). Similarly, peer rejection in childhood is a good predictor of delinquent behaviour in adolescence (Parker and Asher, 1987). A situation can therefore be envisaged in which, for whatever reasons, some children fail to form conventional attachments to conventional agents of socialization such as school, family, or conforming peers. The failure to establish social bonds and rejection by peers, means that social contact must be sought elsewhere — the obvious place being with others outside the mainstream. We arrive at the apparent paradox of some young people being accepted and popular within a delinquent counter-culture, yet at the same time rejected and unpopular among their conforming, socially bonded, peers.

Now, as Agnew (1991) points out, empirical investigations of peer influences on delinquency have been rather simplistic. The typical strategy in such research is to identify individual adolescents and then count the number of delinquent friends they have and the frequency with which these friends commit delinquent acts. However, by their very nature, social groups consist of more than just numbers of people and their frequency of contact. Agnew highlights three dimensions of group dynamics that play an important role in mediating the group effect on the individual; these are *attachment, contact* and the *extent* of peer delinquency. The argument for attachment as an important influence is that with high attachment and emotional closeness to a delinquent peer group, so the delinquents will be more attractive role models and more powerful sources of reinforcement for delinquent behaviour and punishment for being straight and conforming to social rules. Similarly, the more contact there is between the adolescent and the delinquent group and the greater the extent of the delinquent behaviour, the greater the likelihood of the delinquents modelling, observing and rewarding any display of delinquent attitudes and behaviour. Further, it might be anticipated that the relationship between these dimensions would be interactive; for example, greater amounts of contact might lead to greater levels of attachment.

In order to search for such interactive effects Agnew (1991) carried out a study of delinquent peer group functioning looking at variables such as peer attachment, time spent with friends, peer approval for delinquency, and peer pressure for deviance. In addition, delinquent peers were classified as 'minor', that is they carried out crimes such as vandalism, petty theft and bullying, or 'serious' in that they sold hard drugs, committed burglary and stole substantial amounts of money. The data were gathered from the National Youth Survey, conducted in the state of Colorado in the USA, based on self-reported information from a sample of 1,725 young people aged 11 to 17 years. Agnew carried out a thorough and sophisticated analysis of the data, arriving at two key findings. The first is that 'The results are compatible with previous research: peer delinquency is the best predictor of delinquency' (p. 62). However, the second key finding indicates that this relationship is not so straightforward as it might appear:

> The impact of Delinquent Friends (Serious) on delinquency is strongly conditioned by the measures of peer interaction. When the peer interaction variables are at their mean or lower levels, Delinquent Friends (Serious) has no effect or in some cases a negative effect on delinquency. When these variables are at high levels, Delinquent Friends (Serious) has a strong positive effect on delinquency. The measure of Delinquent Friends (Minor), however, is largely unaffected by the peer interaction variables (p. 68).

Thus delinquent peers do have an influence, but only in certain circumstances: it is when an adolescent forms strong relationships — as defined and measured in Agnew's study — with delinquents who commit serious offences that peer group influence exerts its strongest pull. Adolescents who associate with peers who perform minor delinquent acts or who do not form strong attachments to their delinquent peer group do not appear from Agnew's findings to be at increased risk of becoming delinquent themselves. In order to look more closely at this pattern of findings, Agnew conducted further analyses looking at the influence of a range of control variables such as the demographic factors of age, sex, race, community size and socioeconomic status, and measures of parental attachment and school achievement. Even when the effects of these factors were added to the equation they had a minimal impact on the results — the finding remains that the prediction of delinquency is dominated by the effects of peers.

Another recent study by Brownfield and Thompson (1991) looked at the relationship between attachment to peers and delinquent behaviour. Once again the main finding emerged that measures of peer involvement in delinquency, such as friends being picked up by the police, are strongly related to measures of self-reported delinquency. However, Brownfield and Thompson failed to find a significant association between attachment to delinquent peers and self-reported delinquency. In other words, contact with delinquents did predict involvement in crime, but this did not appear to be explicable by level of attachment. At face value this appears to contradict the force of Agnew's research discussed above. However, Agnew showed that attachment interacts with the level of delinquent activity displayed by the peer group and this was not a variable accounted for in the Brownfield and Thompson study. While Agnew was able to specify the conditions under which attachment became of influence, this is not the case in the Brownfield and Thompson study and this may account for the variation in findings between the two studies.

While there can be little doubt that peers exert a considerable influence, it would be a mistake to assume that *all* the acts a delinquent performs are due to peer group pressure. Agnew (1990) offers another piece of exemplary empirical research investigating offender accounts of the origin of delinquent events. The methodology used in this study was perfectly straightforward: a sample of 1,395 adolescents was interviewed and asked if they had engaged in any of seventeen different delinquent acts (grouped for the purpose of analysis into the four categories of violent offences, property offences, drug offences, and the status offence of running away). When a positive reply was given, the adolescent was asked the question, 'What led you to do this?' and their reply duly recorded. The majority of collected responses fell into one of three categories: 1) responses that reflect a rational choice in that the delinquent act was carried out to reap some positive benefit such as money or kicks; 2) responses that are a reaction to a negative event such as anger or provocation; 3) responses that suggested the delinquent behaviour was carried out because of peer pressure to conform, or to impress friends and gain their approval. The main part of the analysis therefore was to see if the delinquents' explanations for their offences varied according to the type of criminal act they committed. Indeed, this was found to be the case. Violent offences were most often committed for motives of retaliation or revenge following an insult or other provocation (see the account of Luckenbill's work in Chapter 9). Property offences are most often carried out in a rational search for personal gain, although the gain was more often fun and thrills than hard cash. Drug offences were most often explained by the young offenders as being committed because of social pressure. Finally, running away was most often precipitated by some negative event and carried out to avoid punishment or to exact revenge on other people. The explanations for the different crimes held more or less the same when seriousness of the offence was taken into consideration.

In summary, while delinquents mix with other delinquents and, of course, commit some crimes with their delinquent friends, it would be a mistake to assume that all delinquent acts are carried out because of peer pressure. While delinquent peers are a strong predictor of delinquency, it is clear that much remains to be uncovered about the dynamics of this relationship.

School and Delinquency

As discussed in Chapter 4, there are reasonably strong arguments for a relationship between low IQ and delinquent behaviour even when factors such as social class are controlled. If this finding is taken a step further, it might be anticipated that some association would be found between educational measures and delinquent behaviour. A large body of research evidence has been gathered on this topic and helpful reviews have been presented by Hawkins and Lishner (1987) and Rutter and Giller (1983). This discussion below draws on research conducted with young people of 'normal' IQ; the particular relationship between very low IQ and learning difficulties is discussed in Chapter 6.

The broad conclusion from many studies, using both self-report and official measures of delinquent behaviour, is of a modest but highly consistent association between academic ability, including IQ, and delinquency. This association between academic ability and delinquency holds true when factors such as socioeconomic status are controlled. Further, as distinct from academic *ability*, there is also the issue of academic *performance*; it is, of course, possible to have high ability but perform at a low level and fail to achieve academically, and to have comparatively low academic ability but achieve a degree of academic success. A further cluster of studies has shown that for both males and females academic performance is a reasonable predictor of delinquency even when other factors are controlled. Indeed, it appears that academic performance has a stronger relationship with delinquency than academic ability; children and adolescents who are successful academically are less likely to engage in delinquent behaviour or to be convicted for criminal behaviour as adults.

Everyday experience would suggest that academic performance is likely to be reflected in the young person's conduct at school and the research confirms that this is the case. Low academic performance in the early school years is a reasonably good predictor of a cluster of later school problems including misconduct at school, truancy, dislike of teachers, low levels of involvement in school activities, and dropping out of school. In total, the young person develops a negative, hostile attitude towards schools, together with low levels of academic aspiration. However, it would be unwise to place the blame for this state of affairs entirely at the door of the young person. There is considerable evidence that rates of delinquent behaviour are not equally distributed throughout the school system, even taking into account considerations such as catchment area there are schools that have much higher rates of delinquency than others. For example, in their study of inner-city secondary schools in London, Rutter *et al.* (1979) found a range of organizational characteristics within the schools that correlated with pupil conduct. These characteristics included good classroom management procedures, the perceived fairness of the school's system of reward and punishment, prompt feedback and rewards for academic attainment, pupil participation and responsibility for school activities, and the cohesiveness and stability of the teaching staff. While it would be going too far to suggest that schools are the direct cause of delinquent behaviour, it is interesting that finally giving up school (i.e., dropping out) does not lead to more offending but to a stabilization or even reduction in delinquent behaviour (Elliott and Voss, 1974).

In summary, it is plain that in seeking to understand the development of criminal behaviour school influences cannot be discounted. A cluster of factors including low academic ability, low school performance, negative attitudes to school, low academic aspirations, school misconduct, truancy, and school organization have all been implicated as playing a role in delinquent behaviour. The nature of the relationships between these factors remains to be clarified but two points can be made. The first is that it is highly unlikely that school performance in itself causes delinquency, the developmental chain of events predicting delinquent behaviour stretches back to pre-school ages. It is more likely that the school acts as an environmental catalyst in which rather than originate, conduct problems develop, intensify and take on new forms. In addition the conduct problems become more and more public as they come to the attention of teachers, educational psychologists and so on, and the child becomes labelled as a 'problem'. The second point is that it would be disingenuous to neglect the role of parents and peer group alongside school factors. Reid's (1985) research into the family backgrounds of truants and school absentees — two measures of school dissatisfaction that correlate highly with delinquency — showed that such young people 'do not normally receive proper parental encouragement and support at home, emanate from backgrounds where books or learning are valued or find themselves with the financial back-up necessary to equip them properly for their education' (Reid, p. 53). Once drawn into a delinquent peer group, the young person may become part of a social group in which educational achievement is neither valued or reinforced. On the other hand, it would be over-stating the case to blame the schools absolutely; levels of resources, the sophistication of staff training, the ability to respond to special needs pupils, and educational standards are, to a greater or lesser extent, imposed on schools by local and central government. Thus we see a complex interaction between the individual, the school, family and peers, and the state. In other words, an interaction between the individual, social processes, and social structure. The role of the last of these factors, social structure, is perhaps most sharply highlighted when considering the relationship between poverty and criminal behaviour.

Poverty

Alongside individual, family, and peer group influences, many studies have pointed to indices of poverty, such as low income and poor housing, as important antecedents to the onset of criminal behaviour (e.g., West, 1982). A disadvantaged economic position, as typically found in the lower social classes (the term 'lower' is telling in itself), is seen by social structure theorists as the primary cause of criminal behaviour. Within this broad school of thought, however, there are two main perspectives on the nature of the relationship between social structure and crime.

The first approach is *cultural deviance theory* which holds that subcultures form in which criminal behaviour is normal and accepted as legitimate within the values of that subculture. Within delinquent subcultures, the theory suggests, non-conventional, antisocial values are passed from generation to generation. The classic work in this tradition was carried out in Chicago during the 1920s and 1930s by Clifford Shaw and Henry McKay, examining the crime rates in different parts of the city (e.g., Shaw and McKay, 1942). They found that well-defined zones had formed within Chicago, some of which had considerably higher crime rates than others. The crime zones were the inner-city zones which had the poorest housing, the most health and safety hazards, and the greatest levels of poverty. The people who lived in these high crime zones happened to be foreign-born immigrants, Germans, Irish, Italians, and Poles, and migrating southern black families. Now, the thinking of the time might well have been to explain the criminal behaviour in terms of the characteristics of the inner-city dwellers; that is, the criminal behaviour is a function of belonging to a particular ill-educated racial or ethnic group. However, Shaw and McKay turned the argument around, proposing that the cause of crime lies not in the individual but in the ecological system itself. As the city's social structure denies disadvantaged people access to financial and social privileges, so they are forced to find ways to overcome this disadvantage. Thus criminal behaviour is seen as a *normal* response to adverse environmental conditions. The social and cultural resources available in a given zone make it more or less likely that crime will take place. Areas marked by wealth and luxury are less likely to contain criminals (at least the type that get caught!) than areas of poverty. The problem from the point of view of the advantaged side of the city is one of loss of finance and a rise in fear of victimization. The solution, of course, is to construct rules and laws to forbid such actions and make them illegal, and to have places to put the offenders well out of sight when they are caught. If there is no change in the social structure, then criminal values and traditions are then passed from one generation to the next, preserving the criminal subculture. In turn, the forces of law and order continue to impose the will of the privileged, again contributing to the maintenance of the criminal subculture and fostering conflict between cultures within society. Of course, this view is not without its specific technical difficulties and its critics generally. Technically, there are problems with the assessment of criminal activity, problems with separating out the effects of high levels of police attention and ecological factors, and in describing exactly how criminal behaviour is transmitted from generation to generation. At a broad level there are criticisms of sweeping statements about conflict between cultures, for example Braithwaite (1989) is blunt in his comment that

> Crude conflict theorists who contend that the criminal law is a manifestation of ruling class interest are simply wrong ... working class support for the criminal law is widespread and better explained by the interests which the criminal law does to some extent serve for the working class then by any glib resort to 'false consciousness' (p. 40).

Nonetheless, the work of researchers in this area has highlighted the need to consider the role of social structure in explanations of criminal behaviour.

As noted previously, cultural deviance theory offers one way to consider the impact of social structure. Another theoretical view is based on the premise that social structure can deny some people access to social and financial success; this denial leads to anger and frustration, and hence to criminal behaviour. This approach to understanding the effect of social structure is known as *strain theory*. The main difference between cultural deviance and strain theories is that the former suggest that criminal values and goals are part of lower-class culture; the latter maintain that the lower classes have the same goals and aspirations as the higher social classes but are denied access. Thus strain theories suggest that the disadvantaged within a given society are faced with the choice between accepting their impoverished lot in life, or attempting to gain success either by legitimate or criminal means. One of the most quoted strain theories was developed by Robert Merton, generally known as the theory of *anomie* (e.g., Merton, 1938). Merton argues that the legitimate ways to acquire wealth are not equally distributed across society. Those with little or no access to education and economic resources are highly disadvantaged when it comes to competing for social success, wealth, and power. This, in turn, produces strain and a sense of anomie, that is a feeling of being apart from mainstream society and hence not committed or bound by its rules of conduct. As detailed by Heidensohn (1989), strain theories came under considerable criticism on a number of fronts, perhaps most tellingly in that strain is obviously experienced by members of all classes, not just the working class.

Social structure theories did set into train a line of enquiry concerned with the relationship between crime and, for example, delinquent subcultures, differential opportunity, gangs, and unemployment (see Hagan, 1987; Siegal, 1986). In many cases it is difficult to establish how the relationship between social structure and individual behaviour functions — this is illustrated in the long-running debate about whether economic factors such as unemployment cause crime (Field, 1990) — and it seems to me that this is an area ripe for collaboration between psychologists and sociologists. As a generalization, psychological theories have underplayed the importance of social structure, while sociological theories have failed to develop the role of individual differences. It might be anticipated that if genuine multidisciplinary work, of the type described by Tonry *et al.* (1991), can be developed, this will lead to a more complete understanding of criminal behaviour, an understanding that includes the individual, social process, and social structure in an integrated, not piecemeal, manner.

Chapter 6

Explaining Criminal Behaviour:
The Special Case of Mental Disorder

The term 'mental disorder' is used here in the sense that it is used in the 1983 Mental Health Act for England and Wales; that is, mental disorder refers to 'mental illness, arrested or incomplete development of the mind, psychopathic disorder and any other disorder or disability of mind' [s. 1(2)]. In practice there are three categories from the Mental Health Act that assume importance: *mental illness*, in most cases schizophrenia and depression; arrested or incomplete development of the mind, perhaps more familiar when referred to as *mental handicap* or *learning difficulty*; and *psychopathic disorder*. The relationship between mental disorder — particularly mental illness and mental handicap — and criminal behaviour has been a topic that has concerned criminologists, lawyers, and psychiatrists for many years (Walker, 1968; Whitehead, 1983). In considering the nature of the association between mental disorder and criminal behaviour three relationships can be defined: there are people who experience mental illness and mental handicap who do not commit offences; there are offenders who are not mentally disordered; and there is a third group who display mental disorder and criminal behaviour. It is this third group, sometimes referred to as mentally abnormal offenders (e.g., Craft and Craft, 1984), that is of interest here. However, before looking at mentally disordered offenders it is important to deal with the confusion that sometimes arises when discussing this topic — namely the view that psychological theories assume that *all* criminals are mentally disordered.

The view that criminal, antisocial behaviour is analogous to mental disorder might have one or two proponents (e.g., Washbrook, 1981) but is not one that would be entertained by the majority of those, psychologists included, who study criminal behaviour. In their review of concepts of the criminal and the mentally ill in the nineteenth century, Long and Midgley (1992) document how the blurring of the boundaries between the two phenomena came to pass. At that time the notion of insanity was, as Long and Midgley document, expanded to include all of those who survived on the margins of society — the decrepit, the physically malformed, the socially inept and incompetent, and those who transgressed against the law of the land. The same social policy was applied to all these social outcasts, criminals included, based on the central tenet of removing the person from decent society. As the mentally ill and criminal were thrown together, literally and metaphorically, so explanations and theories for the two different phenomena began to merge. As Long and Midgley note, this was not to the advantage of either group; both became tarred with the same brush of unpredictability, dangerousness and violence. Criminals became like the insane; the insane became as criminals.

Given this, it is hardly surprising that studies of prison populations in the nineteenth century consistently showed high levels of mental disturbance among inmates. The interpretation of such findings was not made in terms of the consequence of a social policy that put the mentally ill into prison; rather, such findings were often interpreted as evidence for close links between mental disorder and criminality. Thus the criminal came to be portrayed in medical terms, as mentally and morally pathological and diseased, and crude biological explanations of criminal behaviour began to dominate the theorizing of the time (see Chapter 3). Some early psychological theorizing followed this line of explaining criminal behaviour in terms of psychopathology. The rest, as they say, is history. A view was constructed of criminal behaviour in terms of a sickness or disease of the mind that afflicts the criminal from inside and, as Long and Midgley show, this belief still pervades our modern day culture. It is unfortunate that this psychopathological approach still colours the views of contemporary criminology theorists and writers when it comes to psychologically based explanations of criminal behaviour. For example, Siegal's (1986) excellent textbook *Criminology* is marred by the comment:

> Psychological theories are useful as explanations of the behaviour of deeply disturbed, impulsive, or destructive people. However, they are limited as general explanations of criminality. For one thing, the phenomenon of crime and delinquency is so widespread that to claim all criminals are psychologically disturbed is to make that claim against a vast majority of people (pp. 177–176).

If we follow the logic of this statement, it appears that psychological theories are only of value as accounts of disturbed behaviour, therefore when applied to criminal behaviour they must be advocating that criminal behaviour is evidence of psychological disturbance. Of course, most psychological theories are accounts of human behaviour generally, not just of disturbed behaviour. If this book does nothing else, it should show that psychological contributions to understanding criminal behaviour are no longer rooted in the language of psychopathology and psychological disturbance.

Instead of the outdated view that criminal behaviour is evidence of mental disorder, the alternative position can be adopted that the relationship between mental disorder and crime is one where the two phenomena coexist. Within this broad position two options have received particular attention: mental disorder can be a *cause* of criminal behaviour — which, of course, is not the same as saying that crime is evidence of mental disorder; or that the relationship between mental disorder and crime is *correlational*. What does the empirical research tell us about which of these positions is likely to be true? There are two broad classes of studies that can be drawn on to attempt to make some general statement about the relationship between mental disorder and criminal behaviour. The first considers mental disorder in offender populations; the second criminal behaviour in psychiatric populations.

Mental Disorder in Prisoners

In a typical study Gunn, Robertson, Dell, and Way (1978) assessed the psychiatric status, using questionnaires and interviews, of a sample of 600 prisoners held in custody. Gunn *et al.* found that over one-fifth of the prisoners had a marked or severe psychiatric condition, a figure much higher than would be expected in the general population. In most cases the prisoners were presented as depressed, with anxiety states the next most common complaint. Addiction to drugs and alcohol were also common, but schizophrenia was seldom found. McManus, Alessi, Grapentine, and Brickman (1984) found a similar pattern of disorders — i.e., a predominance of alcohol addiction and mood disturbances — with delinquent adolescents held in custody.

There have been a number of reviews and summaries of the extent of various types of mental disorder in offender populations (e.g., Prins, 1980, 1986). While there are differences across studies — influenced by factors such as the date when the study was reported, the age and type of offender, and the style of psychiatric diagnosis — the general consensus is that psychiatric problems are common in penal populations. Indeed, a recent study of male and female prisoners serving life sentences reported by Taylor (1986) found that approximately two-thirds of these prisoners appeared to be psychiatrically disordered. Depression and personality disorder were most common, with an estimated 10 per cent being schizophrenic.

As Feldman (1977) argues, a higher prevalence of mental disorder in offender populations than in the rest of the population is not in itself evidence for a causal link between mental disorder and criminal behaviour. Alternative explanations are that mentally disordered people may carry out their offences more clumsily, leading to easier detection; or that the authorities may be more willing to charge the mentally disordered and accept pleas of guilty, perhaps in an attempt legally to gain some form of treatment. Further, as Feldman also notes, because a prisoner exhibits a mental disorder in prison it does not follow that the disorder was extant at the time of the crime. As most people who have been inside a prison will testify, penal establishments are distinctly unpleasant places. It is not unlikely that such aversive surroundings could trigger the onset of a disorder in vulnerable prisoners. While it appears that prison populations are characterized by higher than average levels of mental disorder, as Gunn (1977) suggests, 'This may be more closely related to their function as institutions than to any special relationship between crime and mental disorder' (p. 327).

Criminal Behaviour in Psychiatric Populations

The broad consensus from the relevant studies is that criminal behaviour is higher in psychiatric populations than in the general population (Howells, 1982; Prins, 1980, 1986). There are a number of caveats to this sweeping statement, however. The first is that there is a marked fluctuation in findings according to when individual studies were carried out; such variations over time most probably reflect changes in social policies for the use of psychiatric hospital facilities for offenders. Inspection of type of offence reveals that for some offences, mainly non-violent offences, the rates are similar in both psychiatric populations and the general population. For more serious offences, such as robbery and possibly rape, the incidence is higher in psychiatric populations than in the general population. Again it is important not to accept this finding at face value; while most studies finding a higher incidence of criminal behaviour in psychiatric populations are American, a German study found much *lower* rates of serious crime in a sample of mentally disordered offenders (Häfner and Böker, 1982). In addition, the *prevalence* and *incidence* distinction may once again be important. The higher levels of offending in psychiatric populations may not be a function of a high incidence of offending, but the result of an exceptionally high prevalence of offending by a small proportion of the whole of the in-patient psychiatric population. Further, it is almost certainly the case that in-patient populations are a heavily skewed sample of the mentally disordered population. Therefore in trying to make sense of the research findings we are faced with the same three-way tangle — between mental disorder, criminal behaviour and institutionalization — that made it difficult to draw any definite conclusion from the studies with prisoner populations.

We can say with some degree of confidence, on the basis of the evidence discussed thus far, that there is some overlap between criminal behaviour and mental disorder. Whether this overlap is causal or correlational is impossible to say. Another way to approach this issue is to look more closely at the relationship between specific mental disorders and criminal behaviour.

Mental Illness and Criminal Behaviour

While mental illness is referred to in the Mental Health Act it is not, as Ashworth and Gostin (1985) note, legally defined, meaning that in practice much depends on medical opinion. With particular reference to serious offenders, as indicated by rates of admission to the Special Hospitals (see Chapter 8), by far the greatest number of mentally ill offenders are diagnosed as schizophrenic, with depression the next most frequent diagnosis (Hamilton, 1985). Does any special relationship exist between these two forms of mental illness and criminal behaviour?

Schizophrenia
The most important indicators of schizophrenia, which would *not* all be found in one person, include disturbances of thought, perception, affect and motor behaviour. A number of broad types of schizophrenia can be identified: disorganized or hebephrenic schizophrenia is marked by hallucinations, delusions, and inappropriate affect; catatonic schizophrenia by motor disturbances; and paranoid schizophrenia by delusions of persecution, incorporating 'ideas

of reference' in which personal significance is seen in the words and actions of other people. Given this diversity, schizophrenia is perhaps best thought of as a group of disorders rather than a single disorder. The incidence of schizophrenia is close to 1 per cent in the general population, and this therefore sets a level against which to compare the rates of schizophrenia in offender populations.

Spry (1984) reviews the evidence on the incidence of schizophrenia in offender populations and notes that with studies of normal offender groups (usually prisoners) the incidence of schizophrenia is around the 1 per cent mark. With samples of offenders selected on the basis of referral for psychiatric treatment, typically after committing serious, violent offences, the incidence is much higher. Similarly, Taylor's (1986) figures for the incidence of schizophrenia among a sample of life-sentenced offenders (the majority of whom had killed) were substantially higher than the 1 per cent baseline. Does this indicate, as is popularly believed, that schizophrenia is closely associated with violent criminal behaviour? Häfner and Böker (1982), for example, indicated the possibility of a relationship between paranoid ideas and violence, in that the victims of violent attacks are often those who figured in the schizophrenic person's delusions. There are a number of infamous examples; in the case of Ian Ball it appeared that delusional thoughts were manifest in a plot to kidnap a member of the royal family, while with Peter Sutcliffe, the 'Yorkshire Ripper', it seemed that his paranoid schizophrenia may have played a role in his crimes (see Prins, 1986). It should be stressed, however, that the amount of publicity generated by these cases bears little relation to their low frequency among deluded and paranoid people.

While these extreme cases are infrequent, the suggestion remains that schizophrenics are more likely to commit violent offences than other disordered groups or the general population (Taylor and Gunn, 1984). A recent study by Lindqvist and Allebeck (1990) looked at the offence history of 644 schizophrenic patients discharged from Swedish hospitals in 1971. Using a retrospective longitudinal design, Lindqvist and Allebeck were able from police records to see what offences had been committed by their study population during the period 1972–1986. The first level of analysis was concerned with the incidence of criminal offences. They found that of the 644 discharged patients, 45 out of 330 men and 9 out of 314 women had committed offences. If the crime rate for the schizophrenic offenders (i.e., the number of offences over the period spanned by the study) is compared to crime rate in the general population, the crime rate among men was very similar to the norm but was almost double for women. However, as Linqvist and Allebeck caution, given the small numbers involved for women it would be unwise to read too much into this particular finding. With regard to the type of offence committed by the schizophrenic population: 'Violent crimes were four times more frequent among schizophrenics than "normals"' (Lindqvist and Allebeck, p. 348).' However, to put this in context, the schizophrenic group committed far more non-violent than violent crimes, mainly theft and petty theft, and the violent offences were almost exclusively minor in nature, mostly assault with no cases of manslaughter or murder.

While schizophrenia may have some association with violent behaviour, it is important to emphasize that the majority of people with schizophrenia are not violent, and that when violence is evident it is mostly trivial in nature. For those people with schizophrenia who do commit violent offences, the nature and function of delusional and paranoid beliefs appears to be of importance in arriving at an understanding of the act. Certainly, a simple relationship between schizophrenia and criminal behaviour is unlikely to be the case. As Taylor (1982) observes:

> It is not unusual to find that the violent act of a schizophrenic cannot be directly explained by the current psychopathology. This does not, however, negate the relevance of the illness ... social and illness variables must be considered together (p. 280).

Taylor's observation is important because it means that when considering the association between schizophrenia and violence, attention should be directed not only to the person but also to the environment. There are marked similarities in the social and environmental antecedents that characterize *both* violent behaviour and schizophrenia. In other words, rather than conceiving of schizophrenia as somehow directly causing violent behaviour, the schizophrenia and violence should be seen as the interactive products of common adverse environmental conditions. Thus from a survey of psychotic offenders, Taylor (1985) was able to conclude that in about one-fifth of the cases in her sample the psychotic symptoms played an active part in the offence. However, when environmental factors such as homelessness were taken into account so that 'the direct and indirect consequences of psychosis are considered together, then over 80 per cent of the offences of the psychotic were probably attributable to their illness' (Taylor, 1985, p. 497). As the research continues to unfold, it is becoming more and more obvious that in order to understand the relationship between schizophrenia and criminal behaviour it is not sufficient simply to focus on the illness and on the offence. To generate an accurate picture of schizophrenia and crime, it will be necessary to account for the interactive effects of the relevant organic, psychological, social, environmental and legal variables.

Depression

Contemporary diagnostic schemes distinguish two types of depression, termed *major* (or *unipolar*) *depression* and *bipolar disorder*. Major depression is characterized by profoundly sad mood, overwhelming feelings of self-blame, guilt, and worthlessness, appetite disturbances, fatigue and long periods of sleep, lethargy, and recurrent thoughts of death and suicide. Bipolar disorder is typified by bouts of mania as well as periods of depression; the manic phase is characterized by elated or irritable mood, high levels of furious physical activity, long periods without sleep, and inflated self-esteem. Major depression is the most common, with estimates of 8 to 11 per cent of men and 18 to 23 per cent of women experiencing this form of clinical depression at least once in their life; bipolar disorder is less common, being found in about 1 per cent of the population.

As with schizophrenia there are difficulties in establishing the nature of the association between depression and criminal behaviour. There are a range of possibilities; the offence may have been committed because the offender was depressed; the offender's guilt after the offence may have precipitated the depression; or the offender may have been depressed when committing the crime, but the depression was not a direct cause of their criminal behaviour. In terms of a direct link, one of the more familiar and tragic associations between depression and criminal behaviour is seen when a person becomes convinced that life is hopeless and not worth living. Before committing suicide the depressed person kills their children and other members of their family. West (1965) reports on seventy-eight cases of murder followed by suicide and estimates that in twenty-eight of these cases the offender was depressed at the time of the killing. It is tempting to conclude in this type of tragedy that the depression caused the offence but, as with schizophrenia, the broader picture must be considered. Studies of the general pattern of murder by people who have become depressed suggest that adverse social factors, such as a breakdown in a long-term relationship, may play an important role (Lawson, 1984).

As well as murder, depression has been linked with other crimes including shoplifting and violence (particularly towards relatives), with the additional suggestion of a particular link between a manic state and arson. Given that depressed in-patients are not generally thought of as a violent population, it seems likely that the relationship between depression and criminal behaviour is mediated by social factors, especially those concerned with close personal relationships.

The research on mental illness and criminal behaviour does little more, in one sense, than the research discussed earlier on mental disorder generally and criminal behaviour; mental illness, particularly schizophrenia and depression, is found in criminal populations but the nature of the relationship between the illness and the criminal behaviour remains unclear. However, recent studies are beginning to extend our thinking away from the notion of a simple relationship in which mental illness causes criminal behaviour, towards a view of the association in terms of a complex psychosocial phenomena. However, perhaps the most important issue concerns responsibility; can a person with schizophrenia or depression be held responsible for their criminal behaviour?

Mental Handicap and Criminal Behaviour

The Mental Health Act seeks to define a group of offenders characterized by 'arrested or incomplete development of mind which includes . . . impairment of intelligence and social functioning' [s.1(2)]. The Act notes the classification of 'severe' and 'significant' mental impairment, although the difference between these two categories is not defined (Ashworth and Gostin, 1985). The population referred to as being of impaired intelligence is more generally referred to as mentally handicapped, although other terms such as mentally retarded and mentally subnormal are sometimes used. It should be emphasized that mental *handicap* is not the same as mental *illness*; the former refers to the person's enduring level of intellectual and social ability; the latter is an episodic disturbance which does not necessarily affect intellectual functioning. The term *learning disability* which is currently in vogue, and which will be used from this point, makes such confusion less likely. The assessment of learning disability depends on a combination of results from tests of intellectual and social ability. While there is no legal level of IQ score by which to define intellectual impairment, in clinical assessment it is generally taken that an IQ in the region of 70 points (on IQ tests with a 'normal' score of 100) is taken as 'borderline'. Thus an IQ score of 70 or below, in conjunction with a low level of social functioning, may be indicative of some degree of learning disability (having eliminated any other explanations such as memory loss, trauma, and so on). IQ scores below 50 usually indicate a substantial degree of impairment, typically with an organic basis as, for example, following head injury or with a genetic or chromosomal abnormality such as Down's Syndrome.

In the discussion of IQ and criminal behaviour in Chapter 4, the point was made that on average, offenders tend to show a lower IQ score than non-offenders. However, the magnitude of this difference — about 8 IQ points averaged across studies — does *not* mean that offenders as a group are learning disabled. Offenders may display a lower IQ on average, but this means that some offenders will have normal or above normal IQs, while an 8-point difference in IQ scores would hardly plunge offenders into the 'below average' classification. The proper area of concern here is with that group of people with genuinely low IQ scores (i.e., 69 and below) and problems with social functioning.

A number of studies have been concerned with the relationship between low IQ scores and criminal behaviour. Craft (1984) reports that in convicted prisoners the percentage with IQ scores less than 70 varies over time, from a high of 31 per cent in a 1931 study, to about 10 per cent in 1940s studies, to a low of 4.2 per cent in a study carried out in 1950. While drawing on a different set of studies, Prins (1980) nonetheless describes a similar pattern, with a high of 28 per cent of convicted offenders deemed 'subnormal' in a 1918 study, falling to 2.4 per cent in a study reported in 1964. These differences over time almost certainly reflect changes in social policy and practice regarding the criminalization of people with a learning disability. More recent American studies have found that about 2.5 per cent of the prison population have IQ scores below 70 (Denkowski and Denkowski, 1985).

While most of the research is based on IQ scores, the importance of social functioning in the assessment of learning disability is seen from the survey by Denkowski and Denkowski (1985) of the prevalence of learning disabled inmates in the prisons of twenty states in America. From their figures on individually tested prisoners, it can be calculated that 2.25 per cent of prisoners are classified as learning disabled in those states which rely solely on IQ testing. However, in the five states where IQ *and* adaptive behaviour was assessed (using a standard psychometric test) the percentage of learning disabled prisoners was 1.28 per cent. Overall, these lower figures — in the region of 2–2.5 per cent — are close to the incidence of learning disability in the general population. Lund (1990) summarizes the evidence as showing that there is a slightly increased prevalence of mild and borderline learning disability among offender groups, but a very low rate of crime among the severely and profoundly learning disabled. Rather than learning disability being a strong factor in the aetiology of crime, it is probable that the slightly increased prevalence is due to the easier detection of crimes committed by this group. Having said that, it is the case that some people with a learning disability do commit crimes — is there anything remarkable about these offences?

There is a suggestion that learning disability is associated with a range of offences, including arson and babysnatching, in which the offence is an expression of emotional turmoil. However, the bulk of the research has been concerned with sex offences in learning disabled populations. Walker (1965) compared the indictable offences over a one year period of 305 males ordered to be committed to hospital by the courts as mentally handicapped, with the offences of all other male offenders dealt with by the courts in the same year. While there were no differences between the two groups of offenders in the frequency of violent and property offences, the percentage of learning disabled offenders sentenced for sexual offences was six times as great as that for the other offenders. Other studies have similarly reported a rate of sex offending among male learning disabled offenders anywhere between four and six times the rate in the normal offender population (e.g., Shapiro, 1969; Tutt, 1971). The type and pattern of sex offending appears to be somewhat different to that in the normal population. For example, the sex offences are less carefully planned and executed, and the offenders are less likely to know their victim than is the norm with such attacks (Gilby, Woolf and Goldberg, 1989). One interpretation of these findings is that the sex offences are clumsy, impulsive expressions of sexual feelings rather than violent acts as is the case with sex offences such as rape that are perpetrated by 'normal' sex offenders. In females with a learning disability the most common sex offence is soliciting.

Robertson (1981) carried out a follow-up study of a group of over 300 learning disabled offenders who had committed a criminal act, received and completed a hospital order, and had been released into the community. Most of the offences after release, for both males and females, involved petty larceny and breaking and entering. The rate of sex offences for males was relatively high, as was the rate of soliciting for the females. Robertson also compared the male learning disabled offenders with male mentally ill offenders. The learning disabled offenders were much younger and less likely to have been married, had fewer hospital admissions, were younger when receiving their first conviction, and had committed more offences as juveniles. On the other hand, the mentally ill group of offenders had more court appearances and had spent longer in prison. While the incidence of theft was similar in the two groups, the mentally ill offenders had been convicted of more (non-sexual) violent offences but there were more sexual offences in the learning disabled group. As Robertson notes, leaving the sexual offences to one side, the pattern evident in the learning disabled group of petty juvenile crime turning in later life to acquisitive offences is very like that found in the general offender population. This contrasts sharply with the atypical pattern observed in the mentally ill population in which juvenile offending is not common and criminal behaviour appears as part of a general social deterioration associated with chronic mental illness.

There are many areas of life in which a person with a learning disability may have failed to learn the rules that define acceptable and unacceptable behaviour. A lack of social skills may mean that acts intended to be friendly are seen by others as aggressive or hostile; sexual experimentation may be more visible than convention allows; sexual advances may be clumsy, reflecting a paucity of skills in making acceptable sexual approaches. While such acts of social and sexual naivety may be perceived by the 'victim' as assault, is it proper to define these as 'criminal' acts when the 'offender' does not hold the concept of 'right' or 'wrong' and it is debatable whether they can knowingly break the law?

Psychopathic Disorder

The 1983 Mental Health Act defines psychopathic disorder as 'a persistent disorder or disability of mind (whether or not including significant impairment of intelligence) which results in abnormally aggressive or seriously irresponsible conduct' [s.1(2)]. This is clearly an imprecise definition as it does not specify the meaning in practice of terms such as 'persistent', 'abnormally aggressive', or 'seriously irresponsible'. Thus researchers and clinicians have devoted a considerable amount of time and energy to attempts to devise diagnostic criteria for psychopathy. It should be noted, however, that the research has almost exclusively been concerned with male offenders.

Assessment

The most influential early work in this area was that of Cleckley (1964, 1976) who attempted to define the psychopath from the characteristics most frequently observed in clinical practice. These characteristics included a singular lack of guilt and remorse for their offences, egocentricity and impulsiveness, an inability to form close relationships, and a failure to learn from experience. In total, the psychopath is marked by emotional and social emptiness in the way in which they behave towards other people. Hare (1980) conducted a factor analysis of data derived from Cleckley's criteria and found five factors that describe the typical picture of the psychopath: 1) an inability to develop warm, empathic relationships; 2) an unstable life-style; 3) an inability to accept responsibility for antisocial behaviour; 4) an absence of intellectual and psychiatric problems; 5) weak behavioural control. Based on Cleckley's criteria, Hare (1980) developed a twenty-two-item *Psychopathy Checklist* (PCL) to allow for a more precise assessment of psychopathy; Hare (1986) subsequently shortened this checklist by removing two items to produce a revised version, termed PCL–R. A summary of the PCL–R is shown in Table 6.1.

Harpur, Hakstian, and Hare (1988) administered the PCL–R to almost 1,200 male prison inmates in Canada, the United States and England. The resultant data were then factor analyzed to determine the structure inherent in

Table 6.1:   Synopsis of the Hare Psychopathy Checklist–Revised (PCL–R) (after Hare, 1991)

1   Superficial charm
2   Grandiose sense of self-worth
3   Need for stimulation/easily bored
4   Pathological lying
5   Manipulative
6   Lack of remorse or guilt
7   No emotional depth
8   Callous
9   Parasitic lifestyle
10 Poor behavioural control
11 Promiscuous sexual behaviour
12 Early behaviour problems
13 Lack of long-term planning
14 Impulsive
15 Irresponsible
16 Failure to accept responsibility for own actions
17 Frequent marital failures
18 Delinquent as a juvenile
19 Poor record on probation or other conditional release
20 Versatile as a criminal

the PCL–R. A one factor solution, as might have been expected, would indicate that all the items on the PCL–R are measuring the same construct; multiple factor solutions would indicate that the trait measured by the inventory (i.e., psychopathy) is actually an amalgam of separate constructs. Harpur *et al.* report that their analysis favoured a two-factor solution:

> *Factor 1: Selfish, callous, and remorseless use of others* ... describes a constellation of personality traits that many clinicians consider to be at the heart of psychopathy, including habitual lying, lovelessness, and guiltlessness; *Factor 2: Chronically unstable and antisocial lifestyle* ... defines a life-style that is aimless, unpredictable, and parasitic (Harpur *et al.*, 1988, p. 745).

Thus Harpur *et al.* suggest that in essence the concept of psychopathy consists of two correlated factors, one concerning personality traits, the other reflecting chronic antisocial and criminal behaviour. However, a high score on just one factor would not indicate psychopathy; the factors do overlap and above average scores would be needed on both in order to diagnose psychopathy. Hare's most recent work has been to continue to refine and develop understanding of these two factors, for example by investigating their relationship with other personality measures (e.g., Hare, 1991; Hare *et al.*, 1990; Harpur, Hare and Hakstian, 1989).

   Thus the approach taken by Cleckley and Hare to defining the psychopath relies first on clinical observation to pick out the characteristics of the psychopath, followed by the use of sophisticated statistical techniques to develop a reliable psychometric instrument (i.e., the PCL–R). Another approach to the same task is to use psychometric measures that have already been tried and tested to search for the defining characteristics of a 'psychopathic personality'.

For example, a considerable body of research has used the Minnesota Multiphasic Personality Inventory (MMPI) to study the personality profiles of violent, including psychopathic, offenders. A number of studies by Blackburn have indicated that there is a distinction to be drawn between *primary psychopaths* and *secondary psychopaths* (Blackburn, 1971, 1986). The primary group shows a personality profile of high levels of hostility, low levels of anxiety, and few psychiatric problems; the secondary psychopaths, on the other hand, display high levels of hostility but accompanied by high levels of anxiety, guilt, and psychiatric problems. The main difficulty with these two approaches is that when administered to the same group of offenders they do not show exact agreement as to which offenders display psychopathy (Harpur *et al.*, 1989).

A third way of reaching a definition, which is rather more informal from the point of view of research design but none the less important for that, is to examine the criteria practitioners use to diagnose psychopathy. Davies and Feldman (1981) asked a sample of over thirty 'forensic specialists' to rate the importance of twenty-two signs of psychopathy. The five most important reported criteria were; 1) not profiting from experience; 2) lacking control over impulses; 3) chronically or recurrently antisocial; 4) lacking a sense of responsibility; 5) their behaviour is unaffected by punishment.

These three methods of assessment clearly have areas of agreement and disagreement in seeking to identify the defining characteristics of the psychopath. Another approach to the problem of assessment and definition is to study the correlates of psychopathy, thereby seeking an empirical means of differentiating the psychopath from the non-psychopath. The relevant research has looked at background factors, physiological functioning, cognitive-behavioural measures, and criminal history.

Background factors

As with criminal behaviour generally, background factors in psychopathy are the familiar ones of family functioning, childhood behaviour, and genetic influences. A number of studies have pointed to a variety of child and adolescent behavioural factors strongly associated with adult psychopathic behaviour (e.g., McCord and McCord, 1964; Robins, 1966). These background factors included early clinical referral for theft or aggression, a history of truancy, lying, non-compliance, a lack of guilt or remorse, and general irresponsibility with respect to school and family routines, together with a lack of parental affection, severe parental rejection, little or no discipline at home, and paternal antisocial behaviour. However, as noted previously, such patterns are to be found in the backgrounds of many offenders who are not psychopaths; indeed, they are aetiological factors in many disorders ranging from neuroses to psychoses. It is doubtful therefore that these background factors are specific antecedents of psychopathy.

Physiological functioning

There is a considerable body of research looking at physiological functioning — mainly the central nervous system (CNS) and the autonomic nervous system (ANS) — in psychopathy (Blackburn, 1983; Raine, 1985). As discussed in Chapter 3, studies of CNS functioning frequently use EEG recordings and this is also true in this area of investigation. While there are indications of high frequencies of EEG abnormality in psychopaths, not all psychopaths show EEG abnormalities, and in those that do the pattern of abnormality is not consistent (Syndulko, 1978). Blackburn (1975, 1979) found little evidence to support the notion of a general association between EEG and aggression. However, Blackburn did suggest that EEG differences may exist between primary and secondary psychopaths; primary psychopaths show the lowest levels of EEG arousal, while secondary psychopaths appeared more alert.

Studies of ANS functioning in psychopaths have indicated that when resting, psychopaths have unduly *low* levels of electrodermal reactivity, but in stressful situations they exhibit very *high* levels of cardiac reactivity (Hare, 1978). This arousal pattern can be interpreted as a fast heart rate being an indication of the 'gating out' of sensory input and so lowering cortical arousal, meaning that the psychopath is effectively 'tuning out' unpleasant environmental cues. Skin conductance is therefore low because to all intents and purposes environmental stimuli, especially aversive stimuli, are being ignored. This interpretation of the physiological evidence assumes greater significance when considered alongside the cognitive-behavioural evidence.

Cognitive-behavioural measures
Cleckley suggested that one of the main characteristics of the psychopath was a failure to learn from experience — evident in the psychopath's failure to avoid the negative consequences of antisocial behaviour. Experimental investigations of this aspect of learning ability in psychopaths have employed the technique of *passive avoidance learning*. This procedure typically requires the subject to learn to respond to anticipatory cues in order to avoid some unpleasant outcome (usually electric shock in laboratory studies). Psychopaths typically perform poorly on passive avoidance learning tasks, indicating that they have a low state of ANS arousal and are relatively anxiety-free (Chesno and Kilmann, 1975). The physiological evidence on ANS functioning offers an explanation; high cardiac arousal 'gates out' the environmental signals of a forthcoming unpleasant event, leading in turn to lower arousal and impaired avoidance learning. However, this hypothesis is complicated by findings that show an effect of the *type* of aversive event. If the aversive consequence of poor learning is physical pain or social disapproval psychopaths perform less well than non-psychopaths; if the consequence is financial penalty then psychopaths learn more efficiently than non-psychopaths (Schmauk, 1970). In other words, what most people consider to be aversive punishments may have little or no meaning for psychopaths.

If the experimental learning task is made more complex by including the competing goals of monetary reward for good performance and avoiding monetary loss for poor performance, then psychopaths perform at a lower level than controls (Newman and Kosson, 1986). As psychopaths are equal to controls with financial loss only, it may be that psychopaths have difficulty attending to competing contingencies once they are trying to gain a reward.

Newman, Patterson and Kosson (1987) employed an experimental task in which money could be gained and lost; they found that while controls were able to make allowances for increases in the probability of losing, psychopaths failed to make such adjustments and so lost accordingly. This pattern of behaviour is termed 'response perseveration' — the continuation of the same pattern of behaviour regardless of the consequences it produces. In other words, a failure to learn from experience.

These peculiarities of learning found in experimental tasks may, perhaps together with physiological functioning, be linked with the under-socialization and poor social performance of psychopaths. While psychopaths do commit violent crimes, such behaviour is not limited by environmental constraints. Blackburn (1982) found that even in a hospital ward psychopaths were rated by nurses as more aggressive, more likely to use threatening behaviour to both staff and other patients, and less likely to follow institutional rules than other patients. Similarly, Hare and McPherson (1984) found that psychopaths held in an institution showed higher levels of verbal abuse and physical violence than other inmates. This pattern of non-conformity to social rules — remembering that criminal behaviour can be seen as breaking social rules — and subsequent lack of remorse can be viewed as a failure to learn to avoid social censure, while response perseveration ensures repetition of the behaviour regardless of the situational demands.

Criminal behaviour

A body of evidence has accumulated that shows that psychopaths are the most persistent and serious offenders. Hare, McPherson and Forth (1988) note from their study that 'Psychopaths generally had significantly more convictions for assault, theft, robbery, fraud, possession of a weapon, and escaping custody than did non-psychopaths' (p. 711). There are few who would disagree with the conclusions of Hare *et al.* with respect to the offence pattern of male psychopaths: they engage in a far wider range of types of criminal behaviour than most offenders, attract more convictions, and spend more time in prison than other offenders. This same point holds true when comparisons are made with mentally ill and learning disabled offenders; psychopaths are much more 'criminal' in that they have committed more offences, particularly theft and assault, received more prison sentences, and spent more time in prison (Robertson, 1981). Yet further, there may be differences *within* the psychopathic offender population. Blackburn (1982) suggests that primary psychopaths are more likely to commit violent offences; secondary psychopaths are more likely to commit sex offences. With respect to numbers of psychopathic offenders, the official statistics for England and Wales in 1984 showed that there were 410 restricted patients classified as psychopathic detained in hospital. Of this number, 200 had been convicted of homicide or other offences against the person, ninety of arson and seventy of sexual offences (DHSS and Home Office, 1986). The number of unclassified psychopaths is, of course, unknown. However, given the history of imprisonment in the backgrounds of many psychopathic offenders, it is not unreasonable to suggest that the prison population may contain substantial numbers of psychopathic offenders.

After conditional release from prison, psychopaths are likely to present with the greatest supervisory problems and to be reconvicted within one year (Hart, Kropp and Hare, 1988). However, as Hare *et al.* (1988) report, there are indications that this high level of criminal activity begins to 'burn out' after the age of forty years. The offence patterns of psychopaths are dissimilar to those found in most offenders. As will be discussed in Chapter 9, a great deal of violence takes place in the context of a heated social exchange between offender and victim. However, Williamson, Hare and Wong (1987) found that psychopaths rarely conform to this picture of crimes of passion. The violence perpetrated by psychopaths was typically cold and callous, without the emotional arousal so typical of similar crimes committed by non-psychopaths.

Psychopathy: Concept or chimera?

Prins (1980), who asks the question concept or chimera, documents the sometimes heated debate about the usefulness of the notion of psychopathy. As can be gleaned from the evidence discussed above, psychopathy is difficult to assess, define, and distinguish. On one hand this can be seen as a technical problem for researchers and clinicians to solve; on the other hand, however, it can be argued that the term is simply a legal and medical convenience. Grounds (1987) gives a flavour of the latter position:

> Walker and McCabe's (1973) examination of how the legal term is used led them to conclude that as a 'diagnosis' 'psychopathic disorder' had no explanatory, descriptive, prognostic or therapeutic function. In practice it is used as a pseudo-diagnosis; a label attached to offenders with a group of abnormalities to help the psychiatrist 'get his patient through the customs-barrier of the courts if he wants to' (p. 474).

In essence, the objection to the concept of psychopathy hinges on a tautology: psychopaths are dangerous highly antisocial people who commit violent offences; the diagnosis of psychopathy is made on the basis of dangerous, highly antisocial, and violent criminal behaviour. The crux of the matter therefore is that there are no criteria — medical, biological, or psychological — by which to identify psychopaths as a type of offender distinct from and different to other offenders.

Perhaps, for the present at least, the conclusion reached by the Department of Health and Social Security and the Home Office (1986) offers a pragmatic compromise:

> The consensus view is that psychopathic disorder is not a description of a single clinical disorder but a convenient label to describe a severe personality disorder which may show itself in a variety of attitudinal, emotional and inter-personal behaviour problems. The core problem is impairment in the capacity to relate to others — to take account of their feelings and to act in ways consistent with their safety and convenience (p. 4).

Mental Disorder and Criminal Behaviour: Theory and Practice

It is clear that mental disorder and criminal behaviour do, at times, coexist. The nature of this relationship is, however, altogether less clear. In some cases, as perhaps with paranoid schizophrenia, the relationship appears, in part at least, to be causal. As Taylor has stressed, however, both disorder and crime must be placed in a broad social context. If paranoid delusions are one cause of violent conduct, what causes the delusions and determines their content? Anticipating future research, it is unlikely that hard and fast theoretical laws will be made regarding mental disorder and crime. It is more likely that cases will have to be considered on their individual merits to determine, in that particular instance, the nature of the relationship between the mental disorder and criminal behaviour. This is not only a theoretical point, but is also one of some practical significance when the courts have to decide on mental state in order to determine whether the offender can be held accountable and therefore punishable for their actions. A brief discussion will illustrate the complexity of the issues involved.

The mentally disordered offender poses special problems for a legal system, such as that in Great Britain, which (as discussed in Chapter 1) relies on the concept of *mens rea*. For a person to be held fully responsible for their behaviour it must be shown that they acted with criminal intent, exercising their free will in so doing. The crucial question, raised several times during the preceding discussion of mental disorder and criminal behaviour, is how responsible for their actions can mentally disordered individuals be held? The legal thinking on this topic has gone through several stages as briefly discussed below.

At one time the position was that it was necessary to show a causal relationship between the individual's mental state and their criminal behaviour before a plea of not guilty by reason of insanity could be offered. This requirement of proof of causality changed with the 1959 Mental Health Act. As Feldman (1977) comments, the Act allows that '*Any* offender committed by a higher court may be detained in hospital or made subject to a guardianship order. It makes no *requirement* for a causal link between the abnormality and the offence' (p. 163). Thus if an offender is shown to be mentally disordered, as defined by the Act, then he or she passes into the world of hospitals rather than prisons (although psychopaths do go to prison on the grounds of being untreatable). The 1959 Act allowed the court a range of sentencing options, from a hospital order which might entail out-patient treatment, to enforced detention in a Special Hospital. The more serious crimes were, of course, more likely to lead to compulsory detention in a secure hospital. A revised Mental Health Act was introduced in 1983 that made amendments to some of the definitions of mental disorder, changed the rules for compulsory admission to hospital, and reviewed matters regarding consent to treatment and discharge procedures.

As Bean (1980) has suggested, the 1959 Act was a landmark in legislation, in effect diminishing judicial control over mentally disordered offenders and handing that power over to the medical, particularly psychiatric, profession.

The trial of Peter Sutcliffe, the 'Yorkshire Ripper', illustrates the difficulties this has caused. In Sutcliffe's trial the jury was required to decide on the accuracy of the diagnosis of four psychiatrists who had diagnosed Sutcliffe as mentally ill. The jury decided that Sutcliffe was fit to stand trial; he was duly tried, found guilty of murder and sentenced to life imprisonment. Three years later he was transferred to a Special Hospital because of his mental illness (see Prins, 1986). While there were many reasons for these manoeuvres, one contributory factor is the reliance in both law and psychiatry on concepts such as mental responsibility, mental disorder, state of mind, and free will. However, there are no tests of normality of mind, no assessment tools for the quality of mind and no measures of free will. Thus decisions about mental state have to be inferred from the individual's verbal and non-verbal behaviour, albeit within the boundaries of a psychiatric diagnosis. It follows that such decisions will always be subjective, and so open to argument and controversy. Thus there are great debates about the *mental* state of individuals such as Sutcliffe who commit the most appalling *acts* against other people. Of course, the question of outcome, that is treatment or punishment, remains a fundamental moral question. Whether it is lawyers or psychiatrists — or psychologists! — who are best placed to decide on that issue remains a topic for debate.

Chapter 7

Preventing Criminal Behaviour: Punishment, Deterrence and Retribution

Suppose you are the victim of a crime, let's say that your car is broken into and the radio stolen, what should happen to the person who committed the offence? What message would you want to send to the rest of society about what will happen to them should they dare to break into your car?

In answer to the first question, you might well want the criminal justice system to respond to the crime in a manner that will achieve a number of outcomes. You might want the offender to suffer some pain or unpleasantness in return for the damage to your property and your feelings; and you might want to try to make sure that the offender does not break into more cars in the future. With regard to the rest of society, you might want the courts to make it plain that other would-be vandals should think twice before breaking into people's cars. In other words, you want *punishment*, and you want that punishment to achieve the twin goals of *retribution* and *deterrence*.

The concepts of punishment, retribution, and deterrence are enshrined in the system of justice that operates in Great Britain and has done so for centuries past. In this chapter the aim is to examine the assumptions about criminal behaviour inherent in these goals, to discuss the practical methods by which they are implemented, and to consider their effectiveness.

Punishment and Retribution

It will be recalled from previous chapters that classical theories of crime are the oldest explanations of criminal behaviour; it is not surprising therefore that they hold a central place in modern day systems of justice in Western society. Classical theories hold that those who commit crimes do so of their own free will, seeking to gain the benefits that their unlawful behaviour will produce for them. In these terms the individual is portrayed as an accountant, coolly calculating and balancing the costs and benefits of their criminal acts in terms of the net gains of their lawbreaking against the penalties should they be caught (see for example Van Den Haag, 1982, discussed in Chapter 4). It follows from this argument that if offenders wilfully break the law, then they must accept the consequences that society has decided should follow criminal acts. Punishment is intended to act as a retribution; it is society's revenge for the wrongdoing it has suffered and it is the offender's right to be punished.

How should we go about the business of delivering punishment and retribution for criminal behaviour? In the first place the punishment must be unpleasant for the offender, perhaps involving personal loss of any or all of wealth, power or liberty. The delivery of punishment cannot be random, however, it cannot be imposed arbitrarily as an exercise of power; nor is it advisable that punishment is meted out by vigilantes undertaking their own private vendettas. Some means of regulating the administration of punishment is clearly needed, yet at the same time making sure that punishment is delivered publicly and effectively. Thus we have a criminal justice system with elaborate checks and safeguards to ensure, as well as possible, that the *appropriate* punishment and retribution is delivered to those who break the law. In this context the term *appropriate* is interesting. At one time the belief was widely held that the punishment for any crime should be of the maximum severity; accordingly, history is studded with tales of the torture, flogging, branding, mutilation, burning, and killing of those who broke the law of the land. It was not until the eighteenth century that social reformers, such as Cesare Beccaria and Jeremy Bentham, began to argue successfully that the severity of the punishment should match the severity of the crime. This basic tenet has become ingrained into our thinking about crime; it seems unlikely that many people today would argue that the person who stole their car radio deserves the same punishment as another person who murders a child.

In order to achieve this goal of appropriate punishment and retribution we have a complex legal code that seeks to define both criminal behaviour and the penalties to be administered to those who transgress. There are, of course, a range of penalties or *sentences* that the court can deliver to those who break the law. For example, the court can impose a fine, inflicting financial penalty; it can place conditions on the offender's behaviour such as attending hospital, seeing a probation officer, or not meeting certain people; it can order the offender to complete a period of supervised community service; and it can impose a period of custody, thereby depriving the offender of their liberty. The administration of such a web of sentencing alternatives is a highly complex task; reviews and discussions are provided by, among others, Prins (1986), Thomas (1979) and Walker (1985).

If we return to the theme of appropriate punishment, legislators are not only faced with the task of deciding what punishment matches what crime, but also with decisions about the quality of the experience of punishment. To take one example, if we agree that a criminal commits an act that deserves loss of liberty, then under what conditions should that person be held? If the loss of freedom is the punishment and retribution, should all the offender's other rights and privileges be held intact, or should these be forfeited along with liberty? In other words, once the court has reached its decision, should criminals be sent to prison *as* a punishment or in order to *receive* punishment? As will be discussed in due course, until quite recently the former view was the official line (which is not to say that it invariably translated into practice); that is, offenders were sent to jail as a punishment but while they were held in custody positive effort would be made to help them return to a good and useful life once their sentence was served. (However, over the past decade or so there has been a marked change in this sentiment; the rise of the *justice model* of correction has coincided with the advent of policies aimed at 'getting tough' with offenders (Hudson, 1987).) To return to the example of prison regimes, this new toughness has translated into practice in a number of ways: custodial aims are no longer directed at positive change but at humane containment in which the offender simply serves their time; harsh custodial regimes, such as the 'short, sharp shock' regime, have been implemented (see below); and prison conditions have been allowed to deteriorate considerably, both in terms of the fabric of many prisons and levels of over-crowding.

The question remains, however, do sentences have the desired effects of delivering punishment and retribution? In truth, the answer is likely to vary from individual to individual. If the court delivers a sentence then, from the public's point of view, retribution has clearly been handed out. Whether or not we think sufficient (or, indeed, too much) retribution has been delivered is another matter. It is not difficult to think of cases in which courts have been severely criticized in the media for being either too lenient or too harsh in the degree of retribution exacted by the sentence passed. However, we must also look to the offender; do criminals find the penalties imposed for their crimes to be punishing?

It is tempting to assume that the confines of penal life would be a highly aversive and punishing experience but, like beauty, punishment is both relative and in the eye of the beholder. For myself, I am sure that I should find imprisonment highly aversive; I can think of few worse things than being separated from my family, taken away from my work, and placed in a cramped, insanitary cell. I am sure that other people, perhaps most other people, feel the same way. However, it would be a mistake to assume that *all* people feel that way. Two pieces of evidence, one a personal anecdote, the other a piece of empirical research, support this view of mixed reactions to imprisonment.

Some time ago I worked as a prison psychologist in an institution for young offenders and one of the tasks on which I worked was a programme to attempt to reduce institutional offending. Specifically, the idea was to target young offenders who continually got into fights in order to help them gain some skills that would allow them to negotiate their way out of the situations that were giving rise to the fights. The justification for this intervention was that the fights were not in anyone's best interest, least of all the young people who would continually be put on report and run the risk of 'losing time'. Accordingly we designed and ran skill-based courses to change institutional behaviour, with some degree of success (Hollin and Courtney, 1983). In running these courses we made great play of the fact that not only would participants run less risk of 'losing time', there was also the additional possibility of earning 'time back' and so securing an earlier date of release. (Changes in sentencing that have abolished the old Borstal Training sentence would probably now make it more difficult to arrange this degree of flexibility; whether that is a good or bad thing is open to debate.) We found that this incentive of time back against sentence worked well for some young offenders, in that their institutional behaviour improved; it had little impact on others; while for a small number of young people it appeared to make matters worse as their levels of discipline deteriorated still further. The reason for this lack of success, as I discovered simply by asking, was that these young people did not want to leave the institution. What was on offer when they left — family problems, unemployment, probation, poor housing, little money — was considerably worse than their current plight. So what if they got into fights and lost time? At least they had three square meals a day and the company of some good mates. This, of course, pointed to the fatal flaw in my own thinking. I had assumed that, like me, the young people would find custody aversive and would want out as fast as possible. However, the experience of an aversive environment is defined both by where you have come from and where you are going to — my own circumstances and those of these intractable young offenders obviously had little in common.

Faced with such a position, what steps can be taken to try to reassert the experience of custody as an aversive, punishing experience? A perfect example is to be found with the reintroduction (in the early 1980s) of the 'short, sharp shock' regime for young offenders. With neoclassical views in the ascendency and the government of the day dedicated to a crackdown on crime with a firm policy of law and order, the decision was made to reintroduce the sharp, short shock regime at several young offender penal institutions in England.) Parenthetically, it is worth noting that while much is made of the 'fact' that the public are in favour of tough sentences and, indeed, demand tougher ones, the evidence both in this country and the United States fails to support the view of a public baying for harsh measures (Cullen *et al.*, 1990; Hough and Mayhew, 1985). As Hough, Moxon, and Lewis (1987) note in their summary of attitudes to sentencing among respondents to the British Crime Survey: 'Policy makers and the courts can treat with a degree of scepticism the claims often made by the media that public opinion demands a tougher line with offenders' (p. 128). Similarly, it does not seem that public fear of crime corresponds with demands for punitive sentences (Ouimet and Coyle, 1991). To return to the early 1980s, the thinking behind the short, sharp shock regime is that the offender's experience of imprisonment should be as punishing as possible to administer a stiff lesson to those who break the law.)The tougher regime was implemented at several penal establishments for young offenders; the effects of the new regimes were monitored and evaluated by a team of psychologists in the Young Offender Psychology Unit at the Home Office (Thornton *et al.*, 1984; see also Thornton, 1987a).

The short, sharp shock regime incorporated a number of distinct features including strict discipline, kit inspections, drill, brisk routines, extended physical exercise and close supervision. The evaluation of the effects of this supposedly shocking regime were assessed by gathering interview and questionnaire data from the young offenders both before and after the introduction of the change. One point of interest was whether the young offenders felt they were having an 'easy time'; it was found that the new regime had no impact in one institution, while in another more young offenders felt the regime was easier *after* the change. The regime may have been different but it was most certainly not shocking! There are a number of possible explanations for this finding: the brisk regime helped time to pass more quickly; the young people enjoyed the hard physical exercise; the regime was not administered by prison staff in a punitive manner; or the changes were not punitive in themselves. If we follow the last point, although allowing some degree of plausibility to the others, it is possible that there was a carbon copy on a much larger scale of my own mistake discussed above. That is, whoever designed the shocking regime, designed one that they personally would find aversive, but which met with the approval of the young people for whom it was intended.

There are many other examples of 'get tough' policies including *shock probation, boot camp prison regimes,* and *scared straight* programmes, none of which have a strong track record (Gendreau and Ross, 1987). This general lack of success with the get tough initiatives can be responded to in one of two ways: we need either a complete rethink of the whole system; or we need more of the same, only harder and tougher. The former option of a rethink will be discussed later, the present emphasis is on 'getting tougher'. If we are serious about punishing criminals, why compromise with drill and brisk routines? Why not use what we all really know to be aversive — physical pain and the threat of death?

Capital Punishment

This is not an easy topic to discuss and it is easy to lose sight of reality in the arguments and counter-arguments that must necessarily be rehearsed. However, it is chastening to begin with a quote from Gerald Gardiner Q.C.: 'Capital punishment is a convenient phrase: but what it means is that once a month they take some man, woman or youth out of a cell and kill him or her on a gallows' (Gardiner, 1956, p. 7).

A little while ago I published a paper on the topic of worry about the threat of nuclear war (Hollin, 1991a). When the paper was returned by the referees after the initial submission the comment was made that my paper should include a declaration of my personal views on nuclear disarmament. While naturally I do have views on that topic, I failed to see their relevance to that particular paper — which was a 'neutral' empirical investigation of the relationship between worry about nuclear war and worry about life's other hazards — and therefore I did not add them to that piece of research. However, what follows on the next few pages is neither empirical nor neutral and I feel that I should declare my hand accordingly:

> I am absolutely opposed to the use of capital (and corporal) punishment.

Before examining the arguments, however, what is known of the current use of the death penalty? Hood (1989) provides the most comprehensive and up-to-date summary of the use of the death penalty around the globe. With respect to the willingness to sentence criminals to death, Hood places each of

the world's countries into one of four classes: 1) *abolitionist*, that is not providing the death penalty for any crime at all (thirty-five countries); 2) *abolitionist
for ordinary crimes only*, that is retaining the death penalty for crimes such as
those committed under military law or in wartime (eighteen countries, including the UK); 3) *abolitionist de facto*, that is retaining the death penalty for ordinary crime but not having executed anyone in the past decade or more
(twenty-six countries and territories); 4) *retentionist*, that is retaining and using
the death penalty (101 countries and territories). Hood provides a listing of the
countries in each of the four categories, noting that for some countries reliable
information is difficult to obtain, and that globally the picture continually
shifts as some countries change their position. Bearing in mind that this is an
area in which it is impossible to gather watertight estimates, with respect to
world figures Hood notes that: 'In the years 1979–83 Amnesty International
recorded an annual average of 1,627 death sentences and 1,758 executions. . . .
Amnesty rightly regards its figures as substantial underestimates' (p. 47).
Further, it should not be thought that once the death penalty has been
abolished it will stay abolished, again to quote Hood:

> In the United States, where executions resumed in 1977, the annual
> number remained low until 1984, when 21 persons were executed.
> Although it has settled around this number in subsequent years — 25
> in 1987 — the number of persons on death row has risen to over
> 2,000, many of whom are reaching the point where no more appeals
> can be made (p. 50).

What then are the arguments for and against the use of the death penalty?
Gardiner (1956), writing at the time when the UK had a death penalty for
ordinary crimes, suggests that the case for the death penalty is based on four
arguments: 1) its deterrence value; 2) that there is no satisfactory alternative
punishment; 3) public opinion demands its retention; 4) with crime levels as
they were at that time, the moment for abolition had not arrived. With respect
to the first point, the deterrence argument will be examined presently, while
with regard to the last point, clearly the moment for abolition has come and
gone in this country. So what are the arguments based on there being no suitable alternative, and on the demands of public opinion?

With respect to the latter line of argument, Gardiner delivers a crushing
riposte to those who seek to bolster their arguments with claims of speaking
for the people: 'To some politicians too, it may not be unfair to say that public
opinion is "the clamour of the ignorant mob" when they do not support the
politician's view, and "the voice of the people" when they do' (p. 68). I think
we can dispense quickly with any argument in favour of the death penalty
based on claims to have inside knowledge of the demands of public opinion.
As noted previously, the public are probably far less punitive then we are led
to believe and, in any case, it is far more likely that public opinion will be
deeply divided on this issue.

We are left then with the argument, used throughout history and one of
the stock arguments in favour of its retention, that there is no alternative

sentence that can deliver the equivalent retribution to the death penalty. If we accept that the punishment should fit the crime, then which crimes should be punished by execution? In the last century the abolition of the death penalty for minor offences was opposed on the grounds that the alternative punishments, including both imprisonment and transportation, were not satisfactory. However, if in the 1990s it was suggested that the death penalty be brought back for theft, most people would think this to be highly unjust; committing an act of theft does not warrant losing your life. It follows from this that there is no absolute or fixed standard of criminal conduct that merits the death penalty. Therefore the question becomes 'for which crimes is the death penalty an appropriate punishment to which no alternative can be found'? This question seems most often to draw the response that crimes that involve taking another life deserve punishment by death. If a member of society is killed, then society should exact retribution by taking the offender's life. We are left therefore with a moral argument. In order to exact retribution (or, as is the current fashion, 'just deserts', or better, an eye for an eye and a tooth for a tooth, or even better, plain old-fashioned revenge — it all amounts to the same thing: once a month a body at the end of a rope) is it morally justifiable to take a life?

The philosophical issues in debating moral theory and capital punishment are somewhat involved (see Sorrell, 1987), I have attempted below to offer a synopsis of the competing points in the debate.

For the retributionists, such as Newman (1983), the moral argument is straightforward; the offender has knowingly broken the law and therefore physical pain is justified, indeed it is the offender's right, because it is fair and just that the offender suffers. This position is consistent with neoclassical theories of crime, in which the offender is said to act of their own free will.

The abolitionist position has several strands, moral, ethical and practical, that tax lay people and professionals alike. The moral argument, quite simply, is that it is absolutely wrong to take life. If this is held to be true, it follows that if it is wrong for the individual, then it is also wrong for the state to commit legalized murder. In one sense the debate stops here. Having considered the arguments, you either believe absolutely that it is wrong to take life, or you believe that, perhaps within a set of rules, it is permissible to kill another human being. While this moral position can stand in its own right, and is, I think, the crux of the matter, there are a number of further considerations.

At another level we are simply trading theories. If positivist or constructional theories are correct then this places a quite different light on the concept of responsibility and hence retribution for one's actions. Suppose the environmentalists are right; what if behaviour is largely determined by environmental forces — what then, hang schoolteachers and parents? Further, we know that many acts of violence, including murder, are committed in the heat of the moment in an emotionally laden social context (see Chapter 9). This image of violent crime as an emotional act contrasts starkly with the prospect of the state deliberately and coolly killing a person which is, for me, a brutal and horrifying act. As an aside, I think we can dispense with the notion of a 'humane' method of killing. As documented in the booklet *The Case Against*

Capital Punishment, published by the Howard League for Penal Reform, all methods of execution, including hanging, electrocution, lethal gas, and lethal injections, are brutal and can go horribly wrong:

> *Electrocution* produces 'visible destructive effects as the body's internal organs are burned; the prisoner often leaps forward against the restraining straps when the switch is thrown; the body changes colour; the flesh swells and may even catch fire; the prisoner may defecate, urinate or vomit blood. Witnesses always report that there is a smell of burning flesh' (Amnesty International 'USA Death Penalty briefing' 1987). In 1983 it took three charges of electricity over a period of fourteen minutes for a prisoner to be declared dead (Howard League for Penal Reform, *The Case Against Capital Punishment*, p. 3).

What if a mistake is made and the wrong person is executed? There are many well-documented cases of wrongful execution (see for example Hain, 1976) and it is likely that there are others that will forever remain undetected. Indeed, if the death penalty were still in force, would the Guildford Four and the Birmingham Six be alive today? (Further, as discussed by Hood, 1989, is it significant that minority groups appear to attract the death sentence in disproportionate numbers?) This seems to me to be the bottom line; if you want the death penalty then you have to be prepared to tolerate errors in the system. Some proponents of the death penalty are perfectly happy with this prospect. Pawsey, cited by Sorell (1987: p. 47), said:

> We must have a balance sheet with, on the one hand, the loss of one or perhaps two innocent lives through judicial procedure, and, on the other, the loss of innocent lives by acts of murder that would have been prevented had an effective deterrent been in existence.

This seems to me to be arrogant, high-handed nonsense: leaving aside the deterrence argument (see below), 'one or two' (but probably more) human lives are not items on a 'balance sheet'; my life, the lives of my children, your life, is not something that can be written off as an unfortunate bookkeeping error should any of us be wrongfully executed.

An additional ethical dilemma is also present for psychiatrists and clinical psychologists. In countries where the death penalty is used, should clinical treatment be made available to a psychotic prisoner so that when he or she is returned to normal functioning they can be executed (Sadoff, 1990)? In a similar vein, Newbold (1990) movingly documents the adverse impact of the death penalty on those charged with its administration.

I believe that the question of whether or not to use the death penalty is a moral question, not likely to be solved by empirical methods (see below). In this light, beliefs about the death penalty raise interesting issues at a psychological level. Harvey (1986) reports a study of the belief systems and attitudes of those for and against the death penalty. Those most strongly in favour of the death penalty were characterized as the most frequent church goers, the most conservative, and most likely to have concrete, less complex belief systems holding faith in 'good' and 'bad' as given truths. Those against the death penalty were more likely to be liberal and to espouse complex and abstract belief systems in which causality is viewed as depending on changing personal and environmental influences, and hence any conception of truth can only be tentative in nature. It is not to difficult to see how this contrast in belief systems is reflected in some of the theoretical differences underpinning retention and abolition, as well as on retribution and the form it should take.

Punishment and Deterrence

It is important to make the distinction between retribution and deterrence. As discussed above, retribution is the response that society makes to criminal behaviour, it is an acknowledgment of the offender's behaviour and the imposition of consequences to punish the wrongdoing. For retributionists, the delivery of fair and just retribution should be the goal of the justice system: to punish criminals for their behaviour, no more no less. Deterrence, on the other hand, is to punish offenders to attempt to produce some change in their behaviour; that is, to administer a penalty with the aim of stopping that offender from committing more crimes. Many retributionists are opposed to the principle of deterrence; the argument is advanced that punishment is administered because it is deserved by past acts, it should not be delivered on the nebulous basis of doing 'good' at some time in the future.

Proponents of deterrence, on the other hand, argue that if our future actions are influenced by our experience then the administration of punishment should have the aim of reducing the crime rate. Again we see the influence of classical theories of crime; if we have free will, then we can choose to commit a crime and take the gains or suffer the penalties. If we accept this way of thinking about criminal behaviour then the solution is elementary; Van Den Haag (1982) again provides a concise statement, drawing once more on the 'balance book' analogy:

> Our only hope for reducing the burgeoning crime rate lies in decreasing the expected net advantage of committing crimes (compared to lawful activities) by increasing the expected severity of the punishments and the probability of suffering them (p. 1035).

In other words, we are back to arguing for sharper, even more shocking sentences.

The concept of deterrence extends beyond the individual offender, with the proposition that punishment sets an example for the whole population as to the consequences should they commit an offence. The first level of deterrence, that is for the individual receiving the punishment, is properly termed *special deterrence*; the second level of deterrence, that is for society is a whole, is termed *general deterrence*.

Special deterrence

Are offenders prevented from committing more offences by the administration of punishment? Clearly this is a very difficult question to answer; it would demand an exhaustive and extensive research programme to come up with anything like a reasonable conclusion. We know, for example, that prison sentences appear to deter some offenders in that they do not, officially at least, reoffend; however, we also know that substantial numbers of those imprisoned will return to prison. With respect to the short, sharp shock regime discussed previously, reconviction data were gathered and it was clear that the tougher regimes did not produce any notable effects on reconviction (which was around the 50 per cent mark). It is probably fair to conclude that there is, at present, no compelling evidence that the delivery of punishment has a consistent special deterrent effect.

General deterrence

Does the creation of a 'threat system' deter would-be criminals because of the fear of the penalties should they be caught? At one level this is undoubtedly true; in most circumstances I will resist from parking my car on double yellow lines because I do not want a ticket, my wheel clamped, or my car towed away. I have seen this happen to other people and I do not want it to happen to me. (This is an excellent example of vicarious learning through modelling.) My actions are perfectly rational; I have decided not to break the law because I fear the consequences. This fits well with deterrence theory, although it is not the whole story; I also do not park on double yellow lines because it blocks traffic, can be dangerous, and is generally antisocial. Following the latter argument, I obey the law because I agree with it and wish to comply for the general good. It is interesting that studies of why people obey the law have shown that in many cases people obey not for fear of the consequences of breaking the law, but from a sense of community and moral agreement with the spirit of the law (Tyler, 1990).

As with special deterrence it is likely that the threat of punishment does produce some curtailment of criminal behaviour across the general population. How great an effect or for what criminal acts remains a matter for debate. To return to the death penalty, however, does execution act as a general deterrent as often claimed by its proponents? Hood (1989) provides an excellent summary of the general deterrence arguments associated with the death penalty and of the ways by which it can be assessed. A substantial body of research evidence has now been amassed on the deterrent effect of the death penalty and across these studies there is no conclusive evidence of a general deterrent effect. Hood offers the following conclusion:

> Most of those who favour abolition (assuming they are not opposed to execution under any circumstances) would demand proof that executions have a substantial marginal deterrent effect. Those retentionists who rely on their intuitive belief in deterrence would require substantial proof that there was no additional risk to the lives

of citizens before sparing murderers from execution. The balance of evidence, looked at in this way, favours the abolitionist position (p. 148).

I agree. The general deterrence arguments lack support in the case of the death penalty (Peterson and Bailey, 1991). The debate, as discussed above, must therefore hinge on the case for retribution.

The concept of punishment is traditionally based on the administration of penalties to the offender *after* they have committed a crime. However, if we accept the view of the individual as a rational decision-maker, might it not be possible to implement strategies that would influence the potential offender's decision-making thereby deterring him or her *before* offending? This line of thought has received particular attention in the last few years, having become known as *situational crime prevention*. This then provides the topic for the final section of this chapter.

Situational Crime Prevention

As discussed above, one of the aims in punishing convicted offenders is to deter that individual from committing further crimes — the case of special deterrence. The notion of special deterrence implicitly assumes that the propensity for criminal behaviour lies within the individual offender. In the early 1980s this 'dispositional' view of crime began to come under scrutiny, particularly in light of the emergence of the 'rational choice' perspective on understanding crime. As discussed in Chapter 4, the rational choice perspective takes the position that for a crime to occur two events must coincide. First the opportunity for crime must present itself; second the individual must decide that the gains to be had from seizing the opportunity outweigh both the chances of being caught and the penalty should they be apprehended. Thus, in these terms, a criminal is a person who takes advantage of the opportunity to carry out a criminal act, believing that personal advantage or gain will follow from their actions. The logical extension of this position is that the prevention of criminal behaviour is as likely, if not more likely, to be successful by changing the environment prior to the crime taking place, than by attempts to change the criminal after the act. This approach is neatly summarized by Hough, Clarke, and Mayhew (1980) who state the case against concentrating on the individual offender:

> This [dispositional] theoretical emphasis has had an unfortunate consequence. It has encouraged a view of crime whereby criminality in some way inheres in the personality of offenders, so that, come what may, they will seek out their opportunities for crime. In terms of prevention too much effort has been extended on unproductive attempts to change the 'criminal disposition' of offenders (p. 3).

Following rational-choice arguments, the alternative to trying to prevent crime by changing the offender is to change the environment. Such environmental change can have the twin aims of reducing the opportunity for crime and increasing the risk of detection. This approach to crime prevention, now widely known as *situational crime prevention,* has attracted a great deal of attention over the past decade. This attention has come not only from researchers (e.g., Clarke, 1985; Heal and Laycock, 1986), but also crucially from policy makers who have invested a great deal of public resources in situational crime prevention measures. As will become apparent as the discussion unfolds, many of the initiatives that have sprung from this financial and political investment have become part of our daily lives. Indeed, many of the examples of situational crime prevention measures discussed below are taken from three publications prepared by government departments and widely circulated and freely available: these are *Your Car is at Risk: Police Advice on Keeping Your Car Secure,* prepared for the Home Office by the Central Office of Information, 1990; *Crime Prevention Week,* 15 April 1991, produced by the Home Office and the Central Office of Information, 1991; and *Practical Ways to Crack Crime: The Handbook* (4th edition), produced by the Home Office and the Central Office of Information, 1991.

Reducing Opportunity

Hardening the target

One way to make it more difficult to commit a successful crime is simply physically to harden the target by the use of stronger materials and the implementation of security devices. The British Post Office has virtually eliminated theft of money from pay telephones by replacing aluminium coin boxes with steel boxes. Car theft is another area in which target hardening has been encouraged; many new cars now include as a matter of course stronger and more sophisticated door locks, car alarms, lockable wheel nuts, security coded cassette-radio equipment and lockable fuel caps (so that thieves are forced to abandon the car when it runs out of petrol). There is little doubt that such measures can be effective; for example, the introduction of steering column locks had a marked effect on car theft (Mayhew, Clarke and Hough, 1980a).

Similarly, the publication *Practical Ways to Crack Crime* lists a number of ways to increase the security of your home. These measures include the obvious ones such as good locks, door chains, high gates, burglar alarms, time switches that make house lights come on at night when no one is at home, and security lighting, as well as perhaps less obvious strategies such as not planting bushes and shrubs where they will provide cover for a burglar trying to enter through a door or window, and gluing the slats in louvred windows (easily removed to gain entry). Commercial properties can, of course, be similarly protected, while goods in shops can be chained together or placed in security cabinets.

Removing the target

In some cases it is possible to eliminate crime by removing the target altogether. Examples of this include the removal of coin boxes from telephone kiosks and the use of credit cards, and the replacement of coin-operated gas and electricity meters with a billing system. Some shops and garages operate a system by which money is regularly removed from tills so that large, tempting sums do not accumulate. Yet further, the payment of wages by cheque or direct bank credit removes the need to transport large amounts of cash and so eliminates the opportunity for robbery. Target removal can also be used with human as well as material targets. A number of institutions such as hospitals and universities have introduced late night transport systems, thereby cutting down the chances of violent and sexual assaults on people returning home after a late shift or an evening's entertainment.

Increasing the Risk of Detection

Formal surveillance

The most obvious people to detect crime are those placed in a position of authority with the designated task of increasing security and detecting crime. The police are the most well known figures of authority with respect to crime, and it is probably true that if there were a police officer on every street corner crime levels would fall. However, the financial costs alone are prohibitive for such a measure, while the prospects of living in an environment with a police officer always in sight might not appeal to everyone, criminal or otherwise! One feasible strategy is therefore to target a police presence and surveillance at areas in which there is judged to be an increased risk of crime. This might be, for example, at football matches and other large-scale public events, in specific areas of towns and cities, in places such as public lavatories where certain types of crime are known to take place, and in amusement centres and video arcades where truants from school may go during school hours.

However, it is not just the police who are perceived by the public as agents of authority who might detect criminal acts. Research has shown, for example, that buses with a conductor are less likely to be vandalized than buses without a conductor (Sturman, 1980). In a similar vein, extra ticket inspection staff, doorkeepers and porters, car park attendants, and shop assistants can, in the appropriate setting, reduce the incidence of crimes of acquisition and violence. However, surveillance does not have to involve people. Many banks and building societies have installed video cameras that not only monitor the activities of their customers but also provide a permanent record — indeed closed circuit television (CCTV) has become widely used in many settings from football matches to supermarkets. A controlled study of the use of CCTV on the London Underground was reported by Burrows (1980). CCTV was installed at four stations to allow surveillance of those areas of the station — escalators, platforms, ticket halls — where crimes of robbery and theft are most likely to occur. In those four stations with CCTV there were 252 reported offences in the year prior to the instalment of the CCTV; this fell to seventy-five offences in the year after installation, a reduction of 70 per cent. This fall in crime was significantly greater than the general fall of 38 per cent on 238 other stations over the Underground system as a whole.

The use of CCTV illustrates the application of technological advances in measures to combat crime. Another use of technology to allow surveillance, in this case of known offenders, lies in the procedure termed *electronic monitoring* or, as it has come to be called, *tagging*. The principle that informs tagging relies on the offender wearing on their body, usually on an ankle, arm or wrist, a small transmitter or *tag*. The transmitter can be used in a number of ways to monitor the offender's whereabouts. The offender can be required to log in to a central computer via a telephone link placed in their home; failure to do so would mean that monitoring officers are sent to investigate. Another system allows for constant monitoring via a device attached to the telephone that constantly picks up signals and transmits them to the computer. If the offender moves out of range of the telephone, about thirty metres, the monitoring officers are alerted. The range of the offender's movements could, given the right technology, be predetermined and so set at whatever boundary was deemed appropriate.

As documented in recent papers from both British (e.g., Nellis, 1991) and North American (e.g., Maxfield and Baumer, 1990) sources, electronic monitoring has become more and more widely used over the past few years. From the standpoint of those in authority, tagging has a number of potential benefits in terms of financial costs, reduction in the prison population, and crime detection. Individuals awaiting trial or on bail can be monitored without recourse to custody, thereby lowering financial costs and reducing the prison population. In addition, the court has an additional non-custodial measure at its disposal so that, for example, tagging allows curfews on individual offenders to be effectively policed. In terms of crime prevention, monitoring of known offenders may well reduce that person's opportunities for engaging in criminal acts. If a tagged offender does commit a crime, then monitoring might well increase the chances of detecting a given offence. There are also hopes that tagging might lead to a growth in the offender's self-discipline, making the offender a better person for the experience. While this might be somewhat optimistic, it is undoubtedly true that tagging has the potential to keep offenders out of the prison system and so allow them continued contact with families, employment and the community in general.

Whether or not tagging achieves any or all of these objectives is impossible to say. From a practical point of view there are a number of difficulties. The technology is moving so fast that the range of options changes continually, making its use exceedingly difficult to evaluate. The judiciary has yet to settle on a policy for the use of tagging, meaning that only pilot schemes can be run, thereby limiting the real life application of tagging and hence the generalizability of any evaluation. Similarly, other organizations concerned with offenders, such as the Probation Service, have yet to agree with the principle of tagging thereby contributing to a general sense of artificiality about its use at present. From the researcher's point of view there are the practical difficulties already noted, with the additional issues of what to measure and the reliability of any data that can be gathered. However, as will be discussed in due course, these practical and research problems are secondary to the human rights and civil liberty arguments posed by tagging.

Informal surveillance

One of the problems in all formal surveillance is that it demands resources in terms of people and time, both of which are very expensive financially. How much better therefore if the public at large could be persuaded to take on the surveillance task, looking out for crime and reporting it when it happens. A number of initiatives have taken place over the past few years to encourage the public to perform this task.

There can be little doubt that Neighbourhood Watch (or Block Watch, as it is sometimes called) has proved enormously popular with the public over the past few years. In both the USA and Canada such schemes have proliferated (Brantingham and Brantingham, 1990); while the impact in this country has been documented by Mayhew *et al.* (1989):

> Neighbourhood Watch has made more of an impact, in terms of its visibility if nothing else, than any other community crime prevention effort in Britain. In 1984, just over half of the BCS [British Crime Survey] sample had heard of Neighbourhood Watch and by 1988 the figure was 90 per cent. Potential support is widespread with two-thirds of those currently not members expressing willingness to join a scheme if one were set up in their area. Actual schemes have proliferated and the time and resources in launching and implementing them has increased accordingly. From BCS estimates, 14 per cent of households were members of schemes at the beginning of 1988, some two and a half million households in England and Wales. The figure may well now be higher (p. 51).

The principle informing Neighbourhood Watch is perfectly straight-forward. With the support of the police, people living in close proximity will take responsibility for the surveillance of each other's property, watching out for suspicious characters, cars being tampered with, or any other unsavoury incidents. Members of the scheme are encouraged to report any signs of criminal activity to the police. Indeed, the liaison between public and police is a prime example of the slogan 'Crime: Together We'll Crack It' that appears in many of the crime prevention publications aimed at the general public. In many schemes a local coordinator is appointed with the role of organizing local groups, distributing information and keeping schemes in touch with new developments and so forth. In many cases signs are placed on lampposts and in windows advertising the fact that a street is part of a Neighbourhood Watch Area.

Does Neighbourhood Watch work? Well, the answer very much depends on the definition of 'work'. There are several possible indexes of success: the number of incidents reported to the police; the use of security devices; the impact on fear of crime; feelings of security and a sense of community; and the actual number of crimes in a Neighbourhood Watch Area. The outcome research suggests that Neighbourhood Watch Schemes are in general successful in terms of fostering a sense of community spirit, making people feel more secure, increasing both awareness of crime and the use of security measures, and in making it more likely that suspicious incidents will be reported to the police. However, almost paradoxically, Neighbourhood Watch Schemes appear to have little impact on worry and fear of victimization; perhaps the constant reminders through Watch meetings of the risks of crime and consequences of victimization act to maintain awareness of crime at a level beyond what is 'healthy'. The question about crime reduction awaits a definitive answer, and when it comes it is likely to be complex, depending on finer points of measurement such as type of crime and type of neighbourhood. However, there is a very real possibility that Neighbourhood Watch Schemes may in truth be acting to make people feel easier about being victimized (which is not necessarily a bad thing). As Brantingham and Brantingham (1990) note:

> The weight of evidence accumulated through evaluation studies conducted in North America and Britain now suggest that Watch programs may substantially improve participants' general attitudes about their neighbourhoods and may reduce participants' fear levels, but may not have much impact on crime (p. 24).

Nonetheless, it may well be prudent to reserve judgment on Neighbourhood Watch until stronger, longitudinal research evidence is gathered.

Some crimes can be guarded against by increasing the odds of informal surveillance. For example, Mayhew *et al.* (1980b) found that there was less vandalism of telephone kiosks when they were overlooked by private housing. The obvious lesson from this is that when new telephone kiosks are being installed they should be placed in spots where informal surveillance is more likely to be at hand. Another approach to informal surveillance is to give people ownership of part of the environment, so that they take responsibility for what happens in that place. For example, it is well established that public areas with no defined owners are the areas where crime is most likely to occur. Therefore if public places — such as entrances, corridors, lifts, stairways, and underground car parks — can be turned into someone's *defensible space* it is much more likely that this particular area will be watched over. This new surveillance will, in turn, act to lower the probability of crime in that area.

Environmental design

The notion of defensible space, as discussed by Newman (1980), is an important one in situational crime prevention. To create defensible space it is necessary to modify the environment in some way. A number of environmental design features have flowed from the recognition of the importance of physical features in criminal events. Poyner (1991) notes lighting, fencing, road closure or street changes, modernization of housing, and landscaping as environment design strategies that have met with some success in lowering rates of crime. It is likely that such strategies have their effects in a complex fashion. Increased lighting is more likely to make detection more probable, thereby acting as a deterrent; fencing may well define defensible space, making reporting more likely; while improvements in the quality of housing may give residents something worth defending and increase their sense of community. Of course, such measures do not have to be carried out in isolation; it is perfectly feasible that several different environmental improvements could be made at once, while at

Table 7.1:   *Strategies to 'strengthen children' to prevent child sexual abuse (after Daro, 1991)*

* Direct instruction to the child on the distinction between good, bad and questionable touching
* Concept of body ownership and the right of children to control who touches them
* Concept of keeping secrets and telling when touched even if told not to tell
* The ability to act on one's intuition when a touch or action makes a child feel uncomfortable even if he or she does not know why they feel uncomfortable
* Gaining assertiveness skills — from saying 'no' to physical self-defence
* The existence of support systems to help the maltreated child

Table 7.2:   *Strategies to 'strengthen parents' to prevent child sexual abuse (after Daro, 1991)*

* Increasing parental knowledge of child development and the demands of parenting
* Developing parental skill in coping with the stresses of child care
* Enhancing parent-child bonding, emotional ties, and communication
* Developing parental skills in coping with the stresses of caring for children with special needs
* Increasing parental knowledge of home and child management
* Reducing the burden of child care
* Increasing access for all the family to social and health services

the same time, residents are encouraged and given the resources to initiate a Neighbourhood Watch Scheme.

Personal skills

While crime can be prevented by changing the environment, another approach is to change the potential victims. This strategy relies upon giving likely victims skills and strategies by which they can reduce the likelihood of personal attack. The two main groups for which such strategies have been devised are women and children.

Practical Ways to Crack Crime: The Handbook offers a number of self-protection strategies for women. These include trying to avoid isolated bus stops after dark; when travelling on trains sit in carriages with several other passengers; when driving alone not stopping for hitch-hikers (if there appears to be an emergency, drive on and telephone the police); park in well lit areas; in the event of a breakdown do not accept a lift from a stranger; if finances permit, a mobile telephone is a considerable advantage. Of course men can also take positive actions. There is no need to walk behind a woman on a quiet road, cross to the other side of the street; do not sit too close on trains and buses, or strike up casual conversations at bus stops; give lifts to friends and family members or walk them home when possible.

Like women, children are also the target for attacks, both physical and sexual, and over the past few years considerable steps have been made in the development of prevention programmes for children. One way of approaching such prevention programmes is through 'strengthening the child'; a summary of strengthening strategies is shown in Table 7.1.

Alternatively, the focus can be on strengthening parents or guardians to alert them to ways of better caring for the children they are charged with the task of protecting and nurturing (see Table 7.2). For example, Daro (1991) offers a review of the evidence on the effectiveness of prevention programmes, together with a thoughtful consideration of the moral and practical issues involved in designing comprehensive strategies for preventing child sexual abuse.

Problems and Objections

Displacement

Does situational crime prevention stop crime, or does it simply move it to another setting? Does the installation of thief-proof telephone kiosks mean that the crime rate falls, or do frustrated thieves select another target? In other words, does situational crime prevention merely *displace* the offence to other settings, times, targets, or types of criminal act?

The possibility of displacement was noted at an early stage in the development of situational crime prevention strategies (e.g., Gabor, 1981; Reppetto, 1976), and a number of studies were carried out to see if displacement occurred when situational measures were implemented. Some of the first studies suggested that displacement did occur. Mayhew *et al.* (1976) presented data that suggested that the introduction of steering column locks on new cars displaced car theft to older, less well protected vehicles. Similarly, the study monitoring the introduction of CCTV on the London Underground hinted that crime had been displaced to those stations without CCTV geographically close to those with the increased surveillance (Burrows, 1980). However, the major problem in seeking to establish whether displacement has occurred lies in disentangling the crime statistics. Patterns of crime can be influenced by many factors, and rises and falls in rates of crime can make it difficult to detect both the exact impact of situational prevention measures and the extent, if any, of displacement. Yet further, as Cornish and Clarke (1987) explain, the notion of displacement harks back to dispositional theories of crime. If we think of crime as the product of a criminal drive within the individual, then it is not unreasonable to suppose that the individual with that criminal propensity will seek out fresh opportunities for crime. However, as Cornish and Clarke (1987) point out, rational-choice theory does not see criminal behaviour as a product of some internal disposition, but as a consequence of an interaction between environmental characteristics and individual choice. In this light, a change in the environment should act to remove the opportunity, thereby not engaging the person's decision-making, and hence reduce crime. For example, many car thefts occur because someone needs to get from one place to another, usually late at night when public transport has ended. Faced with the prospect of a long walk home on a cold wet night, some people will consider stealing a car; if a vulnerable car presents itself then the opportunity will be seized, the car stolen, and a long walk averted. However, if that same person finds that all the cars in the vicinity have central locking and alarms, then the theft becomes too difficult and the long trudge homeward begins. Given this scenario, it would make little sense to argue that the next day that person will go to a car park, search for a vulnerable vehicle, and steal it. Thus Cornish and Clarke (1987) argue that sensitive measures of displacement must look to the impact of preventative measures on the evaluations individuals make when faced with the opportunity to offend.

On the other hand, it could be argued that there are some people who are, for whatever reason, motivated to steal cars and that if they cannot get a vehicle in one place they will go elsewhere until they are successful. Trasler (1986) has expanded on this point, arguing that *two* strategies are needed: one to deter occasional offenders, such as the car thief who has missed the bus; the other to deal with persistent, high-rate offenders, such as professional car thieves. As Trasler suggests, situational measures may be effective for the occasional offenders, but a different strategy is likely to be called for in the second case.

Objections

While displacement is, in one sense, a technical issue for researchers to resolve, situational crime prevention measures also raise questions about the quality of environment in which we wish to live. Do you want to carry a personal identification card?; do you really want to be recorded on videotape every time you go into a shop or bank or building society?; do you want to live surrounded by security fences, guard dogs, and police officers? Do we want a criminal justice system that uses electronic surveillance methods? The moral and political issues raised by tagging, succinctly discussed by Nellis (1991), are staggering; with the application of technological advances already underway, electronic tagging using transmitters implanted under the skin in conjunction with CCTV could be used to monitor and control people with a precision hitherto undreamed of by the criminal justice system. It is not too difficult to evoke images from an Orwellian nightmare as the population's movement is prescribed, monitored and controlled in the name of crime prevention. Lest this be thought fanciful, twenty years ago how many people would have thought that cars and houses would be fitted with electronic sensors that detect an intruder's movements to sound an alarm? As Nellis (1991) observes, once someone realizes that there's a profit to be made, it is astonishing how quickly today's wonder becomes tomorrow's commonplace.

In summary, this chapter has focused on attempts to prevent crime by punishment, by retribution, and by situational measures. We are left with the practical question of whether such measures work, and with the moral issue of whether these are the acceptable ways to respond to crime. As Clarke (1982) notes, we may have to tolerate certain levels of crime in order to preserve existing freedoms. The issue of whether punitive measures work — that is, whether they lower the crime rate — remains unanswered, although perhaps there is little in the way of compelling evidence. The issue of whether such measures are both privately and publicly acceptable is a matter of choice; punishment and retribution is one approach, the other is rehabilitation and it is to that topic that attention is now turned.

Chapter 8

Preventing Criminal Behaviour: Rehabilitation

In a perfect world there would be no crime. In a slightly less than perfect world there would be highly effective prevention programmes that tackled the causes of crime and stopped criminal acts from taking place. In the world in which we live there are people who commit crimes, there are victims of crime, and there is a criminal justice system that produces substantial numbers of criminals. It would be wonderful if a perfect world existed, or even a slightly less than perfect world, but the truth is that it does not. The fact is that many people will commit one or more criminal acts and, while most crimes are relatively trivial, substantial numbers of offenders are brought before the court and sentenced as deemed appropriate. As most offences are trivial, the outcome of a court appearance for most offenders is a fine or some other minor sentence; for serious or persistent offenders there might be a period of incarceration.

As discussed in the previous chapter, the prevailing ethos in the contemporary justice system is one of 'just deserts' in which the offender takes the punishment for their offence. The exception is offenders deemed to be mentally disordered and who are dealt with under mental health legislation rather than criminal law. A separate system has evolved for such offenders as will be discussed later. Within the criminal justice system, however, there has been over the past decades a struggle between proponents of punishment and proponents of rehabilitation. The rise of the notion of rehabilitation for offenders became widely accepted earlier this century with the rise of theories of crime that emphasized the role of individual and social factors in offending. As psychological theories of offending were formulated that portrayed criminal behaviour in pathological terms, so policies for managing offenders became more and more treatment orientated. If, for example, criminal behaviour is conceived of as the outcome of the flourishing of the adolescent's latent delinquency, itself stemming from a failure of socialization allied to the child's early emotional experiences, then it is not difficult to argue that some therapeutic intervention is called for to put right what has gone wrong in the offender's life (Aichhorn, 1955). This determinist, positivist view of crime grew throughout this century as psychological and social theories of criminal behaviour changed and evolved. Accordingly, as the theories developed, a range of psychological therapies and social policies were put into operation to attempt to correct what had gone awry.

It is often thought that psychological and sociological theories stand opposed, however, as West (1980) notes:

> The crucial importance of economic, social and political factors in the definition and incidence of crime is undeniable, as is the need for socio-political change, but the part played by individual characteristics in determining who becomes labelled a criminal should not be neglected (p. 619).

While psychologists and sociologists might squabble about territory, the real argument is between those who stand for what we might call 'human science' explanations of crime, stressing the importance of empirically informed, constructive strategies in the formulation of policies for managing criminals, and those who argue on the basis of ideology and non-empirical analysis for classical and neoclassical explanations of crime and the need for punishment, retribution and deterrence.

For a number of years the advocates of human science held sway, even prison sentences maintained the ethos (if not always the the practice) of working in a constructive manner to return the prisoner to a good and useful life. The 1940s, 1950s and 1960s saw a proliferation of treatment approaches for offenders young and old — psychotherapy, education, group therapy, behaviour modification, counselling ... the list is long and the literature exhaustive (and exhausting). As time passed so more and more evaluative reviews were published of the rehabilitation literature, culminating in the landmark academic paper by Lipton, Martinson, and Wilks (1975) of 231 treatment outcome studies with offenders. It was from this research base that in 1974 one of the authors, Robert Martinson, published a paper titled 'What Works? — Questions and Answers about Prison Reform'. This one article, perhaps more than any other single publication, cast a dark shadow over the light of treatment. The message taken from Martinson's paper, which is not strictly accurate, was that when it comes to the rehabilitation of offenders, what works is 'nothing works'. This doctrine of nothing works has, in the time since Martinson's paper, become an article of faith, accepted by both academics and policymakers alike.

While the substance of this position will be discussed in due course, it is interesting to speculate as to why the nothing works doctrine found such ready acceptance.

If we follow the arguments of researchers such as Don Andrews (e.g., Andrews, 1989, 1990; Andrews and Wormith, 1989), then rehabilitation programmes for offenders must necessarily include a substantial psychological component. In order to design and conduct effective rehabilitation programmes, some sophistication in the skills needed to work with individual offenders is needed. This focus on the individual is clearly an area in which psychologists might claim some expertise. Yet further, the concept of rehabilitation implicitly contains the assumption, with all the associated theoretical connotations, that criminal behaviour can be changed by working with the offender. As Andrews points out, this focus on the individual offender — in both a practical and theoretical sense — runs counter to the sociological and political dominance evident in a great deal of mainstream criminology. The concept of rehabilitation, with its emphasis on understanding and working with the individual offender, stands in stark contrast to theories of crime that emphasize, for example, on one hand the role of a capitalist economy in creating crime, and free will and rational choice on the other. Theories such as these have no time for rehabilitation, their solutions to the problem of crime prevention lie in political revolution at one extreme, and ever harsher punishment at the other. Thus the nothing works position entirely suited those theorists who espoused theories of crime that paid little attention to the finer social and psychological aspects of criminal behaviour.

At a political level the view that nothing works in offender rehabilitation received a favourable reception in the political climate of the 1970s and 1980s. The marked political swings to the right in America, Great Britain, and parts of Europe brought about changes in the criminal justice system based not on the soft liberal ideal of rehabilitation, but on policies steeped in the hard conservative neoclassical assertions of the need for deterrence and justice through punishment. Thus, as Cullen and Gendreau (1989) note, the nothing works doctrine perfectly suited the mood of the times, and was rapidly elevated from the status of theoretical premise to that of socially constructed reality. Against this academic and political backdrop the policies generated by a belief in the futility of rehabilitation were easy to implement — where, after all, was the opposition? Who was there to produce the evidence to state the case for effective rehabilitation (assuming, of course, that policies are based on reasoned empirical debate — which might be a very large assumption to make)?

In fairness there was always a voice of opposition with a number of writers — most notably Paul Gendreau and Robert Ross (e.g., Gendreau and Ross, 1979, 1987; Ross and Gendreau, 1980) — holding the line that effective rehabilitation was not an impossible goal and pointing to examples of success. Indeed, this point is reinforced by Thornton's (1987b) searching re-examination of the studies cited by Martinson (1974), although Martinson (1979) had himself begun to withdraw from the nothing works position. Nonetheless, one of the problems faced by the champions of rehabilitation lay in making a coherent case from a myriad of research findings. In the field of offender rehabilitation, reviewers are faced with many different types of intervention, conducted in different settings, with different measures of 'success'. As there are literally hundreds of outcome studies, it is very difficult, if not impossible, to draw meaningful conclusions about what works, for whom, and under what conditions simply by pooling the results of several hundred studies and 'vote counting'. As remarked elsewhere in this text (see Chapter 5), however, the recent development of the statistical technique of *meta-analysis* has gone some way towards providing a means by which to produce a standardized overview of a large number of empirical studies. Over the past six years there has been a number of meta-analytic studies of the offender rehabilitation literature and a summary of their findings is given below.

The Meta-Analysis Studies: A Short Summary

In the first meta-analysis in this field Garrett (1985) included 111 studies reported between 1960 and 1983, involving a total of 13,055 young offenders who participated in residential treatment programmes. Garrett's analysis showed that the residential programmes have a small but consistent effect in reducing delinquency, with cognitive-behavioural programmes faring particularly well compared to other approaches such as psychodynamic and life skills programmes. In the following years a number of further meta-analysis studies were reported (Andrews *et al.*, 1990a; Gottschalk *et al.*, 1987; Izzo and Ross, 1990; Lipsey, in press; Roberts and Camasso, 1991; Whitehead and Lab, 1989), while Gendreau and Andrews (1990) have offered an overview of the findings from the meta-analyses. As in most research, later studies are able to build upon what has gone before, therefore the conclusions listed below are drawn from the most recent meta-analytic studies. In particular I have drawn upon the studies reported by Andrews *et al.* and by Lipsey; the Andrews *et al.* study addresses several points raised in earlier work, while the Lipsey study is a major piece of work, involving an analysis of 443 outcome studies in the field of juvenile delinquency.

However, before considering the findings of the meta-analytic studies, it is important to make the distinction between what might be called *clinical/personal* and *criminogenic* outcome variables. The former can be thought of as some dimension of personal functioning — such as psychological adjustment, cognition, anger control, educational ability, social skills, and so on — while the latter refers specifically to variables concerned with crime — recidivism, type of offence, and so on. As a generalization, it is the case that programmes with a specific clinical aim tend to produce beneficial outcomes in terms of personal change. Thus, for example, programmes designed to improve academic standards with offender populations do generally lead to positive changes in educational ability (e.g., Filipczak and Wodarski, 1982); similarly, social skills training can increase offenders' levels of social competence (Hollin, 1990b). However, it is possible for intervention programmes to produce significant outcomes in terms of positive personal change, but for that personal change to have no impact on criminogenic variables (Hollin and Henderson, 1984). One of the contributions of the meta-analytic studies is that their results begin to untangle the confusion in the literature between these two types of outcome measure.

The first point to emerge from Lipsey's large-scale meta-analysis is that there is a substantial variability of criminogenic outcome in the literature. As Lipsey notes, some studies show high effects of intervention on recidivism, in keeping perhaps with the position of writers such as Paul Gendreau and Robert Ross, while a considerable number of studies show either no treatment effect or even a negative effect, in line with the views of the advocates of nothing works. Given this large distribution of treatment effects it is understandable that different reviewers, depending on their sampling of the distribution and their own definitions of 'success', have arrived at different conclusions.

To paraphrase Lipsey's metaphor, if the diversity of treatment effects in delinquency is as large as an elephant, it is little wonder that the reviewer who grasps the trunk describes a different creature to the reviewer clutching an ear.

Given that programmes designed to foster personal change will, by and large, be successful in producing that particular change, the issue remains of what contributes most to changes in offending? It is with this issue uppermost in mind that the following points are taken from the most recent meta-analysis studies; the list below outlines the factors that characterize intervention programmes that show a high effect *in terms of a reduction in criminal behaviour*.

1   Indiscriminate targeting of treatment programmes is counter-productive in reducing recidivism; important predictors of success are that medium to high risk offenders should be selected, and that programmes should focus on criminogenic areas.

2   The type of treatment programme is important: 'More structured and focused treatments (e.g., behavioural, skill-orientated) and multimodal treatments seem to be more effective than the less structured and focused approaches, e.g., counseling' (Lipsey, in press).

3   The most successful studies, while behavioural in nature, include a cognitive component in order to focus on the 'attitudes, values, and beliefs that support antisocial behaviour' (Gendreau and Andrews, 1990).

4   With respect to the type and style of service, Andrews *et al.* (1990a) suggest that some therapeutic approaches are not appropriate for general use with offenders. Specifically, they argue that 'traditional psychodynamic and nondirective client-centered therapies are to be avoided within general samples of offenders' (p. 376).

5   Treatment programmes conducted in the community have a stronger effect on delinquency than residential programmes. While residential programmes can be effective, they should be linked structurally with community based interventions.

6   The most effective programmes have high 'treatment integrity' in that they are carried out by trained staff and the treatment initiators are involved in all the operational phases of the treatment programmes. In other words, there is effective management of a sound rehabilitation programme.

7   Roberts and Camasso (1991) found that interventions targeted at the family appear to be successful: 'Rigorous studies of family treatment, involving large groups of 200 or more juveniles demonstrated that this method of intervention was effective in reducing recidivism for at least one year post-treatment' (p. 438).

When the above conditions are met, the meta-analysis studies suggest that the high effect studies can produce decreases in recidivism of the order of 20 to 40 per cent over and above the baseline levels from mainstream criminal sanctioning of offenders. On this basis it is fair to conclude that it is not the case that 'nothing works' in attempts to rehabilitate offenders. It can be stated with confidence that rehabilitation programmes, when based on the principles detailed above, can be effective in significantly reducing recidivism. It goes without saying that this conclusion has a number of practical benefits: it offers the potential to reduce victimization; it can take the offender out of the criminal justice system, to the potential benefit of both the individual offender and their family; and it can also reduce the financial burden on the taxpayer.

Having said all this, the technique of meta-analysis is not foolproof. For instance, the analysis can only be as good as the quality of the data the researchers choose to analyze, and the way in which the data is coded for analysis, while the meaning and interpretation of the findings is again a point for debate rather than a given truth. Indeed, the meta-analysis reported by Andrews *et al.* (1990a), drew a critical response from Lab and Whitehead (1990), responded to in kind by Andrews *et al.* (1990b). Nevertheless, it is the case that meta-analysis allows a fresh look at the data and from the findings discussed above it is possible to make positive recommendation for the design of successful rehabilitation programmes aimed at reducing offending.

Designing Successful Rehabilitation Programmes

In seeking to plan for success, it is necessary to identify the key areas necessary to be successful and then, in as informed a manner as possible, devise strategies to achieve these goals. It seems to me that there are two key areas to consider: the client group selected for rehabilitation, and the delivery and content of the programme.

Client Issues

The meta-analyses firmly suggest that rehabilitation is best delivered to high risk groups; that is, those offenders whose patterns of offending strongly indicate that they are highly likely to reoffend in the future. There are problems with programmes targeted at low risk groups, some of which appear to be counter-productive (e.g., McCord, 1978). Any of several explanations might account for this at a theoretical level (cf. Palamara *et al.*, 1986), and the position might change when better early predictors of risk are developed, but it would seem prudent for the present to take heed of this finding. At a practical level, however, the selection of a high risk group may well produce a cohort of offenders who are unwilling to participate in rehabilitation programmes. At one time such client resistance might have been a cause for despair, however the development of techniques such as motivational interviewing now increasingly offer practitioners a means by which to engage and work with client resistance (Miller, 1985). The application and refinement of this technique with offender populations is beginning to emerge as witnessed by the work of Perkins (1991) with sex offenders — a group characterized by denial and resistance to change — that uses strategies based on the psychology of persuasion to encourage participation in rehabilitation programmes.

Treatment Integrity

Treatment integrity was another highly important point to emerge from the meta-analysis studies. Quay (1987a) has forcefully made this very point, commenting on a study in which:

> The majority of those responsible for carrying out the treatment were not convinced that it would affect recidivism (the major dependent variable of the study), and the group leaders (not professional counsellors) were poorly trained. The treatment was not well implemented (see Quay, 1977) (p. 246).

Given this, it is not surprising that this 'treatment' programme was unsuccessful, although it is doubtful whether it ever had any chance of success.

In order to achieve high treatment integrity it is clearly necessary to overcome organizational resistance. The concept of organizational resistance refers to the obstacles, be it in a community or residential setting, that impede the progress that might be made with a properly implemented rehabilitation programme. Laws (1974) has described the barriers he faced in attempting to implement a residential treatment programme with offenders. Essentially the barriers were about control: control over admission of offenders to the programme; control over the timing of offenders leaving the programme; control over finances and other resources; and control over training for the staff engaged in running the programme. Laws, as have others, documented professional clashes with both administrators and fellow practitioners.

Of course it would be foolish to suggest that such organizational issues will be easily resolved, but if we look to the principles defined by Reppucci (1973) some solutions begin to appear. Reppucci suggested that the chances of treatment integrity can be greatly increased if organizational policies can be formulated along the following lines: 1) a clear guiding philosophy that is understood by *all* those involved in the rehabilitation programme; 2) an organizational structure that facilitates communication and accountability; 3) an involvement of staff in decision-making; 4) maintaining a community orientation; 5) setting time constraints in developing and 'tuning' programmes, thereby resisting the pressure to try to deal with too much in too short a time.

There are, I think, three points to be taken from this list: the need to train staff in the theory and practice of effective rehabilitation; the need for an organizational structure that facilitates rehabilitation work; and the need for management systems that monitor the design, implementation, and progress of rehabilitation programmes. All three are prerequisites for treatment integrity and, in line with Reppucci's suggestions, are indicated by the meta-analysis studies.

These are some of the practical issues to consider in the delivery of effective rehabilitation programmes, but what of the content?

Effective Rehabilitation: Programme Content

The meta-analyses clearly point to programme content that utilizes behavioural, skill based strategies that incorporate a cognitive component. Such strategies are more likely to be successful when used in a community, particularly family, context than within the confines of an institution. The areas of personal functioning that such programmes might attempt to work with are those described in Chapter 4 as characteristics of offender groups. The following section offers a brief overview of behavioural, skills training, and cognitive-behavioural programmes with offenders. More extended discussions are given by Gendreau and Ross (1987), Hollin (1990a, 1991b), and Morris and Braukmann (1987).

Rehabilitation programmes for offenders can be divided into two broad types — individual programmes and residential and community programmes. The former are individual in the sense of *individualized*, in that the programme is designed for a particular young offender, in contrast to community and residential programmes designed for, say, *all* young offenders in a particular institution (although in practice these two approaches are not exclusive).

Individual Programmes

The literature on individually-focused interventions for young offenders can be classified into three broad types — individual behaviour therapy, social skills training, and cognitive-behaviour modification.

Individual Behaviour Therapy

Traditionally drawing on classical and operant learning theory, behaviour therapy is widely practised with a vast range of client populations (Bellack, Hersen and Kazdin, 1989). The recent major reviews of behavioural intervention suggest that individual behaviour therapy is not a popular option with offender populations (Blakely and Davidson, 1984; Gordon and Arbuthnot, 1987; Milan, 1987). However there are some relevant studies and typical examples are given below.

Fo and O'Donnell (1974, 1975) devised the 'Buddy System' in which trained adult volunteers were paired with young offenders to increase (i.e., reinforce) socially acceptable behaviour. A two year follow-up (O'Donnell, Lydgate and Fo, 1979) found mixed results; serious offenders appeared to improve, while those who had committed only minor offences showed an increased arrest rate. While the Fo and O'Donnell studies were based on the promotion of acceptable behaviour, another strategy is to use an approach based on making the offender face the consequences of their offence. This can take the form of restitution and reparation programmes in which the offender makes financial recompense and a personal apology to the victim. Blagg (1985) described the effect of personal reparation on offenders; the young offenders required to face their victims to apologize spoke of being 'terrified', 'feeling sick', and 'finding it difficult to talk'. The offenders' parents complained that this personal reparation was *too* punitive and humiliating, although the offenders themselves said they felt they had benefited enormously from the experience. While the outcome evidence is not extensive, there are indications that restitution can have an impact on offending (Schneider and Schneider, 1985).

Social Skills Training (SST)

There is a considerable body of research on the use of SST with young offenders for which detailed reviews are available (Henderson and Hollin, 1983, 1986). These SST programmes have focused on micro-skills such as eye contact, body posture, and tone of voice, macro-skills such as negotiating with parents and handling encounters with the police, and institutional behaviour such as avoiding getting into fights. The effectiveness of SST has been assessed using measures of discrete skill performance, behaviour ratings, changes in cognition, institutional performance, and recidivism. Broadly speaking, SST has been found to be effective as assessed by the behavioural and cognitive measures, but its effects on recidivism are altogether less certain with little in the way of convincing evidence that SST on its own can lead to a later reduction in offending. As discussed by Hollin (1990b), however, this might well reflect an ill-considered use of SST in terms of both the style and application of training.

Cognitive-Behavioural Programmes

While behaviour therapy is associated with operant theory and SST with Argyle's (1967) skill model, cognitive-behavioural programmes draw on both social learning theory and cognitive theory to inform practice. A range of cognitive-behavioural programmes for young offenders have been reported in the literature of which a sample are discussed below.

Self-control and self-instruction

We use inner speech, or self-statements, in a number of ways: we carry out self-observation of our actions; we make self-evaluations of how well we performed; and we indulge in self-reinforcement when things go well, and self-punishment when things go badly. The modification of self-statements to achieve increased self-control, by for example being less critical of one's own performance and by making more positive self-statements, can be attempted through use of the technique of *self-instructional training* (SIT) (Goldstein and

Keller, 1987). A number of studies have employed SIT with young offenders and have found that it can be used successfully to increase self-control and hence decrease aggressive behaviour (Snyder and White, 1979).

Anger control

A further application of self-control procedures is in programmes specifically designed for anger control. As formulated and developed by the social psychologist Raymond Novaco (e.g., Novaco, 1975, 1979; Novaco and Welsh, 1989), a typical anger management programme consists of three stages — cognitive preparation, skill acquisition, application training — aimed not at eliminating anger but at lowering the incidence of aggressive behaviour through increased self-control over angry arousal. There have been a number of studies of anger control with offenders. A typical study by McDougall *et al.* (1987) with eighteen young offenders held in prison found that the anger control programme was instrumental in lowering the level of institutional offending.

Role-taking

Chandler (1973) describes a programme designed to encourage young offenders to see themselves from the perspective of other people and so to develop their own role-taking abilities. The study was a clear clinical success, enhancing the young offenders' role-taking skills. Chandler found that at an eighteen-month follow-up the young offenders trained in role-taking skills had committed significantly fewer offences than controls. A similarly successful programme in training social perspective taking skills, carried out with female offenders, has been reported by Chalmers and Townsend (1990).

Social problem solving

Spivack, Platt and Shure (1976) suggest that a number of cognitive problem solving skills are necessary for successful social interaction. Such cognitive skills include sensitivity to interpersonal problems, consequential thinking, alternative thinking and means-end thinking. A variety of skills training techniques, including modelling, role-play, and discussion, are blended with cognitive techniques, principally SIT, to train social problem solving skills. A number of studies have provided clear evidence that this type of training can assist young offenders to generate more solutions to social problems (e.g., Hains, 1984).

Moral reasoning development

A typical study aimed at increasing the powers of moral reasoning of a group of young offenders was reported by Gibbs *et al.* (1984). The intervention took the form of small group discussions on a range of sociomoral dilemmas. The offenders not only gave their views, but were required to justify their opinions and to attempt to reach a consensus on the best solution. As assessed by a measure of Kohlberg's moral judgment stages, the intervention led to a significant upward shift in moral reasoning ability.

Multimodal Programmes

A number of programmes have incorporated a number of the methods discussed above. Gross *et al.* (1980) used a combination of SST, behaviour therapy and self-management training with ten female young offenders. The programme improved self-control, reduced levels of problem behaviour and reduced school absenteeism. There are a number of similar programmes with one of the most comprehensive being *Aggression Replacement Training* (ART) developed by Glick and Goldstein (1987). ART uses three main approaches: structured learning training, including SST and social problem solving training; anger control training; and moral education. The outcome studies show that ART does lead to improved skills, greater self-control and improved institutional behaviour. Another multimodal programme, with something of a cognitive slant, has been described by Ross and Fabiano (1985). The outcome data from a controlled trial with adult offenders of this 'Reasoning and Rehabilitation' programme strongly suggested that it had a significant impact on recidivism (Ross, Fabiano and Ewles, 1988).

Institution and Community

In contrast to individually-focused approaches, another approach is based on change via some agency such as a residential establishment or family. Beginning with institutions, the distinction can be made between those in which the emphasis is on custody with rehabilitation as a secondary consideration, generally prisons; and on institutions in which the focus is on treatment with security as a lesser consideration, as in many residential establishments. The main exception to this is to be found in the Special Hospitals for mentally disordered offenders which are high security institutions but with a treatment emphasis. In Britain there are four Special Hospitals: Broadmoor, Rampton, and Ashworth (formed by the amalgamation of Park Lane and Moss Side Special Hospitals) in England, and Carstairs in Scotland (Hamilton, 1985).

Secure Institutions

From the many reviews of behavioural techniques in secure institutions (e.g., Milan, 1987; Nietzel, 1979), it is clear that the token economy programme (TEP) has been the most widely used method of behaviour change in prisons. Simply, the TEP offers a system of reinforcing and punishing identified behaviours by the awarding and withdrawal of tokens that can later be exchanged at an agreed rate for reinforcers such as confectionery and extra privileges. The TEP has been used in two ways: as an aid to management control and as a means of attempting some level of clinical change. There are several examples, mainly American, of the first use of the TEP (Milan, 1987), and a number of treatment studies, exemplified by that of Cullen and Seddon (1981) in a penal institution in England. Few practitioners would disagree that the TEP is an effective means of changing behaviour and TEPs have been used successfully to improve self-maintenance, institutional discipline, and academic standards. However, there are remarkably few follow-up studies and, of those completed, there is little evidence to indicate any systematic effect on reoffending.

While successful in terms of promoting positive behavioural change in the young offenders, the Cullen and Seddon study is fascinating to read as a case study in organizational behaviour. Cullen and Seddon catalogue a stream of examples of organizational resistance. While they saw the TEP as a success, staff were critical of their training; management were unwilling to devote resources to staff development for the project; and some psychiatrists refused to cooperate with the TEP, in some cases being instrumental in transferring young offenders out of the institution, regardless of what had been agreed with respect to the TEP. Cullen and Seddon also expressed concern about their relationship as psychologists with the staff running the programme; they were criticized for their limited effectiveness and understanding of the situation, unlike the staff who saw things as they 'really are'. Cullen and Seddon would no doubt agree completely with the comment made by Burchard and Lane (1982) that, 'with respect to resistance to change ... behavior-modification advocates who do not recognize that much of their time will be spent trying to change the behavior of staff and policy of administrators are in for a rude awakening' (p. 616).

Clearly practitioners working with offenders can face resistance from a number of sources: an emphasis on punishment rather than rehabilitation; conflict between therapists about the 'right' type of treatment; and a lack of resources and management support to run effective treatment programmes. Given this, it says something about the strength of behavioural techniques (and practitioners!) that even with such constraints it is possible, as Cullen and Seddon have documented, to bring about positive change with incarcerated offenders.

It is possible to make a number of suggestions to assist in formulating tactics to overcome resistance — these apply equally well to community and institutional settings. It is necessary to devote time and energy to training for colleagues, involve colleagues in programme planning and design, and write regular, jargon-free reports to keep everyone in touch with what is happening. When challenged about rehabilitation have responses at the ready; Perkins (1987) has used the tactic of costing, in financial terms, the relative cheapness of clinical intervention in preventing offending (see also Roberts and Camasso, 1991). Cite high recidivism rates to support the argument that rehabilitation deserves consideration in the attempt to prevent future victims experiencing crime; and use the meta-analysis findings in support of rehabilitation as an effective means of crime prevention. In particular, challenge false beliefs and stereotypes about cognitive-behavioural rehabilitative methods; invite critics to see work in operation and to talk to those involved in rehabilitation programmes. These strategies can help to establish a cogent, defendable viewpoint on rehabilitation. While not everyone concerned will be convinced, if no attempt is made nothing will change.

Residential Establishments

Achievement Place

There is little doubt that the Achievement Place style of residential provision has generated the most interest in behavioural circles. The first Achievement Place, in Kansas, proved to be a model of residential care later followed by over 200 establishments both in the USA and Great Britain. There are a number of reviews of the wealth of research output from Achievement Place, the most recent by Braukmann and Wolf (1987). Two notable features of Achievement Place are the innovative use of 'teaching-parents' and the use of behavioural methods of change. Achievement Place itself is actually a collection of family-style homes, managed by a specially trained couple, for about six young offenders per home. The couple have the role of teaching-parents; that is, they have responsibility for specific programmes, such as skills training, *and* responsibility for the less-structured care and attention associated with parents. The behaviour change system progresses from a TEP to a 'merit system', together with a peer manager system, alongside which individually-based programmes in social, educational, and self-management skills also take place (see Burchard and Lane, 1982).

The first major outcome study of Achievement Place compared thirteen Achievement Place homes with nine group homes that had not used a teaching-parent approach at a one-year follow-up (Kirigin *et al.*, 1982). It was found that *during* the period in which the programme was running, the young offenders at Achievement Place were at a significant advantage with regard to offending. However, this advantage was not maintained after a one-year period. At least two other outcome studies have reported similar findings (Braukmann and Wolf, 1987; Weinrott *et al.*, 1982). In summary, it appears that the Achievement Place model is successful in reducing offending while it is in operation, but that this success does not transfer in the longer term to the community.

A number of residential establishments for young offenders based on behavioural methods have opened in Britain (Yule and Brown, 1987). There include Gilbey House in Birmingham, Unit 1 at Orchard Lodge in London, Aycliffe School in Durham, and Glenthorne Youth Treatment Centre in Birmingham. The SHAPE project in Birmingham was showing signs of success in lowering levels of offending (Ostapiuk, 1982); it has, however, run into financial difficulties and can no longer accept referrals.

While gains can be made in custody, it is highly desirable that the gains generalize beyond institutional confines (Huff, 1987). Programmes should include real world targets, and as much assessment and treatment as possible should take place in the real world. Given the importance of the family, every effort should be made to include relatives in both planning and carrying out programmes. There should be clear planning throughout the young offender's time in custody to allow targets to be achieved, and links fostered with community agencies to continue treatment after discharge (Burchard and Harrington, 1986; Ostapiuk and Westwood, 1986).

Community Programmes

School-based Intervention

As reviewed by Hawkins and Lishner (1987), there have been a number of projects aimed at reducing delinquency by promoting school achievement and programmes in the literature; the Preparation through Responsive Education Programme (PREP) is described in a number of publications in the late 1970s (for a review see Burchard and Lane, 1982). Based in Maryland, USA, PREP was designed for pupils recommended to the programme because of academic, social and offending problems. The PREP curriculum consisted of academic tutoring, SST and some family work. The outcome data, gathered from over 600 pupils, showed that PREP had a significant impact in improving school discipline and academic performance; however, there was little indication that it had any effect on offending.

Family-based Intervention

As patterns of family interaction and styles of parenting have been shown to be so strongly associated with the onset of offending, it is not surprising that a considerable body of literature has accumulated on family-based interventions. Basically, this literature divides into two categories, one that focuses on parenting skills, another that primarily concerns itself with family functioning (Kazdin, 1987). While most of the research is community based with younger offenders, family therapy has been attempted in much more difficult circumstances as, for example, in a secure environment with violent mentally ill offenders (Robinson *et al.*, 1991).

Parent management training (PMT)
PMT aims to modify, through skills training, the way in which parents interact with their children. Typically, this is achieved by training parents to reinforce their child's or adolescent's appropriate behaviour and to use acceptable methods of discipline for inappropriate behaviour. A number of studies of the effectiveness of PMT have been carried out with young offenders and their families (Bank *et al.*, 1987; Fraser, Hawkins and Howard, 1988). The outcome data clearly show that PMT has beneficial effects on family communication and family relationships, with some indication that a reduction in offending can also be achieved.

Functional family therapy (FFT)
While there are similarities between PMT and FFT, in the latter the emphasis is much more explicitly focused on family interaction. A number of studies

have used *contingency contracting* as a means of changing family interaction in cases of young offenders, with success in reducing offending (Stumphauzer, 1976; Welch, 1985). Other similar studies have used a broader range of techniques; Henderson (1981) used behavioural, cognitive and FFT methods in a programme which was successful in reducing stealing, while Alexander and Parsons (1973) used skills training, contingency contracting and problem-solving training to improve family interaction. A series of follow-up studies found that the FFT had lower offending for both the young offenders themselves (Alexander *et al.*, 1976), and also for the younger siblings of the offender (Klein *et al.*, 1977). The data from FFT studies strongly suggest that the intervention can modify beneficially family interaction, and there are strong indications of an effect upon recidivism.

One of the potential pitfalls in this field of work is to blame the parents and the family for crime — if only parents were better behaved then how much better everything else would be. In a sense this is true; if efforts are made to work with parents as discussed above great strides can be made. However, parents and families are not autonomous and it is necessary to see their functioning in a broader social, economic and political context. Why are some families criminogenic? It is just a coincidence that the families that can benefit from interventions are most likely to be disadvantaged socially and economically?

Broader Schemes

There are, of course, a range of services and type of intervention that are rightly not identified as psychological interventions. However, on occasions these broader schemes do embrace approaches that are identifiable as psychological and two examples of this, briefly discussed below, are to be found in probation and diversion.

Probation

As a number of commentators have noted (e.g., Hudson, 1986), behavioural casework is used by some by probation officers, with SST proving particularly popular. From their review Remington and Remington (1987) suggest that there is enormous scope for the use of behavioural methods in probation work. Many of the problems faced by offenders — anxiety, depression, drug and alcohol abuse — are those in which behavioural intervention has proved effective. Given that training programmes have shown that probation officers can be equipped with the skills to be effective behaviour therapists (e.g., Wood *et al.*, 1982), it is disappointing that Remington and Remington conclude that much of what might be achieved has yet to be realized. The reason for this may lie in the bad press given to behavioural intervention generally, the debate within the probation service whether individual treatment is an appropriate task for the probation officer (Willis, 1986), or with disillusionment about the effectiveness of probation in reducing recidivism (Cohen, Eden and Lazar, 1991).

Diversionary projects

Flowing from concern that early experience of the criminal justice system could have a damaging effect on young people, the concept of diversion has emerged over the past two decades. Since that time it has attracted considerable attention from researchers, with promising outcomes (Davidson *et al.*, 1990). Of the various measures aimed at diverting young offenders from custody and recidivism, *intermediate treatment* (IT) has been widely used. A behaviourally orientated IT scheme based in Birmingham (UK) did produce some reduction in offending (Preston, 1982), and similar programmes in America have also suggested that diversionary schemes can reduce offending (e.g., Davidson *et al.*, 1987).

Effective Rehabilitation: The Next Hurdle

It is more than apparent that the 'nothing works' argument does not hold water; effective rehabilitation programmes aimed at reducing offending have been conducted, and we can go so far as to make very specific recommendations as to the best way to go about designing even more effective programmes. The meta-analyses have reinforced the position of long-standing advocates of rehabilitation that successful programmes can be distinguished from unsuccessful on the basis of the theoretical model they employ, the type of practice they encourage, and the degree of treatment integrity they enjoy. Successful programmes will be based on social learning theory, using cognitive-behavioural techniques of change, and have a high degree of treatment integrity. Given these requirements, can we anticipate that social policy makers and politicians will abandon their current punitive philosophies and practices and introduce constructive rehabilitative strategies for managing offenders?

In the short-term I think the answer is no. Cullen and Gendreau (1989) have identified the core of resistance to rehabilitation as being nested in the widespread adherence to the orthodoxy of 'nothing works'. They comment that acceptance of this orthodoxy 'is especially prevalent among academic criminologists who have jumped in large numbers upon the antitreatment bandwagon. Key policymakers in a variety of states also have come to assume that rehabilitation is a failed agenda' (p. 30). At the root of the refusal to engage the positive findings regarding rehabilitation are fundamental tensions between those who advocate an empirically driven human science approach to the study of criminal behaviour and those who prefer an approach based on ideological and political analysis. In a reasonable world there would be room for both approaches, which in any case should be complementary not competing, but there are historical reasons why this is not the case.

Since the 1920s the study of criminal behaviour has been identified as a sociological topic, and 'mainstream' criminology is heavily reliant on the application of concepts from sociology to formulate theories of criminal behaviour. Other approaches to the study of criminal behaviour — as for example from anthropologists, biosocial researchers and psychologists — that stress the importance of human diversity in formulating theories have mainly been marginalized in criminology texts. While there are, of course, some outstanding empirical researchers in both sociology and criminology, it is fair to say that while empiricism is fundamental to theory formation in the human sciences this appears to be less so in mainstream criminology. Thus while advocates of human science will use the data to support their position, they will meet opposition that uses ideology and non-empirical analysis to inform its arguments. When human scientists present their data they are met not with competing data, but with ideological arguments as to why their data are useless. Andrews and Wormith (1989) have used the term 'knowledge destruction' to describe this devaluation of empirical research. As an example of this process of knowledge destruction, Andrews and Wormith offer an analysis of the 'highly rhetorical and pseudoscientific' criticisms levelled against the research on personality and crime. Similarly, with regard to resistance to rehabilitation, Andrews (1990) has tackled the anti-rehabilitation bias in a report issued by the Canadian Sentencing Commission. Andrews (1989) has assembled a catalogue of myths and half-baked objections to rehabilitation as shown in the list below.

A Sample of Some Anti-rehabilitation Themes: How to Destroy Evidence of the Effectiveness of Correctional Treatment (Andrews, 1989)

(With thanks to Michael Gottfredson)

- *Discount the very possibility of predicting criminal conduct through the big lie and/or outright denial of the evidence. Note that many respected textbooks in mainstream criminology state, as a fact, that there are no differences between offenders and nonoffenders, that any apparent differences really reflect bias against young, lower-class men, that the true roots of crime are buried deep in political economy, culture, and social structure.*
- *Enthusiastically endorse the findings of studies that fail to uncover treatment effects, and promote those findings as scientifically sound evidence that rehabilitation does not work.*
- *Note that crime is socially functional in that it helps define the boundaries of acceptable conduct for society as a whole, and hence the pursuit of effective rehabilitation programs threatens the very existence of society.*
- *Assert that rehabilitation, even if it works, is inherently immoral, evil, ideologically incorrect, and promotes both severe sentences and unwarranted sentencing disparity (relative to the dignity of just punishment and radical nonintervention).*
- *Discount rehabilitation because it involves, by definition, more social control than does absolute freedom.*
- *Discount rehabilitation because it involves, by definition, less social control than does absolute social control.*
- *Discount rehabilitation because any program, upon close inspection, may be found to include elements of sexism, racism, and/or elitism.*

- *Discount rehabilitation programs because they are not primary prevention programs (or some other personally favoured program).*
- *Discount evidence of reduced recidivism because it is not evidence of improvement in the bigger picture of justice.*
- *Discount evidence of reduced recidivism because it is not evidence of effects on community-wide (aggregated) crime rates.*
- *Discount evidence of effects on officially recorded crime because it is not evidence of effects on self-reported crime.*
- *Discount evidence of effects on self-reported crime because it is not evidence of effects on officially recorded crime.*
- *Discount evidence of effects on any measure of recidivism by asserting that the program failed to increase self-esteem or to make the client a better person in some other way.*
- *Discount evidence of positive effects by asserting that rehabilitation is nothing but a successful attempt to make lower-class persons more acceptable to higher-class persons.*
- *Discount any evidence of effectiveness by asserting that it is a shame that offenders get access to quality programs (they deserve just punishment).*
- *Discount evidence of effectiveness over a one-year follow-up period because it is not evidence of effects over a two-year follow-up period; discount evidence of effectiveness over a two-year follow-up period because it is not evidence of effects over a three-year follow-up period; discount . . .*
- *Assert that rehabilitation can't possibly work because criminology has proven that the human science of criminal conduct is nonsense.*
- *Assert that we all know, from prior experience, that rehabilitation doesn't work.*
- *Regardless of the quality of the design or the magnitude of the treatment effect, suggest some ambiguity regarding what really caused the effect, and then note the absurdity of claiming effectiveness when the true cause of reduced recidivism remains unknown.*
- *Regardless of the quality of the research design, note that experimental designs are the tools of criminology's positivistic past, and the mere play-things of ritualistic positivists (I don't know what this means either, but this type of expression is not unusual in mainstream criminological textbooks).*
- *Reject the positive findings of a well-controlled study because it is immoral that the comparison clients did not have access to it.*
- *Reject a treatment program that has been found to be effective with some types of offenders under specific circumstances, because it doesn't work for everyone under all circumstances. (A complex and differentiated world is inconsistent with the universally applicable and morally superior visions of truth with which theoreticians have been privileged).*
- *No matter what number or types of offenders were studied, note that the study failed to work with a sample representative of all types of offenders that one could possibly imagine.*
- *Question the motives and objectivity of scholars and practitioners who speak in favour of rehabilitation.*

- *THE ULTIMATE KNOWLEDGE DESTRUCTION TECH-NIQUE: Remind readers that studies that report positively on treatment 'are based upon the conclusions of the authors of the reports, themselves.'*

In total, as Andrews (1990) concludes:

> We in the human sciences have not been getting our message out to those people who could make use of a rational empirical attitude that is informed by the substance of human science. . . . Not only must we learn to have less faith in the impact of technical research reports, we must realize that many in our intended audience have been trained to be antipsychological (p. 253).

It follows from this that it is incumbent upon psychologists to get out there and press home what they know. This means not just academic publications, but writing for practitioners, giving time to sitting on policy-making committees, giving papers (sometimes to hostile audiences which is not, as I can testify from personal experience, an uplifting experience), and talking to the media. I think that advocates of rehabilitation now have a highly defensible position, and there is every sign that the public is not as anti-rehabilitation as some might have us believe. The challenge for the future is to present the case to influence policy and practice.

Chapter 9

Criminal Behaviour, Explanation and Prevention: The Example of Violence

---

In previous chapters we have looked at the individual factors thought to play a role in criminal behaviour, and at the environmental influences on individual behaviour. When discussing individual factors the point was made that these should be understood with reference to the environmental context in which the behaviour took place. Similarly, when discussing environmental factors the caution was advanced that these factors need to be understood with reference to individual differences. As hinted in the discussion of developmental pathways from childhood troublesomeness, to adolescent delinquency, and ultimately to adult recidivism (Chapter 5), highly complex models are needed to account for the interplay between environmental factors and individual behaviour (Robins and Rutter, 1990). In order to give a flavour of what such a model should encompass — without claiming at all to offer anything like a model, such an enterprise is beyond the scope of this book — I have drawn together in an ordered manner some of the research findings on the topic of violent behaviour. What follows is therefore intended as an illustration of the way in which environmental and individual factors can be combined in a logical way in seeking to advance our understanding of violent behaviour.

Understanding Violent Behaviour

The conceptual basis of the way offered here of understanding violent behaviour in terms of a situation-person interaction can be shown simply, as in Figure 9.1. In this scheme there are three stages to consider: the first is the situation in which the violence takes place; the second, which is the 'person' part of the scheme, is the individual's thoughts, feelings and actions; the third is the impact of the violent behaviour on the world.

This sequence of three stages — situation, person, impact — provides a useful means by which to consider the research findings on violent behaviour. Of course, this is not the only way to understand violent behaviour; clearly there are many different ways to explain the phenomenon of violence. There are any number of attempts, from several disciplines, to account for violent behaviour. For example, biology, anthropology, neurology and sociology have

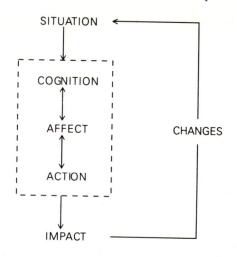

Figure 9.1. Schematic representation of the person-situation interaction.

all made valuable contributions to our understanding of violence, while from psychology alone, there have been a variety of explanations of violence based on psychodynamic theories, instinct and drive theories, behavioural theories and theories from social psychology (for reviews see Archer and Browne, 1989; Goldstein, 1986; Hollin, 1989; Howells and Hollin, 1989; Siann, 1985).

It is important at the outset to be clear with respect to terminology. There are two particular terms in common, sometimes interchangeable, use in the literature — *aggression* and *violence*. Megargee (1982) and Siann (1985) suggest the following use of these terms: aggression refers to the *intention* to hurt or gain physical advantage over other people, without necessarily involving physical injury, while violence involves the use of strong physical force against another person, sometimes but not always impelled by aggressive motivation, that results in the physical injury of the other person. In what follows the terms aggression and violence are used in the sense suggested by Megargee and Siann.

Situational Analysis

Henderson (1986) conducted an analysis of the narratives given by adult male violent offenders about the types of situation in which they behaved in a violent manner. This study is of particular interest as it gives an indication of the settings in which violent incidents, at least those involving adult males, are most likely to be found.

As shown in Table 9.1, Henderson's analysis revealed four broad categories of violent situation: 1) violence in conjunction with another crime — sometimes intentionally as with robbery, sometimes in panic as when discovered committing another non-violent crime such as burglary; 2) family

Table 9.1:   *Violent situations (after Henderson, 1986)*

Type of Violence	Location
Crime Related (Individual)	Domestic
Crime Related (Group)	Domestic
Family	Domestic
Public	Street/Club or Bar
Institutional	Police Station/Prison

violence directed towards both women and children; 3) violence in public places such as clubs and bars; 4) violence in institutions — police stations and prisons in Henderson's study — directed towards fellow inmates, police officers and prison staff. While not part of Henderson's analysis, violence in institutions can be extended to other institutions such as hospitals and to other professional staff such as nurses, social workers and probation officers.

While Henderson looked at violence from the accounts of the offender, Dowds (in press) offers an analysis drawing on the reports of victims of violent attacks. Using data gathered during the course of the British Crime Survey, Dowds identified a range of variables in victim reports including where the incident took place, offender details, level of violence and degree of injury. Dowds then carried out a statistical analysis of the coded data, using the technique of *principal components analysis*, to search for patterns of violent behaviour. By carrying out separate analyses for incidents with female and male victims, Dowds was able to compare the types of violence experienced by men and women.

Dowds's analysis revealed that women victims experienced six main types of violence. The first is *domestic violence* in which the woman is typically assaulted at home by a partner or ex-partner; these assaults often result in serious injury. Alternatively, this category can also include assaults while the woman was travelling or on the street. The second is *leisure related* in which a violent incident takes place in, say, a pub or some setting in which the victim spends their leisure time. The third is *occupational hazard* in which the violence occurs because the nature of the woman's work demands contact with a specific client group or with the general public. The fourth type is *friend/ neighbour disputes* typified by a daylight altercation between the woman and people who live in close proximity. The fifth is an incident in which the victim felt that she *provoked* or was responsible for the violence. Finally, the sixth type of incident Dowds called *defended/chased* in which the victim defended herself by using force against the attacker or by chasing the offender(s) — this type of incident was most common among young people who had been involved in violence before.

If we turn to male violence, Dowds's analysis also revealed six patterns of male victimization. The first is *pub fights* in which the victim might be part of a group in which a fight breaks out, or might be in the vicinity of the pub and become caught up in the violence. The second and third are *fights between friends*, similar to the friend/neighbour disputes for women, and *occupational hazard*, again similar to the corresponding type for female victims. The fourth

Table 9.2: Examples of situational factors associated with violence

---

Physical Factors
  High Temperature
  Air Pollution
  Over-crowding

Social Factors
  Verbal Provocation
  Physical Intimidation
  Breaking Social Rules

---

is *minor fracas* in which the victim was not seriously injured and did not defend themselves, as in cases of common assault. The fifth is *serious unprovoked wounding* which is similar in nature to a minor fracas but where the victim receives extensive injuries. Finally, the sixth type of incident is *domestic violence* where the man was injured by a female offender who was likely to be a partner or ex-partner; in such incidents the men often felt that they had acted in some way to provoke the incident.

In offering a conclusion to the study, Dowds makes the point that for women domestic assaults were the most frequent forms of violence, while for men pub fights were the dominant form of violent incident. While great discussion takes place about so called 'street violence', this type of violence does not emerge strongly from the analysis; it seems that most 'everyday' violence is safely tucked out of public view.

If we return to Henderson's (1986) study, we find here an illustration of the long-held distinction between premeditated or 'instrumental' violence, as for example in the case of robbery, and 'angry' or 'hostile' violence which is impulsive and unplanned (Buss, 1961). If we concentrate on hostile violence, situational analysis has pointed to a number of factors that increase the likelihood of this type of violent outburst.

The first group of influences are *physical* in nature; that is they are the aspects of the situation that do not involve social interaction with other people. These physical correlates include high temperature, air pollution, and over-crowding. There is strong evidence to suggest that all these factors are related to rises in the number of violent acts over a given period (Anderson, 1989; Rotton and Frey, 1985). In this vein, a study by Jarrell and Howsen (1990) investigated the effects of transient crowding on rates of criminal behaviour. Transient crowding refers to increases in the population density caused by an influx of 'strangers' such as tourists, students or shoppers into a given area. Jarrell and Howsen report that an increase in the numbers of strangers in an given area has the effect of increasing the rates of burglary, larceny and robbery, but had a negligible effect on rates of assault, murder and rape. An explanation for this pattern of results might be that the crimes that increased in frequency are crimes of acquisition, which may involve instrumental violence. The more people there are in an area, the greater the number of opportunities, sometimes involving violence, for taking another person's property. On the other hand, offences typically involving angry violence, such as murder, assault and sexual offences, are often closely bound in with close personal relation-ships; the number of strangers passing into and out of an area would therefore be less likely to have an effect on this type of criminal act. In addition, of course, the greater the numbers of people the more stretched police resources become and hence the lower the risk of apprehension.

The second factor is social in nature; that is, it refers to the words and actions of other people that can be experienced either through the media (Wood, Wong and Chachere, 1991) or through personal contact. To follow the line of personal contact, the violent act might be precipitated by verbal provo-cation, such as an insult, physical intimidation, as with jostling or pushing, or the other person's behaviour breaking some social rule. However, these social factors are in the eye of the beholder; my social rule is not necessarily your social rule, so what I find provoking and insulting may not have the same effect on you. When seen in this way, there is an obvious relationship between social factors and personal factors; in order to understand the impact of social factors it is necessary to turn to the person part of the sequence in Figure 9.1.

The Person

An individual's response to situational cues is likely to be influenced by their previous experiences; accordingly a number of studies have looked at the backgrounds of violent people.

Background

The longitudinal studies, such as the Cambridge Study of Delinquent Develop-ment (see Chapter 4), have paid some attention to the issue of background predictors of violent behaviour. Farrington and West (1990) suggest that while there is a significant continuity between childhood forms of violent conduct and violent adult offences, the early predictors of violence were essentially the same as for non-violent offences — economic disadvantage, family criminality, troublesome at school, and so on. Farrington and West conclude therefore that:

> Aggression was merely one element of a more general antisocial tend-ency, which arose in childhood and continued through the teenage and adult years. . . . Violent offenders were very similar to non-violent frequent offenders in childhood, adolescent, and adult features . . . the causes of aggression and violence were essentially the same as the causes of persistent and extreme antisocial, delinquent and criminal behaviour (p. 131).

Stattin and Magnusson (1989) reported a prospective longitudinal study of the relationship between aggressiveness at an early school age and criminal behaviour in later life with a sample of 1,027 young people followed from the age of 10 years through to the age of 26 years. It was found that for both males and females, high ratings by teachers of childhood aggressiveness was strongly associated with later criminal behaviour, both in terms of the seriousness and frequency of these acts. This relation between early aggressiveness and later criminal behaviour was independent of both intelligence and the educational level of the parents. Denno (1990) carried out a study of background, psychological, and biological factors in the development of violent behaviour. Rather like Farrington and West, Denno concluded that a complex admixture of the influences was needed to account for criminal behaviour generally, with the boundaries between violent and non-violent crime somewhat blurred. Widom (1989) reported a thorough examination of the literature concerned with the hypothesis that 'violence breeds violence'; in other words, that abused and neglected children will become the next generation of abusers, that the victims of violence become the violent perpetrators when their turn comes. Despite the intuitive appeal of this notion of intergenerational transmission of violent behaviour, as Widom notes in concluding her review of the evidence:

> Not all children who grow up in violent homes become violent adults. . . . Certainly a wide variety of environmental stresses, potential triggering mechanisms, and many other factors are involved in the learning process. Nevertheless, because many children appear not to succumb to the adverse effects of abuse or neglect, it is important to determine why this is so and what it is that protects them from those negative consequences (p. 24).

While DiLalla and Gottesman (1991) followed Widom's (1989) paper with an argument for a strong genetic component to the transmission of violence, Widom (1991) suggests that the evidence may not be so compelling after all. In summary there appears to be little difference in the broad sociodemographic backgrounds of violent and non-violent criminals, although whether there are more subtle psychological and neuropsychological differences, perhaps acting in conjunction with styles of parenting, remains an open area of research activity. In seeking to understand violence perhaps there is something to be learned from the violent person's immediate response to situational cues. This response to situational cues can be divided into three components — cognition, emotion, and action.

Response: cognition

Dodge (1986) defined a sequence of steps in the effective processing of social information: 1) encoding social cues; 2) the cognitive representation and interpretation of these social cues; 3) searching for appropriate ways to respond; 4) deciding on the best way to respond. The first part of this cognitive sequence involves the person in perceiving and interpreting situational cues, particularly the words and actions of other people. There is a body of research evidence to suggest that aggressive and violent people, perhaps especially aggressive and violent children and adolescents, search for and perceive *fewer* social cues than non-violent people (e.g., Dodge and Newman, 1981). Further, it is also clear that violent people are much more likely to interpret cues in a hostile fashion (Slaby and Guerra, 1988). This hostile, aggressive interpretation of social cues may well be a fundamental component of violent behaviour.

Indeed, a study by Stefanek *et al.* (1987) demonstrated that this tendency is evident even in aggressive young children. Stefanek *et al.* recorded the self-statements of groups of young children as they were faced with social contact with other children. They found that aggressive children were much more likely to describe to themselves social encounters in an aggressive fashion: 'That child doesn't like me', or 'They want to take my toys'. If we follow this line of argument, the violent person must continually perceive other people's actions in a hostile manner, so that the world must appear to be a perpetually threatening place.

The next part of the sequence demands the ability to generate suitable responses to one's understanding of the situation — this cognitive ability is sometimes referred to as *social problem solving*. Effective social problem solving demands the ability both to generate solutions, that is effective courses of action, and to select the most expedient alternative. Some studies have pointed to limited social problem solving skills — in terms of generating solutions and considering the consequences of their actions — for interpersonal conflicts in aggressive and violent populations (e.g., Slaby and Guerra, 1988; Spivack, Platt and Shure, 1976). As discussed in Chapter 4, however, this finding extends to delinquent groups generally and so may not be peculiar to violent individuals. This finding of limited social problem solving ability in violent populations can be counted for in one of two ways. The first possibility is that violent people experience difficulty with social problem solving; that is, they have not mastered the requisite skills to generate effective, socially acceptable solutions to interpersonal problems. Alternatively, it may be that the process of *defining* of the interaction as aggressive — following a limited perception of the situation and a hostile interpretation of what has been seen — naturally cuts down the number of options violent people are able to generate. Thus the argument could be advanced that rather than limited problem solving ability leading to the generation of fewer solutions and their consequences, it is in the nature of violent situations that they offer fewer alternatives for action. Following this line of thought, the eventual decision to act in a violent manner is entirely understandable; if you are being physically threatened then to retaliate in kind is a perfectly reasonable and rational response. It is not surprising, in this light, that aggressive people select a violent response, viewing their violent behaviour as an acceptable, legitimate course of action (Slaby and Guerra, 1988).

Response: emotion
This cognitive sequence of perception, interpretation and problem solving may be influenced significantly by the individual's level of emotional arousal. The widely cited work of the American social psychologist Raymond Novaco has suggested that there can be reciprocal relationships between environmental events, both physical and social, cognitive processes and angry emotional arousal. Specifically, Novaco's (1975) original analysis of anger suggested four stages: 1) external triggering events; 2) angry thoughts; 3) heightened angry emotional arousal, including both physiological and psychological elements; 4) action. Novaco suggested that complex reciprocal relationships might function between these components. For example, another person's remark (triggering

event) might be appraised in a hostile manner, leading to angry thoughts; this heightens emotional arousal, in turn intensifying the angry thoughts. This interplay between cognition and arousal thereby increases the likelihood of the individual acting in a violent manner.

Response: action

In the final part of the response sequence the individual carries out a violent act. Violent behaviour can, of course, take many different forms. Most typically it involves an unarmed physical assault, involving kicking, punching, slapping and strangling; less typically a weapon is used, most often a broken bottle or a knife, sometimes a gun (Henderson, 1986). Most violent incidents are not planned in advance, and often the use of a weapon is the result of one of the people involved in the incident grabbing whatever comes to hand. Thus it is not surprising that countries with the highest level of firearm availability have a higher firearm homicide rate (Lester, 1991). The premeditated use of weapons, particularly firearms, can be seen in crimes such as armed robbery. In this type of crime, the weapon is used to increase the chances of a successful outcome through intimidation and fear — which is not to say that the weapons would not be fired if opposition were encountered.

The sequence of cognition, emotion and action may well not be a single event; there can be a number of interactions and social exchanges, involving changes in thought and deed prior to the violent act. In other words, there might be an escalation of behaviour as an interpersonal exchange becomes more heated and out of control. This possibility is discussed below in considering the impact of the person's behaviour on the other people in the situation.

Impact

The individual's actions have the effect of changing the situation; violent behaviour is, one suspects, often a highly rewarding strategy. A display of violence might produce some financial or social rewards that would otherwise not be forthcoming. For example, a successful robbery can produce both hard cash and peer group status. Violent behaviour is an excellent way to avoid social situations or escape from unwanted tasks; an assault on a teacher is a remarkably effective strategy to avoid lessons and to escape from the constraints of the classroom. For some people, the victim's fear and pain are the rewards; the history of criminology is littered with studies of criminals who performed sadistic acts of torture on their victims, sometimes recording or photographing the results of their actions, to enjoy the power and control afforded by their victim's suffering.

As violent behaviour has an impact on other people, often producing a response to the offender's actions, it follows that to understand violence it is necessary to look at the role of the victim in the violent event. Thus violence between offender and victim can be portrayed as a dynamic interaction, as those involved continually shift and move in response to each other's actions. Such a dynamic interchange is described in a classic paper by Luckenbill (1977) which examines violent acts that culminate in murder.

Based on an analysis of case material, Luckenbill documents the typical pattern of events culminating in murder as a series of 'transactions' between offender and victim (often when one or both have been drinking). Luckenbill notes that in many instances of murder, the opening move comes from the victim; this may take the form of a verbal comment, flirtation with another person, or a refusal to comply with a request. In some cases the provocation was clearly intended, in others the offender interprets the victim's actions as provocative. The next transaction involves the offender in checking his or her perception of insult or refusal; this might be by directly asking the victim or onlookers, or inferred by the offender from the victim's refusal to obey a command to stop. For example, an offender judges his or her perception of refusal to comply as accurate when a screaming child does not obey an instruction to be quiet. In the next stage, the offender opts not to retreat but to engage with the other person to sort things out; in the main this is done through verbal retaliation and the issue of threats, although in a minority of cases the first level of retaliation is physical, resulting in murder. More usually, however, the victim responds in some way to the offender's actions, making a verbal or even physical counter-attack. Luckenbill suggests that such a move by the victim appears to confirm to the perpetrator that violence is appropriate in the context of that social exchange. The offender attacks and in many cases, as Luckenbill notes, 'dropped the victim in a single shot, stab, or rally of blows' (p. 185).

While Luckenbill's analysis exemplifies the social, interactive nature of violent acts, it would be unwise to assume that all violence is 'victim-precipitated'. Indeed, Savitz, Kumar and Zahn (1991) have estimated that of the homicide cases in their study, based in Philadelphia, USA, approximately 60 per cent were 'contests' of the type detailed by Luckenbill. Further, in situations where men are violent towards women or children — for extended reviews by psychologists see Browne (1989) and Frude (1989) — the concept of a situated transaction may not be appropriate. Dobash and Dobash (1984) argue strongly against the notion of victim precipitation of violence; they are of the view that violent episodes of this type should be understood as intentional acts by the man. Indeed, rather than contributing to violence, many women victims seek to avoid or avert the onset of violence, trying to negotiate a safe outcome for themselves and sometimes their children. An understanding of this type of violence, Dobash and Dobash suggest, requires an analysis that involves the male's gender identity and its associated roles and meanings within a social and cultural context. Goldsmith (1990) reported a study of abuser characteristics as perceived by the abused spouse; the most frequently nominated characteristics of the male abuser were that he was easily angered and violent when angered, domineering, accepted violence as a problem solving technique, a heavy drinker, and valued macho type behaviour. Within this list we perhaps see elements of the type of male gender identity referred to by Dobash and Dobash: a constellation of attitudes, beliefs and emotions that for the offender legitimize and even excuse their violent behaviour.

It is clear that different types of violent act are going to demand different levels of explanation, a task that is far from simple. The last words belong to

Widom (1991): 'The study of social problems such as child abuse and violence places a heavy burden on the researcher to cross disciplinary boundaries in developing theories and designing research to address these important questions' (p. 131).

Reducing Violent Behaviour

If we can begin to understand violence using a cognitive-behavioural frame-work as described above, how might this inform strategies aimed at reducing levels of violent behaviour? There are several paths that might be taken: change the situation in which the violence occurs; change the violent person; change the consequences that follow violent behaviour. The first of these may be termed *prevention*; the second *treatment*; the third *sentencing*.

Prevention

There are a number of crime prevention strategies that might be expected to reduce the level of violent crime: environmental design such as better lighting in public places, Neighbourhood Watch schemes, more police patrols, and transport schemes to remove victims from potentially dangerous situations. All of these are examples of ways in which to lessen the chances of violent attacks by muggers, armed robbers and rapists. As discussed in Chapter 8, 'situational crime prevention' has become enormously popular over the last decade. On a note of caution, however, the possibility must be considered that situational measures might 'displace' violent crimes to other more vulnerable targets.

Moving away from these broad social measures to more personal areas, the last few years have seen increasing attention being paid to the prevention of face-to-face violence. Many professional people — nurses, police, probation officers, social workers — are regularly exposed to situations in which violence may erupt with them as victims. A number of researchers have examined such potentially dangerous face-to-face situations and have formulated various strategies to minimize the risks of becoming a victim of a violent assault (Breakwell, 1989; Davies, 1989). These strategies include, for example, developing *personal skills* to heighten awareness of the risk of violence. These can be as basic as familiarizing oneself with case material prior to an initial family visit; or learning the specific non-verbal cues associated with anger so as to recognize the early warning signs of likely violence.

Strategies for managing violent incidents are also important: issues such as effective time management so as not to keep potentially aggressive clients waiting and growing more angry, or provoking anger by cutting short appointments. There are obvious points to be made: guarding one's own address and telephone number; letting colleagues know where you are going and what time to expect to hear from you; paying attention to office design so that there are no heavy objects to hand or easily barricaded doors; paying attention to aspects of one's clothing might also save injury — such as plastic lenses for spectacles, tying back long hair, and not wearing hanging earrings. Perhaps most importantly, there should be clear articulated policies within a group or staff team as to the procedures to be followed should a violent incident occur. In addition, those responsible for the implementation of policy should ensure that *all* staff are aware of and understand the organizational policies on violent incidents. Indeed, given the present mood of some sections of the legal profession, not to have a policy on violent incidents, and staff trained in accordance with that policy, could leave both individuals and their employers in a vulnerable position.

Treatment

The assumption underpinning a treatment approach is that violent behaviour can be stopped by changing the violent person. In this light a range of treatment techniques (Roth, 1987), some based on cognitive-behavioural theory (Goldstein *et al.*, 1989), have proved popular in recent years. These treatment approaches can be broadly divided into those that aim to change cognition, and those that aim to change behaviour.

Of those that seek to change cognition (together with the associated angry arousal), *anger management* has proved enormously popular (Feindler and Ecton, 1986). Of the techniques aimed at changing behaviour, *social skills training* has been widely used with violent people (Henderson, 1989). Both these approaches have, within limits, proved to be moderately successful; however, the next generation of treatment programmes looks even more promising. As discussed in Chapter 8, a number of North American researchers and practitioners — principally Robert Ross in Canada and Arnie Goldstein in the US — are developing *multimodal treatment programmes*. With regard to violent offenders, the *Aggression Replacement Training* (ART) programme developed by Goldstein and his colleagues looks set to be a major innovation in this field (Glick and Goldstein, 1987; Goldstein and Keller, 1987; Goldstein *et al.*, 1989).

Context

It is recognized by most practitioners and indicated by the meta-analyses that context is an important determinant of the success of a treatment approach to working with offenders. In looking specifically at the management and treatment of violent behaviour, Gentry and Ostapiuk (1989) have raised some important issues concerning the relative effectiveness of treatment in institutions and community settings. They suggest that the characteristics of institutions and communities are quite different in a number of important respects. For many reasons, including legal requirements, protection of staff and other residents, and protection of the public, institutions are characterized by security and the predictability of routines. These factors, of course, produce a highly artificial environment when compared to the community which very often lacks such rigid and controlling security, structure, and definitions of rules and boundaries.

Overlaying this dichotomy of institutions and community, Ostapiuk and Gentry also make the distinction between *management* needs and *client* needs.

Management needs, reflected in the characteristics of many institutions, involve an effective means by which to ensure compliance, containment and adherence to routines in order to impose control over the client's behaviour. In contrast, to survive in the community the client needs to develop self-control in order to ensure continued freedom and independence.

It follows that the treatment of violent people in institutions demands that a number of problems be solved. The secure artificiality of the institution may control the violent behaviour, but this does not mean that the violent person has been changed; the problem has not been solved, it has simply been put to one side for a period of time. Further, the artificiality of the institution may lead to a low rate of generalization of treatment gains back into the community after release. In the community the position is reversed; the professional may have such little control over the violent person's environment — friends, family, drinking — that intervention has little chance against such odds. The control offered by the institution is simply not to be found in the community. However, in the community the generalization problem is solved at a stroke — as the intervention takes place in the environment where the behaviour occurs, so generalization is 'built-in'. This leaves two issues: how to construct institutional regimes to move from management imposed external control to person-centred internal control prior to release; how to begin in the community to gain some degree of control over the violent person to engage them in changing their violent behaviour. It is evident that the formulation of practices and policies to meet these demands will continue to tax professionals in this field.

Sentencing

The formulation of effective sentencing policies for violent offenders remains an art form that has yet to be mastered. What is evident is that sentencing practice to date has conspicuously failed — from harsher penal sentences to capital punishment nothing has stemmed the numbers of violent crimes committed each year (although it should be noted that the actual numbers of violent crimes, compared to other offences, is very small). I think it is time for a large-scale radical reassessment of sentencing practice with violent offenders; exactly what might emerge from such an exercise is, of course, unclear although I would anticipate elements from reparation and treatment programmes such as ART would be required.

In summary, this chapter has illustrated how a cogent framework can be applied both to advance our understanding of a phenomenon, in this case violent behaviour, and how that improved understanding can be used to begin to generate means by which to develop strategies for reducing violence. If this exercise can be carried out for violence, then it can be carried out for any criminal behaviour. That remains the challenge for the future.

Postscript

I waited to write this brief postscript until the second draft of the manuscript was complete, my idea being that after having read the text at least twice I would be able to jot down what seemed to me to be the most pertinent issues. In this light I have six main points to make which seem, to me at least, to be important areas for the future.

My first point concerns the status of psychological approaches to explaining criminal behaviour. It is crucial that those within psychology work hard to help those outside psychology appreciate that to construct a model of criminal behaviour that is *psychological* — a term which I use here in the sense of including biological and social variables — is not to impute psychopathology. As this book has hopefully made clear, psychological theories that aspire to explain normal, everyday behaviour are appropriate for explaining criminal behaviour. This brings me to the second of my six points; as mainstream psychological theories develop, witnessed at the moment in a number of areas such as behaviour genetics and cognitive neuropsychology, so psychological explanations of criminal behaviour will need to be revised. In turn, however, if psychological accounts of criminal behaviour must be modified according to developments in psychology, so they must also be sensitive to changes in concern and emphasis in mainstream criminology. Therefore my third point is to suggest areas towards which research in criminological psychology might move.

It is evident that the time has passed when the implicit assumption was made that to study crime was to study male criminals. The forceful arguments of writers on the topic of gender and crime, such as Smart (1976), Carlen (1983), Campbell (1984) and Heidensohn (1985), have begun to have an impact on current thinking and empirical research in mainstream criminology (e.g., Allen, 1989; Berger, 1989; Hill and Crawford, 1990; Worrell, 1990). Indeed, to take this point a stage further, Hill and Crawford (1990) have asked 'Does the explanation of black female criminality involve a causal structure different from that of their white counterparts?' (p. 601). Clearly the challenge that faces psychological contributions to theories of crime is to incorporate issues of gender and race into current psychological thinking about criminal behaviour.

At a practical level, moving to my fourth point, psychology is making a significant contribution to rehabilitation programmes for offenders, as exemplified by the clinical work with violent offenders (Howells and Hollin, 1989) and with sex offenders (Hollin and Howells, 1991). In moving on from this work with offenders, the next important step must be the development of prevention programmes. While there are many excellent examples of preventative work at both community and individual levels (Johnson, 1987), this is an area in which psychologists should play an even more prominent role. One of the research issues raised by prevention is where to target prevention programmes for maximum efficacy. This, in turn, means that we need to develop predictors of delinquency and recidivism; there is relevant work currently being reported (e.g., Greenberg, 1991; White *et al.*, 1990) and over the coming years hopefully psychologists will pay increased attention to this important topic.

To move to my fifth point, this book like many others has concentrated on offenders and, while recognizing the arguments that many offenders are also victims, it is important not to lose sight of the fact that there are victims of crime. While, mainly for reasons of space, victimology has not been addressed here, another book edited by Kevin Howells and myself draws together in a single volume work with sex offenders and victims (Hollin and Howells, 1991). On a much broader level altogether, Wright (1991) has offered a blueprint for a criminal justice system that expresses concern for the rights and needs of both offenders and victims. Wright's book is important because it addresses the basic principles of criminal justice, arguing that the system should be restorative not retributive. This concern with the guiding principles of the way in which society constructs systems of justice brings me to my sixth and final point.

It has always seemed to me that psychologists can bring a fresh approach to old arguments, either by drawing on empirical studies or by the application of psychological theories and principles. On the other hand, my perception is that very often psychologists are less willing to engage publicly in moral or philosophical arguments. Take for example the recent findings on the effectiveness of rehabilitation with offenders. As discussed in Chapter 8, there are now very strong arguments that effective rehabilitation is an achievable goal. Psychologists who have said this for decades should at this very moment be in the vanguard of campaigns to force this message home to politicians and policy makers; the Canadian psychologists offer a perfect example of how this task might be approached. It is not enough to publish papers in academic journals and sit back for the world to take note; administrators, politicians and policy makers are not renowned for rushing to either psychologists or their journals when it come to making decisions; we as psychologists must turn things around and make ourselves one of the first professions policy makers turn to when forming panels and seeking experts. I think psychologists have important things to say and need to create a forum to make their voices heard. This view is not expressed in an attempt to create jobs for psychologists. Indeed, what it will mean in practice is quite the reverse; there will be an increase in the workload of those psychologists whose research and knowledge equips them to make an effective contribution. Nonetheless, it is my view that, with due regard to the limitations and constraints on our knowledge, we are morally bound to participate in the time-consuming world of committees and the like. That is *applied* psychology: that is what psychology and crime should be about.

References

AGGLETON, P. (1987) *Deviance*, London, Tavistock.

AGNEW, R. (1990) 'The origins of delinquent events: An examination of offender accounts', *Journal of Research in Crime and Delinquency*, **27**, pp. 267–94.

AGNEW, R. (1991) 'The interactive effects of peer variables on delinquency', *Criminology*, **29**, 47–72.

AICHHORN, A. (1955) *Wayward Youth*, (trans.) New York, Meridian Books; (originally published in 1925).

AKERS, R.L. (1985) *Deviant Behavior: A Social Learning Approach* (3rd Ed.) Belmont, CA, Wadsworth.

AKERS, R.L. (1990) 'Rational choice, deterrence, and social learning theory in criminology: The path not taken', *Journal of Criminal Law and Criminology*, **81**, pp. 653–76.

ALEXANDER, J.F., BARTON, C., SCHIAVO, R.S. and PARSONS, B.V. (1976) 'Systems behavioral intervention with the families of delinquents: Therapist characteristics, family behavior, and outcome', *Journal of Consulting and Clinical Psychology*, **44**, pp. 223–31.

ALEXANDER, J.F. and PARSONS, B.V. (1973) 'Short-term behavioral intervention with delinquent families: Impact on family processes and recidivism', *Journal of Abnormal Psychology*, **81**, pp. 219–25.

ALLEN, J. (1989) 'Men, crime and criminology: Recasting the questions', *International Journal of the Sociology of Law*, **17**, pp. 19–39.

AMERICAN PSYCHIATRIC ASSOCIATION (APA) (1987) *Diagnostic and Statistical Manual of Mental Disorders*, (3rd Ed., rev.) Washington, DC, American Psychiatric Association Press.

ANDERSON, C.A. (1989) 'Temperature and aggression: Ubiquitous effects of heat on occurrence of human violence', *Psychological Bulletin*, **106**, pp. 74–96.

ANDREWS, D.A. (1989) 'Recidivism is predictable and can be influenced: Using risk assessments to reduce recidivism', *Forum on Corrections Research*, **1**, pp. 11–18.

ANDREWS, D.A. (1990) 'Some criminological sources of anti-rehabilitation bias in the Report of The Canadian Sentencing Commission', *Canadian Journal of Criminology*, **2**, pp. 511–24.

ANDREWS, D.A. and WORMITH, J.S. (1989) 'Personality and crime: Knowledge destruction and construction in criminology', *Justice Quarterly*, **6**, pp. 289–309.

ANDREWS, D.A., ZINGER, I., HOGE, R.D., BONTA, J., GENDREAU, P. and CULLEN, F.T. (1990a) 'Does correctional treatment work? A clinically relevant and psychologically informed meta-analysis', *Criminology*, **28**, pp. 369–404.

ANDREWS, D.A., ZINGER, I., HOGE, R.D., BONTA, J., GENDREAU, P. and CULLEN, F.T. (1990b) 'A human science approach or more punishment and pessimism: A rejoinder to Lab and Whitehead', *Criminology*, **28**, pp. 419–29.

ARCHER, J. and BROWNE, K.D. (Eds) (1989) *Human Aggression: Naturalistic Approaches*, London, Routledge.

ARGYLE, M. (1967) *The Psychology of Interpersonal Behaviour*, Harmondsworth, Middlesex, Penguin.

ARGYLE, M. (1983) *The Psychology of Interpersonal Behaviour* (4th ed.) Harmondsworth, Middlesex, Penguin.

ARGYLE, M. and KENDON, A. (1967) 'The experimental analysis of social performance', in L. BERKOWITZ (Ed.) *Advances in Experimental Social Psychology*, **3**, NY, Academic Press.

ASHWORTH, A. and GOSTIN, L. (1985) 'Mentally disordered offenders and the sentencing process', in L. GOSTIN (Ed.) *Secure Provision: A Review of Special Services for the Mentally Ill and Mentally Handicapped in England and Wales*, London, Tavistock.

BANDURA, A. (1977) *Social Learning Theory*, Englewood Cliffs, NY, Prentice-Hall.

BANDURA, A. (1986) *Social Foundations of Thought and Action: A Social Cognitive Theory*, Englewood Cliffs, NY, Prentice-Hall.

BANK, L., PATTERSON, G.R. and REID, J.B. (1987) 'Delinquency prevention through training parents in family management', *The Behavior Analyst*, **10**, pp. 75–82.

BARTOL, C.R. (1980) *Criminal Behavior: A Psychosocial Approach*, Englewood Cliffs, NY, Prentice-Hall.

BEAN, P.T. (1980) *Compulsory Admissions to Mental Hospitals*, Chichester, Wiley.

BECK, S.J. and OLLENDICK, T.H. (1976) 'Personal space, sex of experimenter, and locus of control in normal and delinquent adolescents', *Psychological Reports*, **38**, pp. 383–7.

BECKER, H.S. (1963) *Outsiders: Studies in the Sociology of Deviance*, London, Macmillan.

BELLACK, A.S., HERSEN, M. and KAZDIN, A.E. (Eds) (1989) *International Handbook of Behavior Modification and Therapy*, (2nd ed.) New York, Plenum Press.

BELSON, W. (1975) *Juvenile Theft: The Causal Factors*, NY, Harper and Row.

BERGER, R.J. (1989) 'Female delinquency in the emancipation era: A review of the literature', *Sex Roles*, **21**, pp. 375–99.

BILLIG, M. (1978) *Fascists: A Social Psychological View of the National Front*, London, Academic Press.

BIRON, L. and LeBLANC, M. (1977) 'Family components and home-based delinquency', *British Journal of Criminology*, **7**, pp. 157–68.

BLACKBURN, R. (1971) 'Personality types among abnormal homicides', *British Journal of Criminology*, **11**, pp. 14–31.

BLACKBURN, R. (1975) 'An empirical classification of psychopathic personality', *British Journal of Psychiatry*, **127**, pp. 456–60.

BLACKBURN, R. (1979) 'Cortical and autonomic arousal in primary and secondary psychopaths', *Psychophysiology*, **16**, pp. 143–50.

BLACKBURN, R. (1982) 'On the relevance of the concept of the psychopath', in D.A. BLACK (Ed.) *Symposium: Broadmoor Psychology Department's 21st Birthday. Issues in Criminological and Legal Psychology, No. 2*, Leicester, The British Psychological Society.

BLACKBURN, R. (1983) 'Psychopathy, delinquency and crime', in A. GALE and J.A. EDWARDS (Eds) *Physiological Correlates of Human Behaviour, Vol. 3: Individual Differences and Psychopathology*, London, Academic Press.

BLACKBURN, R. (1986) 'Patterns of personality deviation among violent offenders', *British Journal of Criminology*, **26**, pp. 254–69.

BLAGG, H. (1985) 'Reparation and justice for juveniles', *British Journal of Criminology*, **25**, pp. 267–79.

BLAKELY, C.H. and DAVIDSON, W.S. (1984) 'Behavioral approaches to delinquency: A review', in P. KAROLY and J.J. STEFFEN (Eds) *Adolescent Behavior Disorders: Foundations and Contemporary Concern*, Lexington, MA, Lexington Books.

BOTTOMLEY, K. and PEASE, K. (1986) *Crime and Punishment: Interpretating the Data*, Milton Keynes, Open University Press.

BOTTOMS, A.F. and MCCLINTOCK, F.H. (1973) *Criminals Coming of Age*, London, Heinemann.

BRAITHWAITE, J. (1989) *Crime, Shame and Reintegration*, Cambridge, Cambridge University Press.

BRANTINGHAM, P.L. and BRANTINGHAM, P.J. (1990) 'Situational crime prevention in practice', *Canadian Journal of Criminology*, **32**, pp. 17–40.

BRAUKMANN, C.J. and WOLF, M.M. (1987) 'Behaviorally based group homes for juvenile offenders', in E.K. MORRIS and C.J. BRAUKMANN (Eds) *Behavioral Approaches to Crime and Delinquency: A Handbook of Application, Research and Concepts*, New York, Plenum Press.

BREAKWELL, G. (1989) *Facing Physical Violence*, Leicester/London, BPS Books/Routledge.

BROPHY, J. (1981) 'Teacher praise: A functional analysis', *Review of Educational Research*, **51**, pp. 5–32.

BROWNE, K.D. (1989) 'Family violence: Spouse and elder abuse', in K. HOWELLS and C.R. HOLLIN (Eds) *Clinical Approaches to Violence*, Chichester, Wiley.

BROWNFIELD, D. (1990) 'Adolescent male status and delinquent behaviour', *Sociological Spectrum*, **10**, pp. 227–48.

BROWNFIELD, D. and THOMPSON, K. (1991) 'Attachment to peers and delinquent behaviour', *Canadian Journal of Criminology*, **33**, pp. 45–60.

BUIKHUISEN, W., BONTEKOE, L., VAN DER PLAS-KORENHOFF, C. and MEIJS, B.W.G.P. (1988) 'Biological, psychological and social factors related to juvenile delinquency', in W. BUIKHUISEN and S.A. MEDNICK (Eds) *Explaining Criminal Behaviour: Interdisciplinary Approaches*, Leiden, E.J. Brill.

BURCHARD, J.D. and HARRINGTON, W.A. (1986) 'Deinstitutionalization: Programmed transition from the institution to the community', *Child and Family Behavior Therapy*, **7**, pp. 17–32.

BURCHARD, J.D. and LANE, T.W. (1982) 'Crime and delinquency', in A.S. BELLACK, M. HERSEN and A.E. KAZDIN (Eds) *International Handbook of Behavior Modification and Therapy*, New York, Plenum Press.

BURROWS, J. (1980) 'Closed circuit television and crime on the London Underground', in R.V.G. CLARKE and P. MAYHEW (Eds) *Designing Out Crime*, London, HMSO.

BURT, C. (1925) *The Young Delinquent*, London, University of London Press.

BUSS, W.A.H. (1961) *The Psychology of Aggression*, New York, Wiley.

CAMPBELL, A. (1984) *The Girls in the Gang*, Oxford, Blackwell.

CAMPBELL, S.B. and WERRY, J.S. (1986) 'Attention deficit disorder (hyperactivity)', in H.C. QUAY and J.S. WERRY (Eds) *Psychopathological Disorders of Childhood* (3rd ed.) New York, Wiley.

CAPLAN, N.S. (1965) 'Intellectual functioning', in H.C. QUAY (Ed.) *Juvenile Delinquency*, Princeton, Van Nostrand.

CARLEN, P. (1983) *Women, Crime and Poverty*, Milton Keynes, Open University Press.

CATANIA, A.C. and HARNAD, S. (1988) *The Selection of Behavior: The Operant Behaviorism of B.F. Skinner: Comments and Consequences*, Cambridge, Cambridge University Press.

CHALMERS, J.B. and TOWNSEND, M.A.R. (1990) 'The effects of training in social perspective taking on socially maladjusted girls', *Child Development*, **61**, pp. 178–90.

CHANDLER, M.J. (1973) 'Egocentrism and antisocial behavior: The assessment and training of social perspective-taking skills', *Developmental Psychology*, **9**, pp. 326–32.

CHESNO, F.A. and KILMANN, P.R. (1975) 'Effects of stimulation intensity on sociopathic avoidance learning', *Journal of Abnormal Psychology*, **84**, pp. 144–50.

CLARKE, R.V.G. (1982) 'Crime prevention through environmental management and design', in J. GUNN and D.P. FARRINGTON (Eds) *Abnormal Offenders, Delinquency, and the Criminal Justice System*, Chichester, Wiley.

CLARKE, R.V.G. (1985) 'Jack Tizard memorial lecture: Delinquency, environment and intervention', *Journal of Child Psychology and Psychiatry*, **26**, pp. 505–23.

CLECKLEY, H. (1964) *The Mask of Sanity*, (4th ed.) St. Louis, MO, C.V. Mosby.

CLECKLEY, H. (1976) *The Mask of Sanity*, (5th ed.) St. Louis, MO, C.V. Mosby.

CLONINGER, C.R. and GOTTESMAN, I.I. (1987) 'Genetic and environmental factors in antisocial behaviour disorders', in S.A. MEDNICK, T.E. MOFFITT and S.A. STACK (Eds) *The Causes of Crime: New Biological Approaches*, Cambridge, Cambridge University Press.

COHEN, B.Z., EDEN, R. and LAZAR, A. (1991) 'The efficacy of probation versus imprisonment in reducing recidivism of serious offenders in Israel', *Journal of Criminal Justice*, **19**, pp. 263–70.

CORNISH, D.B. and CLARKE, R.V.G. (Eds) (1986) *The Reasoning Criminal: Rational Choice Perspectives on Crime*, New York, Springer-Verlag.

CORNISH, D.B. and CLARKE, R.V. (1987) 'Understanding crime displacement: An application of rational choice theory', *Criminology*, **25**, pp. 933–47.

CRAFT, M. (1984) 'Low intelligence, mental handicap and criminality', in M. CRAFT and A. CRAFT (Eds) *Mentally Abnormal Offenders*, London, Baillière Tindall.

CRAFT, M. and CRAFT, A. (Eds) (1984) *Mentally Abnormal Offenders*, London, Bailliere Tindall.

CROWE, R.R. (1974) 'An adoption study of antisocial personality', *Archives of General Psychiatry*, **31**, pp. 785–91.

CULLEN, F.T. and GENDREAU, P. (1989) 'The effectiveness of correctional rehabilitation: Reconsidering the "nothing works" debate', in L. GOODSTEIN and D.L. MACKENZIE (Eds) *The American Prison: Issues in Research and Policy*, New York, Plenum Press.

CULLEN, F.T., SKOVRON, S.E., SCOTT, J.E. and BURTON, V.S. (1990) 'Public support for correctional treatment: The tenacity of a rehabilitation ideal', *Criminal Justice and Behavior*, **17**, pp. 6–18.

CULLEN, J.E. and SEDDON, J.W. (1981) 'The application of a behavioural regime to disturbed young offenders', *Personality and Individual Differences*, **2**, pp. 285–92.

DARO, D. (1991) 'Prevention programs', in C.R. HOLLIN and K. HOWELLS (Eds) *Clinical Approaches to Sex Offenders and Their Victims*, Chichester, Wiley.

DAVIDSON, W.S., SEIDMAN, E., RAPPAPORT, J., BERCK, P., RAPP, N., RHODES, W. and HERRING, J. (1977) 'Diversion programs for juvenile offenders', *Social Work Research and Abstracts*, **13**, pp. 40–9.

DAVIDSON, W.S., REDNER, R., BLAKELY, C.H., MITCHELL, C.M. and EMSHOFF, J.G. (1987) 'Diversion of juvenile offenders: An experimental comparison', *Journal of Consulting and Clinical Psychology*, **55**, pp. 68–75.

DAVIDSON, W.S., REDNER, R., AMDUR, R.L. and MITCHELL, C.M. (1990) *Alternative Treatments for Troubled Youth: The Case of Diversion from the Justice System*, New York, Plenum Press.

DAVIES, W. (1989) 'The prevention of assault on professional helpers', in K. HOWELLS and C.R. HOLLIN (Eds) *Clinical Approaches to Violence*, Chichester, Wiley.

DAVIES, W. and FELDMAN, P. (1981) 'The diagnosis of psychopathy by forensic specialists', *British Journal of Psychiatry*, **138**, pp. 329–31.

DENKOWSKI, G.C. and DENKOWSKI, K.M. (1985) 'The mentally retarded offender in the state prison system: Identification, prevalence, adjustment and rehabilitation', *Criminal Justice and Behavior*, **12**, pp. 55–70.

DENNO, D.W. (1990) *Biology and Violence: From Birth to Adulthood*, Cambridge, Cambridge University Press.

DHSS AND HOME OFFICE (1986) *Offenders Suffering from Psychopathic Disorder*, London, DHSS and Home Office.

DiLALLA, L.F. and GOTTESMAN, I.I. (1990) 'Heterogeneity of causes for delinquency and criminality: Lifespan perspectives', *Development and Psychopathology*, **1**, pp. 339–49.

DiLALLA, L.F. and GOTTESMAN, I.I. (1991) 'Biological and genetic contributors to violence — Widom's untold tale', *Psychological Bulletin*, **109**, pp. 125–9.

DOBASH, R.E. and DOBASH, R.P. (1984) 'The nature and antecedents of violent events', *British Journal of Criminology*, **24**, pp. 269–88.

DODGE, K.A. (1986) 'A social-information processing model of social competence in children', in M. PERMUTTER (Ed.) *Minnesota Symposium on Child Psychology*, **18**, Hillsdale, NJ, Erlbaum.

DODGE, K.A. and NEWMAN, J.P. (1981) 'Biased decision-making processes in aggressive boys', *Journal of Abnormal Psychology*, **90**, pp. 375–9.

DOWDS, L. (in press) 'Victim surveys: Exploring the nature of violent crime', in J.F. RODERO RODRIGUEZ and D.P. FARRINGTON (Eds) *Psychology, Crime and the Law: British and Spanish Research*, Pamplona, Spain, Colegio Oficial de Psicologos.

EHRENKRANZ, J., BLISS, E. and SHEARD, M.H. (1974) 'Plasma testosterone: Correlation with aggressive behavior and social dominance in man', *Psychosomatic Medicine*, **36**, pp. 469–75.

ELLIOTT, D. HUIZINGA, D. and AGETON, S. (1985) *Explaining Delinquency and Drug Use*, Beverly Hills, CA, Sage.

ELLIOTT, D. and VOSS, H. (1974) *Delinquency and Dropout*, Lexington, MA, Lexington Press.

ELLIS, L. (1987) 'Neurohormonal bases of varying tendencies to learn delinquent and criminal behavior', in E.K. MORRIS and C.J. BRAUKMANN (Eds) *Behavioral Approaches to Crime and Delinquency: A Handbook of Application, Research, and Concepts*, New York, Plenum.

ELLIS, L. and COONTZ, P.D. (1990) 'Androgens, brain functioning, and criminality: The neurohormonal foundations of antisociality', in L. ELLIS and H. HOFFMAN (Eds) *Crime in Biological, Social and Moral Contexts*, New York, Praeger.

ELLIS, L. and HOFFMAN, H. (1990) 'Views of contemporary criminologists on causes and theories of crime', in L. ELLIS and H. HOFFMAN (Eds) *Crime in Biological, Social and Moral Contexts*, New York, Praeger.

ERIKSON, K.T. (1962) 'Notes on the sociology of deviance', *Social Problems*, **9**, pp. 307–14.

EYSENCK, H.J. (1964) *Crime and Personality*, London, Routledge and Kegan Paul.

EYSENCK, H.J. (1973) *The Inequality of Man*, London, Temple Smith.

EYSENCK, H.J. (1984) 'Crime and personality', in D.J. MULLER, D.E. BLACKMAN and A.J. CHAPMAN (Eds) *Psychology and Law*, Chichester, Wiley.

EYSENCK, H.J. (1987) 'Personality theory and the problems of criminality', in B.J. McGURK, D.M. THORNTON and M. WILLIAMS (Eds) *Applying Psychology to Imprisonment: Theory and Practice*, London, HMSO.

EYSENCK, H.J. and GUDJONSSON, G.H. (1989) *The Causes and Cures of Criminality*, New York, Plenum Press.

Eysenck, S.B.G. and Eysenck, H.J. (1972) 'The questionnaire measurement of psychoticism', *Psychological Medicine*, **2**, pp. 50–5.

Eysenck, S.B.G., Eysenck, H.J. and Barrett, P. (1985) 'A revised version of the psychoticism scale', *Personality and Individual Differences*, **6**, pp. 21–9.

Fagan, J. (1990) 'Social processes of delinquency and drug abuse among urban gangs', in C.R. Huff (Ed.) *Gangs in America*, Newbury Park, CA, Sage Publications.

Farrington, D.P. (1983) 'Offending from 10 to 25 years of age', in K. Teilmann Van Dusen and S.A. Mednick (Eds) *Prospective Studies of Crime and Delinquency*, The Hague, Kluwer-Nijhoff.

Farrington, D.P. (1986) 'Age and crime', in M. Tonry and N. Morris (Eds) *Crime and Justice: An Annual Review of Research*, **7**, Chicago, University of Chicago Press.

Farrington, D.P. (1987) 'Epidemiology', in H.C. Quay (Ed.) *Handbook of Juvenile Delinquency*, New York, Wiley.

Farrington, D.P. (1990) 'Implications of criminal career research for the prevention of offending', *Journal of Adolescence*, **13**, pp. 93–113.

Farrington, D.P. and Bennett, T. (1981) 'Police cautioning of juveniles in London', *British Journal of Criminology*, **21**, pp. 123–35.

Farrington, D.P. and Dowds, E.A. (1985) 'Disentangling criminal behaviour and police reaction', in D.P. Farrington and J. Gunn (Eds) *Reactions to Crime: The Police, Courts and Prisons*, Chichester, Wiley.

Farrington, D.P. and West, D.J. (1990) 'The Cambridge Study in Delinquent Development: A long-term follow-up of 411 London males', in H.J. Kerner and G. Kaiser (Eds) *Criminality: Personality, Behaviour and Life History*, Berlin, Springer-Verlag.

Farrington, D.P., Loeber, R. and Van Kammen, W.B. (1990) 'Long-term criminal outcomes of hyperactivity–impulsivity–attention deficit and conduct problems in childhood', in L. Robins and M. Rutter (Eds) *Straight and Devious Pathways from Childhood to Adulthood*, Cambridge, Cambridge University Press.

Farrington, D.P., Ohlin, L.E. and Wilson, J.Q. (1986) *Understanding and Controlling Crime*, NY, Springer-Verlag.

Feehan, M., Stanton, W.R., McGee, R., Silva, P.A. and Moffitt, T.E. (1990) 'Is there an association between lateral preference and delinquent behavior?' *Journal of Abnormal Psychology*, **99**, pp. 198–201.

Feindler, E.L. and Ecton, R.B. (1986) *Adolescent Anger Control: Cognitive-Behavioral Techniques*, Elmsford, NY, Pergamon Press.

Feldman, M.P. (1977) *Criminal Behaviour: A Psychological Analysis*, Chichester, Wiley.

Field, S. (1990) *Trends in Crime and their Interpretation: A Study of Recorded Crime in Post-War England and Wales*, London, HMSO.

Filipczak, J. and Wodarski, J.S. (1982) 'Behavioral intervention in public schools: I. Short-term results', in D.J. Safer (Ed.) *School Programs for Disruptive Adolescents*, Baltimore, MD, University Park Press.

Fischer, D.G. (1984) 'Family size and delinquency', *Perceptual and Motor Skills*, **58**, pp. 527–34.

Fishbein, D.J. (1990) 'Biological perspectives in criminology', *Criminology*, **28**, pp. 27–72.

Fishbein, D.J. and Pease, S.E. (1990) 'Neurological links between substance abuse and crime', in L. Ellis and H. Hoffman (Eds) *Crime in Biological, Social and Moral Contexts*, NY, Praeger.

Fo, W.S.O. and O'Donnell, C.R. (1974) 'The buddy system: Relationship and contingency conditions in a community intervention program for youth and non-professionals as behavior change agents', *Journal of Consulting and Clinical psychology*, **42**, pp. 163–8.

Fo, W.S.O. and O'Donnell, C.R. (1975) 'The buddy system: Effect of community intervention on delinquent offences', *Behavior Therapy*, **6**, pp. 522–4.

Foster, J. (1990) *Villains: Crime and Community in the Inner City*, London, Routledge.

Fraser, M.W., Hawkins, J.D. and Howard, M.O. (1988) 'Parent training for delinquency prevention', *Child and Youth Services*, **11**, pp. 93–125.

Freedman, B.J., Rosenthal, L., Donahoe, C.P., Schlundt, D.G. and McFall, R.M. (1978) 'A social-behavioral analysis of skills deficits in delinquent and non-delinquent adolescent boys', *Journal of Consulting and Clinical Psychology*, **46**, pp. 1448–62.

Frude, N. (1989) 'The physical abuse of children', in K. Howells and C.R. Hollin (Eds) *Clinical Approaches to Violence*, Chichester, Wiley.

Furnham, A. (1984) 'Personality, social skills, anomie and delinquency: A self-report study of a group of normal non-delinquent adolescents', *Journal of Child Psychology and Psychiatry*, **25**, pp. 409–20.

Furnham, A.F. and Thompson, J. (1991) 'Personality and self-reported delinquency', *Personality and Individual Differences*, **12**, pp. 585–93.

Gabor, T. (1981) 'The crime displacement hypothesis: An empirical examination', *Crime and Delinquency*, **26**, pp. 390–404.

Gaffney, L.R. and McFall, R.M. (1981) 'A comparison of social skills in delinquent and non-delinquent adolescent girls using a behavioral role-playing inventory', *Journal of Consulting and Clinical Psychology*, **49**, pp. 959–67.

Gardiner, G. (1956) *Capital Punishment as a Deterrent: And the Alternative*, London, Victor Gollancz.

Garrett, C.J. (1985) 'Effects of residential treatment of adjudicated delinquents: A meta-analysis', *Journal of Research in Crime and Delinquency*, **22**, pp. 287–308.

Gendreau, P. and Andrews, D.A. (1990) 'Tertiary prevention: What the meta-analyses of the offender treatment literature tell us about "What Works"', *Canadian Journal of Criminology*, **32**, pp. 173–84.

Gendreau, P. and Ross, R.R. (1979) 'Effective correctional treatment: Bibliotherapy for cynics', *Crime and Delinquency*, **25**, pp. 463–89.

Gendreau, P. and Ross, R.R. (1987) 'Revivification of rehabilitation: Evidence from the 1980s', *Justice Quarterly*, **4**, pp. 349–407.

Gentry, M.R. and Ostapiuk, E.B. (1989) 'Violence in institutions for young offenders and disturbed adolescents', in K. Howells and C.R. Hollin (Eds) *Clinical Approaches to Violence*, Chichester, Wiley.

Gibbs, J.C. Arnold, K.D., Cheesman, F.L. and Ahlborn, H.H. (1984) 'Facilitation of sociomoral reasoning in delinquents', *Journal of Consulting and Clinical Psychology*, **52**, pp. 37–45.

Gibson, H. (1967) 'Self reported delinquency among school boys and their attitudes to the police', *British Journal of Social and Clinical Psychology*, **6**, pp. 168–73.

Gilby, R., Woolf, L. and Goldberg, B. (1989) 'Mentally retarded adolescent sex offenders: A survey and pilot study', *Canadian Journal of Psychiatry*, **34**, pp. 542–8.

Glick, B. and Goldstein, A.P. (1987) 'Aggression replacement training', *Journal of Counseling and Development*, **65**, pp. 356–67.

Glueck, S. and Glueck, E.T. (1934) *One Thousand Juvenile Delinquents*, Cambridge, MA, Harvard University Press.

Glueck, S. and Glueck, E.T. (1950) *Unraveling Juvenile Delinquency*, New York, Commonwealth Fund.

Goldsmith, H.R. (1990) 'Men who abuse their spouses: An approach to assessing future risk', in N.J. Pallone and S. Chaneles (Eds) *The Clinical Treatment of the Criminal Offender in Outpatient Mental Health Settings*, New York, Haworth Press.

GOLDSTEIN, A.P. and KELLER, H. (1987) *Aggressive Behavior: Assessment and Intervention*, Elmsford, NY, Pergamon Press.

GOLDSTEIN, A.P., GLICK, B., IRWIN, M.J., PASK-MCCARTNEY, C. and RUBAMA, I. (1989) *Reducing Delinquency: Intervention in the Community*, Elmsford, NY, Pergamon Press.

GOLDSTEIN, J.H. (1986) *Aggression and Crimes of Violence* (2nd ed.) Oxford, Oxford University Press.

GORDON, D.A. and ARBUTHNOT, J. (1987) 'Individual, group and family interventions', in H.C. QUAY (Ed.) *Handbook of Juvenile Delinquency*, New York.

GORING, C. (1913/1972) *The English Convict: A Statistical Study*, Montclair, NJ, Patterson Smith.

GOTTSCHALK, R., DAVIDSON, W.S., GENSHEIMER, L.K. and MAYER, J. (1987) 'Community-based interventions', in H.C. QUAY (Ed.) *Handbook of Juvenile Delinquency*, New York, Wiley.

GREEN, S. (1991a) 'Physiological studies I', in J. RADFORD and E. GOVIER (Eds) *A Textbook of Psychology*, London, Routledge.

GREEN, S. (1991b) 'Physiological studies II', in J. RADFORD and E. GOVIER (Eds) *A Textbook of Psychology* (2nd ed.) London, Routledge.

GREENBERG, D.F. (1991) 'Modeling criminal careers', *Criminology*, **29**, pp. 17–46.

GRESSWELL, D.M. and HOLLIN, C.R. (in press) 'Towards a new methodology for making sense of case material: An illustrative case involving attempted multiple murder', *Criminal Behaviour and Mental Health*.

GROSS, A.M., BRIGHAM, T.A., HOPPER, C. and BOLOGNA, N.C. (1980) 'Self-management and social skills training: A study with pre-delinquent and delinquent youth', *Criminal Justice and Behavior*, **7**, pp. 161–84.

GROTH, A.N., LONGO, R.E. and MCFADIN, J.B. (1982) 'Undetected recidivism among rapists and child molesters', *Crime and Delinquency*, **28**, pp. 450–8.

GROUNDS, A.T. (1987) 'Detention of "psychopathic disorder" patients in special hospitals', *British Journal of Psychiatry*, **151**, pp. 474–8.

GUNN, J. (1977) 'Criminal behaviour and mental disorder', *British Journal of Psychiatry*, **130**, pp. 317–29.

GUNN, J. and BONN, J. (1971) 'Criminality and violence in epileptic prisoners', *British Journal of Psychiatry*, **118**, pp. 337–43.

GUNN, J., ROBERTSON, G., DELL, S. and WAY, C. (1978) *Psychiatric Aspects of Imprisonment*, London, Academic Press.

HÄFNER, H. and BÖKER, W. (1982) *Crimes of Violence by Mentally Abnormal Offenders: A Psychiatric and Epidemiological Study in the Federal German Republic*, (trans. H. Marshall) Cambridge, Cambridge University Press (originally published in 1973).

HAGAN, J. (1987) *Modern Criminology: Crime, Criminal Behavior and Its Control*, NY, McGraw-Hill.

HAIN, P. (1976) *Mistaken Identity: The Wrong Face of the Law*, London, Quartet Books.

HAINS, A.A. (1984) 'A preliminary attempt to teach the use of social problem-solving skills to delinquents', *Child Study Journal*, **14**, pp. 271–85.

HAMILTON, J.R. (1985) 'The special hospitals', in L. GOSTIN (Ed.) *Secure Provision: A Review of Special Services for the Mentally Ill and Mentally Handicapped in England and Wales*, London, Tavistock.

HARE, R.D. (1978) 'Electrodermal and cardiovascular correlates of psychopathy', in R. D. HARE and D. SCHALLING (Eds) *Psychopathic Behaviour: Approaches to Research*, Chichester, Wiley.

HARE, R.D. (1980) 'A research scale for the assessment of psychopathy in criminal populations', *Personality and Individual Differences*, **1**, pp. 111–19.

HARE, R.D. (1986) 'Twenty years of experience with the Cleckley psychopath', in W.H.

REID, D. DORR, J.I. WALKER, and J.W. BONNER (Eds) *Unmasking the Psychopath: Antisocial Personality and Related Syndromes*, NY, W.W. Norton.

HARE, R.D. (1991) *The Hare Psychopathy Checklist—Revised*, Toronto, Ontario, Multi-Health Systems.

HARE, R.D. and FORTH, A.E. (1985) 'Psychopathy and lateral preference', *Journal of Abnormal Psychology*, **94**, pp. 541–6.

HARE, R.D. and McPHERSON, L.M. (1984) 'Violent and aggressive behavior by criminal psychopaths', *International Journal of Law and Psychiatry*, **7**, pp. 35–50.

HARE, R.D., McPHERSON, L.M. and FORTH, A.E. (1988) 'Male psychopaths and their criminal careers', *Journal of Consulting and Clinical Psychology*, **56**, pp. 710–14.

HARE, R.D., HARPER, T.J., HAKSTIAN, A.R., FORTH, A.E., HART, S.D. and NEWMAN, J.P. (1990) 'The revised Psychopathy Checklist: Reliability and factor structure', *Psychological Assessment: A Journal of Consulting and Clinical Psychology*, **2**, pp. 338–41.

HARPUR, T.J., HAKSTIAN, A.R. and HARE, R.D. (1988) 'Factor structure of the Psychopathy Checklist', *Journal of Consulting and Clinical Psychology*, **56**, pp. 741–7.

HARPUR, T.J., HARE, R.D. and HAKSTIAN, A.R. (1989) 'Two-factor conceptualization of psychopathy: Construct validity and assessment implications', *Psychological Assessment: A Journal of Consulting and Clinical Psychology*, **1**, pp. 6–17.

HARRY, B. and BLACER, C. (1987) 'Menstruation and crime: A critical review of the literature from the clinical criminology perspective', *Behavioral Sciences and the Law*, **5**, pp. 307–22.

HART, S.D., KROPP, P.R. and HARE, R.D. (1988) 'Performance of male psychopaths following conditional release from prison', *Journal of Consulting and Clinical Psychology*, **56**, pp. 227–32.

HARVEY, O.J. (1986) 'Belief systems and attitudes toward the death penalty and other punishments', *Journal of Personality*, **54**, pp. 659–75.

HAWKINS, J.D. and LISHNER, D.M. (1987) 'Schooling and delinquency', in E.H. JOHNSON (Ed.) *Handbook on Crime and Delinquency Prevention*, New York, Greenwood Press.

HAYES, S.C. (Ed.) (1989) *Rule-governed Behavior: Cognition, Contingencies and Instructional Control*, New York, Plenum Press.

HEAL, K. and LAYCOCK, G. (Eds) (1986) *Situational Crime Prevention: From Theory into Practice*, London, HMSO.

HEIDENSOHN, F. (1985) *Women and Crime*, London, Macmillan.

HEIDENSOHN, F. (1989) *Crime and Society*, London, Macmillan.

HENDERSON, J.Q. (1981) 'A behavioral approach to stealing: A proposal for treatment based on ten cases', *Journal of Behavior Therapy and Experimental Psychiatry*, **12**, pp. 231–6.

HENDERSON, M. (1986) 'An empirical typology of violent incidents reported by prison inmates with convictions for violence', *Aggressive Behavior*, **12**, pp. 21–32.

HENDERSON, M. (1989) 'Behavioural approaches to violent crime', in K. HOWELLS and C.R. HOLLIN (Eds) *Clinical Approaches to Violence*, Chichester, Wiley.

HENDERSON, M. and HOLLIN, C.R. (1983) 'A critical review of social skills Training with young offenders', *Criminal Justice and Behavior*, **10**, pp. 316–41.

HENDERSON, M. and HOLLIN, C.R. (1986) 'Social skills training and delinquency', in C.R. HOLLIN and P. TROWER (Eds) *Handbook of Social Skills Training, Vol. 1: Applications Across the Life Span*, Oxford, Pergamon Press.

HENGGELER, S.W. (1989) *Delinquency in Adolescence*, Newbury Park, CA, Sage Publications.

HENNESSY, M., RICHARDS, P.J. and BERK, R.A. (1978) 'Broken homes and middle-class delinquency: A reassessment', *Criminology*, **15**, pp. 505–28.

HERBERT, M. (1986) 'Social skills training with children', in C.R. HOLLIN and P. TROWER (Eds) *Handbook of Social Skills Training, Vol. 1: Applications Across the Life Span*, Oxford, Pergamon Press.

HILL, D. and POND, D.A. (1952) 'Reflections on a hundred capital cases submitted to electroencephalography', *Journal of Mental Science*, **98**, pp. 23–43.

HILL, G.D. and CRAWFORD, E.M. (1990) 'Women, race, and crime', *Criminology*, **28**, pp. 601–26.

HINDELANG, M.J., HIRSCHI, T. and WEIS, J. (1981) *Measuring Delinquency*, Beverly Hills, CA, Sage.

HIRSCHI, T. (1969) *Causes of Delinquency*, Berkeley, CA, University of California Press.

HOLLIN, C.R. (1989) *Psychology and Crime: An Introduction to Criminological Psychology*, London, Routledge.

HOLLIN, C.R. (1990a) *Cognitive-Behavioral Interventions with Young Offenders*, Elmsford, NY, Pergamon Press.

HOLLIN, C.R. (1990b) 'Social skills training with delinquents: A look at the evidence and some recommendations for practice', *British Journal of Social Work*, **20**, pp. 483–93.

HOLLIN, C.R. (1991a) 'Concern about the threat of nuclear war: Just another worry?' *Anxiety Research: An International Journal*, **4**, pp. 51–60.

HOLLIN, C.R. (1991b) 'Cognitive behaviour modification with delinquents', in M. HERBERT (Ed.) *Clinical Child Psychology: Social Learning, Development and Behaviour*, Chichester, Wiley.

HOLLIN, C.R. and COURTNEY, S.A. (1983) 'A skills training approach to the reduction of institutional offending', *Personality and Individual Differences*, **4**, pp. 257–64.

HOLLIN, C.R. and HENDERSON, M. (1984) 'Social skills training with young offenders: False expectations and the "failure of treatment"', *Behavioural Psychotherapy*, **12**, pp. 331–41.

HOLLIN, C.R. and HOWELLS, K. (Eds) (1991) *Clinical Approaches to Sex Offenders and their Victims*, Chichester, Wiley.

HOLLIN, C.R. and TROWER, P. (Eds) (1986a) *Handbook of Social Skills Training: Volume 1: Applications Across the Life Span*, Oxford, Pergamon Press.

HOLLIN, C.R. and TROWER, P. (Eds) (1986b) *Handbook of Social Skills Training: Volume 2: Clinical Applications and New Directions*, Oxford, Pergamon Press.

HOLLIN, C.R. and TROWER, P. (1988) 'Development and applications of social skills training: A review and critique', in M. HERSEN, R.M. EISLER and P.M. MILLER (Eds) *Progress in Behaviour Modification*, **22**, Beverly Hills, CA, Sage Publications.

HOLLIN, C.R. and WHEELER, H.M. (1982) 'The violent young offender: A small group study of a Borstal population', *Journal of Adolescence*, **5**, pp. 247–57.

HOOD, R. (1989) *The Death Penalty: A World-Wide Perspective*, Oxford, Clarendon Press.

HOOD, R. and SPARKS, R. (1970) *Key Issues in Criminology*, London, Weidenfeld and Nicolson.

HOUGH, J.M., CLARKE, R.V.G. and MAYHEW, P. (1980) 'Introduction', in R.V.G. CLARKE and P. MAYHEW (Eds) *Designing Out Crime*, London, HMSO.

HOUGH, M. and MAYHEW, P. (1983) *The British Crime Survey: First Report*, London, HMSO.

HOUGH, M. and MAYHEW, P. (1985) *Taking Account of Crime: Key Findings from the Second British Crime Survey*, London, HMSO.

HOUGH, M., MOXON, D. and LEWIS, H. (1987) 'Attitudes to punishment: Findings from the British Crime Survey', in D.C. PENNINGTON and S. LLOYD-BOSTOCK (Eds) *The Psychology of Sentencing: Approaches to Consistency and Disparity*, Oxford, Centre for Socio-Legal Studies.

HOWELLS, K. (1982) 'Mental disorder and violent behaviour', in P. FELDMAN (Ed.) *Developments in the Study of Criminal Behaviour, Vol. 2: Violence*, Chichester, Wiley.

HOWELLS, K. (1986) 'Social skills training and criminal and anti-social behaviour in adults', in C.R. HOLLIN and P. TROWER (Eds) *Handbook of Social Skills Training, Vol. 1: Applications Across the Life Span*, Oxford, Pergamon.

HOWELLS, K. and HOLLIN, C.R. (Eds) (1989) *Clinical Approaches to Violence*, Chichester, Wiley.

HSU, L.K.G., WISNER, K., RICHEY, E.T. and GOLDSTEIN, C. (1985) 'Is juvenile delinquency related to abnormal EEG? A study of EEG abnormalities in juvenile delinquents and adolescent psychiatric inpatients', *Journal of the American Academy of Child Psychiatry*, **24**, pp. 310–15.

HUDSON, B.L. (1986) 'Community applications of social skills training', in C.R. HOLLIN and P. TROWER (Eds) *Handbook of Social Skills Training, Vol. 1: Applications Across the Life Span*, Oxford, Pergamon.

HUDSON, B. (1987) *Justice through Punishment: A Critique of the 'Justice' Model of Corrections*, London, Macmillan.

HUFF, C.R. (Ed.) (1990) *Gangs in America*, Newbury Park, CA, Sage Publications.

HUFF, G. (1987) 'Social skills training', in B.J. MCGURK, D.M. THORNTON and M. WILLIAMS (Eds) *Applying Psychology to Imprisonment: Theory and Practice*, London, HMSO.

HUNTER, N. and KELLEY, C.K. (1986) 'Examination of the validity of the adolescent problems inventory among incarcerated juvenile delinquents', *Journal of Consulting and Clinical Psychology*, **54**, pp. 301–2.

HURWITZ, S. and CHRISTIANSEN, K.O. (1983) *Criminology*, London, Allen and Unwin.

IZZO, R.L. and ROSS, R.R. (1990) 'Meta-analysis of rehabilitation programs for juvenile delinquents: A brief report', *Criminal Justice and Behavior*, **17**, pp. 134–42.

JARRELL, S. and HOWSEN, R.M. (1990) 'Transient crowding and crime: The more "strangers" in an area, the more crime except for murder, assault and rape', *American Journal of Economics and Sociology*, **49**, pp. 483–94.

JEFFERY, C.R. (1965) 'Criminal behavior and learning theory', *Journal of Criminal Law, Criminology and Police Science*, **56**, pp. 294–300.

JEHU, D. (1988) *Beyond Sexual Abuse: Therapy with Women Who Were Childhood Victims*, Chichester, Wiley.

JEHU, D. (1991) 'Clinical work with adults who were sexually abused in childhood', in C.R. HOLLIN and K. HOWELLS (Eds) *Clinical Approaches to Sex Offenders and their Victims*, Chichester, Wiley.

JESSOR, R. and JESSOR, S.L. (1977) *Problem Behavior and Psychosocial Development: A Longitudinal Study of Youth*, NY, Academic Press.

JOHNSON, E.H. (Ed.) (1987) *Handbook on Crime and Delinquency Prevention*, New York, Greenwood Press.

JONES, T., MACLEAN, B. and YOUNG, J. (1986) *The Islington Crime Survey: Crime, Victimization and Policing in Inner-City London*, Aldershot, Hants, Gower.

KAPLAN, P.J. and ARBUTHNOT, J. (1985) 'Affective empathy and cognitive role-taking in delinquent and non-delinquent youth', *Adolescence*, **20**, pp. 323–33.

KAZDIN, A.E. (1979) 'Fictions, factions and functions of behavior therapy', *Behavior Therapy*, **10**, pp. 629–54.

KAZDIN, A.E. (1987) 'Treatment of antisocial behavior in children: Current status and future directions', *Psychological Bulletin*, **102**, pp. 187–203.

KINSEY, R. (1984) *Merseyside Crime Survey: First Report, November 1984*, Liverpool, Merseyside County Council.

KLEIN, N.C., ALEXANDER, J.F. and PARSONS, B.V. (1977) 'Impact of family systems intervention on recidivism and sibling delinquency: A model of primary prevention and program evaluation', *Journal of Consulting and Clinical Psychology*, **45**, pp. 469–74.

KLOCKARS, C. (1980) 'The contemporary crises of Marxist criminology', in J. INCIARDI (Ed.) *Radical Criminology: The Coming Crisis*, Beverly Hills, CA, Sage Publications.

KORN, J.J., DAVIS, R. and DAVIS, S.F. (1991) 'Historians' and chairpersons' judgments of eminence among psychologists', *American Psychologist*, **46**, pp. 789–92.

KREUTZ, I.E. and ROSE, R.M. (1972) 'Assessment of aggressive behavior and plasma testosterone in a young criminal population', *Psychosomatic Medicine*, **34**, pp. 321–32.

KROHN, M.D., MASSEY, J.L. and SKINNER, W.F. (1987) 'A sociological theory of crime and delinquency: Social learning theory', in E.K. MORRIS and C.J. BRAUKMANN (Eds) *Behavioral Approaches to Crime and Delinquency: A Handbook of Application, Research and Concepts*, New York, Plenum Press.

KRYNICKI, V.E.L. (1978) 'Cerebral dysfunction in repetitively assaultive adolescents', *Journal of Nervous and Mental Disease*, **166**, pp. 59–67.

LAB, S.P. and WHITEHEAD, J.T. (1990) 'From "nothing works" to "the appropriate works": The latest stop on the search for the secular grail', *Criminology*, **28**, pp. 405–17.

LANGE, J. (1929) *Verbrechen Als Soschicksal*, Leipzig, Verlag.

LAWS, D.R. (1974) 'The failure of a token economy', *Federal Probation*, **38**, pp. 33–38.

LAWSON, W.K. (1984) 'Depression and crime: A discursive approach', in M. CRAFT and A. CRAFT (Eds) *Mentally Abnormal Offenders*, London, Baillière Tindall.

LAYCOCK, G. and TARLING, R. (1985) 'Police force cautioning: Policy and practice', *Howard Journal of Criminal Justice*, **24**, pp. 81–92.

LEE, V.L. (1988) *Beyond Behaviorism*, Hillsdale, NJ, Lawrence Erlbaum.

LEMERT, E. (1951) *Social Pathology*, NY, McGraw-Hill.

LEMERT, E. (1967) *Human Deviance, Social Problems and Social Control*, Englewood Cliffs, NJ, Prentice-Hall.

LESTER, D. (1991) 'Crime as opportunity: A test of the hypothesis with European suicide rates', *British Journal of Criminology*, **31**, pp. 186–8.

LEWIS, D.O., PINCUS, J.H., SHANOK, S.S. and GLASER, G.H. (1982) 'Psychomotor epilepsy and violence in a group of incarcerated adolescent boys', *American Journal of Psychiatry*, **139**, pp. 882–7.

LINDQVIST, P. and ALLEBECK, P. (1990) 'Schizophrenia and crime: A longitudinal follow-up of 644 schizophrenics in Stockholm', *British Journal of Psychiatry*, **157**, pp. 345–50.

LINNOILA, M., VIRKKUNEN, M., SCHEININ, M., NUUTILA, A., RIMON, R. and GOODWIN, F.K. (1983) 'Low cerebrospinal fluid 5-hydroxyindoleacetic acid concentration differentiates impulsive from nonimpulsive violent behavior', *Life Science*, **33**, pp. 2609–14.

LIPSEY, M.W. (in press) 'Juvenile delinquency treatment: A meta-analytic inquiry into the variability of effects', in K.W. WACHTER and M.L. STRAF (Eds) *Meta-Analysis for Explanation: A Casebook*, New York, Russell Sage Foundation.

LIPSITT, P.D., BUKA, S.L. and LIPSITT, L.P. (1990) 'Early intelligence scores and subsequent delinquency: A prospective study', *The American Journal of Family Therapy*, **18**, pp. 197–208.

LIPTON, D., MARTINSON, R. and WILKS, D. (1975) *The Effectiveness of Correctional Treatment*, New York, Praeger.

LIPTON, D.M., McDONEL, E.C. and McFALL, R.M. (1987) 'Heterosocial perception in rapists', *Journal of Consulting and Clinical Psychology*, **55**, pp. 17–21.

LOEBER, R. (1988) 'Behavioral precursors and accelerators of delinquency', in W. BUIKHUISEN and S.A. MEDNICK (Eds) *Explaining Criminal Behaviour: Interdisciplinary Approaches*, Leiden, E.J. Brill.

LOEBER, R. (1990) 'Development and risk factors of juvenile antisocial behavior and delinquency', *Clinical Psychology Review*, **10**, pp. 1–41.

LOEBER, R. and STOUTHAMER-LOEBER, M. (1986) 'Family factors as correlates and predictors of juvenile conduct: Problems and delinquency', in M. TONRY and N. MORRIS (Eds) *Crime and Justice: An Annual Review of Research*, **7**, Chicago, University of Chicago Press.

LONG, C.G. and MIDGLEY, M. (1992) 'On the closeness of the concepts of the criminal and the mentally ill in the nineteenth century: Yesterday's professional and public opinions reflected today', *Journal of Forensic Psychiatry 3*, 63–79.

LOOMIS, P.J., BOHNERT, P.J. and HUNCKE, S. (1967) 'Prediction of EEG abnormalities in adolescent delinquents', *Archives of General Psychiatry*, **17**, pp. 494–7.

LOWE, C.F. (1983) 'Radical behaviourism and human psychology', in G.C.L. DAVEY, (Ed.) *Animal Models of Human Behaviour*, Chichester, Wiley.

LUCKENBILL, D.F. (1977) 'Criminal homicide as a situated transaction', *Social Problems*, **25**, pp. 176–86.

LUND, J. (1990) 'Mentally retarded criminal offenders in Denmark', *British Journal of Psychiatry*, **156**, pp. 726–31.

McCORD, J. (1978) 'A thirty-year follow-up of treatment effects', *American Psychologist*, **33**, pp. 284–9.

McCORD, J. (1982) 'A longitudinal view of the relationship between paternal absence and crime', in J. GUNN and D.P. FARRINGTON (Eds) *Abnormal Offenders, Delinquency and the Criminal Justice System*, Chichester, Wiley.

McCORD, W. and McCORD, J. (1964) *The Psychopath: An Essay on the Criminal Mind*, NY, Van Nostrand Reinhold.

McCOWN, W., JOHNSON, J. and AUSTIN, S. (1986) 'Inability of delinquents to recognise facial effects', *Journal of Social Behaviour and Personality*, **1**, pp. 489–96.

McDOUGALL, C., THOMAS, M. and WILSON, J. (1987) 'Attitude change and the violent football supporter', in B.J. McGURK, D.M. THORNTON, and M. WILLIAMS (Eds) *Applying Psychology to Imprisonment: Theory and Practice*, London, HMSO.

McFALL, R.M. (1976) *Behavioral Training: A Skill-Acquisition Approach to Clinical Problems*, Morristown, NJ, General Learning Press.

McGURK, B.J. and McDOUGALL, C. (1981) 'A new approach to Eysenck's theory of criminality', *Personality and Individual Differences*, **2**, pp. 338–40.

McMANUS, M., ALESSI, N.E., GRAPENTINE, M.D. and BRICKMAN, A. (1984) 'Psychiatric disturbance in serious delinquents', *Journal of the American Academy of Child Psychiatry*, **23**, pp. 602–15.

MAGUIRE, M. and POINTING, J. (Eds) (1988) *Victims of Crime: A New Deal?* Milton Keynes, Open University Press.

MARTINSON, R. (1974) 'What works? — Questions and answers about prison reform', *Public Interest*, **35**, pp. 22–54.

MARTINSON, R. (1979) 'New findings, new views: A note of caution regarding sentencing reform', *Hofsta Law Review*, **7**, pp. 242–58.

MAXFIELD, M. (1988) *Explaining Fear of Crime: Evidence from the 1984 British Crime Survey*, London, HMSO.

MAXFIELD, M.G. and BAUMER, T.L. (1990) 'Home detention with electronic monitoring: Comparing pretrial and postconviction programs', *Crime and Delinquency*, **36**, pp. 521–36.

MAYHEW, P., CLARKE, R.V.G., STURMAN, A. and HOUGH, J.M. (1976) *Crime as Opportunity*, Home Office Research Study 34, London, HMSO.

MAYHEW, P., CLARKE, R.V.G. and HOUGH, J.M. (1980a) 'Steering column locks and car theft', in R.V.G. CLARKE and P. MAYHEW (Eds) *Designing Out Crime*, London, HMSO.

MAYHEW, P., CLARKE, R.V.G., HOUGH, J.M. and WINCHESTER, S.W.C. (1980b) 'Natural surveillance and vandalism to telephone kiosks', in R.V.G. CLARKE and P. MAYHEW (Eds) *Designing Out Crime*, London, HMSO.

MAYHEW, P., ELLIOTT, D. and DOWDS, L. (1989) *The 1988 British Crime Survey*, London, HMSO.

MEDNICK, S.A., GABRIELLI, W.F. and HUTCHINGS, B. (1983) 'Genetic influences in criminal behavior: Evidence from an adoption cohort', in K.T. VAN DUSEN and S.A. MEDNICK (Eds) *Prospective Studies of Crime and Delinquency*, The Hague, Kluwer-Nijhoff Publishing.

MEGARGEE, E.I. (1982) 'Psychological determinants and correlates of criminal violence', in M.E. WOLFGANG and N.A. WEINER (Eds) *Criminal Violence*, Beverly Hills, CA, Sage.

MERRILL, M. (1947) *Problems of Child Delinquency*, Boston, Houghton-Mifflin.

MERTON, R. (1938) 'Social structure and anomie', *American Sociological Review*, **3**, pp. 672–82.

MILAN, M.A. (1987) 'Basic behavioral procedures in closed institutions', in E.K. MORRIS and C.J. BRAUKMANN (Eds) *Behavioral Approaches to Crime and Delinquency: A Handbook of Application, Research and Concepts*, New York, Plenum Press.

MILLER, L. (1988) 'Neuropsychological perspectives on delinquency', *Behavioral Sciences and the Law*, **6**, pp. 409–28.

MILLER, W.R. (1985) 'Motivation for treatment: A review with special emphasis on alcoholism', *Psychological Bulletin*, **98**, pp. 84–107.

MODGIL, S. and MODGIL, C. (Eds) (1987) *B.F. Skinner: Consensus and Controversy*, New York, Falmer Press.

MONAHAN, T.P. (1957) 'Family status and the delinquent child: A reappraisal and some new findings', *Social Forces*, **35**, pp. 250–8.

MORRIS, E.K. and BRAUKMANN, C.J. (Eds) (1987) *Behavioral Approaches to Crime and Delinquency: A Handbook of Application, Research and Concepts*, New York, Plenum Press.

MOYER, K.E. (1976) *The Psychology of Aggression*, NY, Harper and Row.

NELLIS, M. (1991) 'The electronic monitoring of offenders in England and Wales', *British Journal of Criminology*, **31**, pp. 165–85.

NELSON, J.R., SMITH, D.J. and DODD, J. (1990) 'The moral reasoning of juvenile delinquents: A meta-analysis', *Journal of Abnormal Child Psychology*, **18**, pp. 231–9.

NEWBOLD, G. (1990) 'Capital punishment in New Zealand: An experiment that failed', *Deviant Behavior*, **11**, pp. 155–74.

NEWMAN, G. (1983) *Just and Painful*, New York, Macmillan.

NEWMAN, J.P. and KOSSON, D.S. (1986) 'Passive avoidance learning in psychopathic and nonpsychopathic offenders', *Journal of Abnormal Psychology*, **95**, pp. 252–6.

NEWMAN, J.P., PATTERSON, C.M. and KOSSON, D.S. (1987) 'Response preservation in psychopaths', *Journal of Abnormal Psychology*, **96**, pp. 145–8.

NEWMAN, O. (1980) *Community of Interest*, NY, Anchor.

NIETZEL, M.T. (1979) *Crime and its Modification: A Social Learning Perspective*, Elmsford, NY, Pergamon Press.

NOVACO, R.W. (1975) *Anger-Control: The Development and Evaluation of an Experimental Treatment*, Lexington, MA, D.C. Heath.

Novaco, R.W. (1979) 'The cognitive regulation of anger and stress', in P. Kendall and S. Hollon (Eds) *Cognitive-Behavioral Interventions: Theory, Research and Procedures*, New York, Academic Press.

Novaco, R.W. and Welsh, W.N. (1989) 'Anger disturbances: Cognitive mediation and clinical prescriptions', in K. Howells and C.R. Hollin (Eds) *Clinical Approaches to Violence*, Chichester, Wiley.

Nye, F.I. (1958) *Family Relationships and Delinquent Behaviors*, NY, Wiley.

O'Donnell, C.R., Lydgate, T. and Fo, W.S.O. (1979) 'The buddy system: Réview and follow-up', *Child Behavior Therapy*, **1**, pp. 161–9.

Offord, D.R. (1982) 'Family backgrounds of male and female delinquents', in J. Gunn and D.P. Farrington (Eds) *Abnormal Offenders, Delinquency, and the Criminal Justice System*, **1**, Chichester, Wiley.

Olweus, D. (1987) 'Testosterone and adrenaline: Aggressive antisocial behavior in normal males', in S.A. Mednick, T.E. Moffitt and S.A. Stack (Eds) *The Causes of Crime: New Biological Approaches*, Cambridge, Cambridge University Press.

Osborn, S.G. and West, D.J. (1979) 'Conviction records of fathers and sons compared', *British Journal of Criminology*, **19**, pp. 120–33.

Ostapiuk, E.B. (1982) 'Strategies for community intervention in offender rehabilitation: A review', in M.P. Feldman (Ed.) *Developments in the Study of Criminal Behaviour, Vol. 1: The Prevention and Control of Offenders*, Chichester, Wiley.

Ostapiuk, E.B. and Westwood, S. (1986) 'Glenthorne Youth Treatment Centre: Working with adolescents in graduations of security', in C. Hollin and K. Howells (Eds) *Clinical Approaches to Criminal Behaviour. Issues in Criminological and Legal Psychology*, No. 9. Leicester, The British Psychological Society.

Ouimet, M. and Coyle, E.J. (1991) 'Fear of crime and sentencing punitiveness: Comparing the general public and court practitioners', *Canadian Journal of Criminology*, **33**, pp. 149–62.

Overholser, J.C. and Beck, S. (1986) 'Multimethod assessment of rapists, child molesters and three control groups on behavioral and psychological measures', *Journal of Consulting and Clinical Psychology*, **54**, pp. 682–7.

Palamara, F., Cullen, F.T. and Gersten, J.C. (1986) 'The effect of police and mental health intervention on juvenile deviance: Specifying contingencies in the impact of formal reaction', *Journal of Health and Social Behavior*, **27**, pp. 90–105.

Parker, J.G. and Asher, S.R. (1987) 'Peer relations and later personal adjustment: Are low-accepted children at risk?' *Psychological Bulletin*, **102**, pp. 357–89.

Patterson, G.R. (1986) 'Performance models for antisocial boys', *American Psychologist*, **41**, pp. 432–44.

Perkins, D.E. (1987) 'A psychological treatment programme for sex offenders', in B.J. McGurk, D.M. Thornton and M. Williams (Eds) *Applying Psychology to Imprisonment: Theory and Practice*, London, HMSO.

Perkins, D.E. (1991) 'Clinical work with sex offenders in secure settings', in C.R. Hollin and K. Howells (Eds) *Clinical Approaches to Sex Offenders and Their Victims*, Chichester, Wiley.

Peterson, J.L. and Zill, N. (1986) 'Marital disruption, parent-child relationships, and behavior problems in children', *Journal of Marriage and the Family*, **48**, pp. 295–307.

Peterson, R.D. and Bailey, W.C. (1991) 'Felony, murder and capital punishment: An examination of the deterrence question', *Criminology*, **29**, pp. 367–95.

Platt, T. (1985) 'Criminology in the 1980s: Progressive alternatives to "law and order"', *Crime and Social Justice*, **22**, pp. 191–9.

Plomin, R. (1990) *Nature and Nurture*, Pacific Grove, CA, Brooks/Cole.

PORAC, C. and COREN, S. (1981) *Lateral Preferences and Human Behavior*, NY, Springer-Verlag.

POWELL, G.E. (1977) 'Psychoticism and social deviancy in children', *Advances in Behaviour Research and Therapy*, **1**, pp. 27–56.

POYNER, B. (1991) 'What works in crime prevention: An overview of evaluations', Paper presented at the British Criminology Conference, University of York, York.

PRESTON, M.A. (1982) 'Intermediate treatment: A new approach to community care', in M.P. FELDMAN (Ed.) *Developments in the Study of Criminal Behaviour, Vol. 1: The Prevention and Control of Offending*, Chichester, Wiley.

PRINS, H. (1980) *Offenders, Deviants, or Patients? An Introduction to the Study of Socio-Forensic Problems*, London, Tavistock.

PRINS, H. (1986) *Dangerous Behaviour, the Law and Mental Disorder*, London, Tavistock.

QUAY, H.C. (1977) 'The three faces of evaluation: What can be expected to work?', *Criminal Justice and Behavior*, **4**, pp. 341–54.

QUAY, H.C. (1987a) 'Institutional treatment', in H.C. QUAY (Ed.) *Handbook of Juvenile Delinquency*, New York, Wiley.

QUAY, H.C. (1987b) 'Intelligence', in H.C. QUAY (Ed.) *Handbook of Juvenile Delinquency*, New York, Wiley.

QUINNEY, R. (1970) *The Social Reality of Crime*, NY, Little, Brown.

RACHLIN, H. (1991) *Introduction to Modern Behaviorism*, (3rd ed.) New York, W.H. Freeman.

RADFORD, J. and HOLLIN, C. (1991) 'Intelligence', in J. RADFORD and E. GOVIER (Eds) *A Textbook of Psychology*, London, Routledge.

RAFTER, N.J. (1990) 'The social construction of crime and crime control', *Journal of Research in Crime and Delinquency*, **27**, pp. 376–89.

RAINE, A. (1985) 'Antisocial behaviour and social psychophysiology', in H. WAGNER (Ed.) *Bodily Changes and Social Behaviour: Theory and Experiment in Social Psychophysiology*, Chichester, Wiley.

RAINE, A., VENABLES, P.H. and WILLIAMS, M. (1990) 'Autonomatic orientating responses in 15-year-old male subjects and criminal behavior at age 24', *American Journal of Psychiatry*, **147**, pp. 933–6.

RANKIN, J.H. (1983) 'The Family Context of Delinquency', *Social Problems*, **30**, pp. 466–79.

REID, K. (1984) 'Some social, psychological and educational aspects related to persistent school absenteeism', *Research in Education*, **31**, pp. 53–82.

REID, K. (1985) *Truancy and School Absenteeism*, London, Hodder and Stoughton.

REMINGTON, B. and REMINGTON, M. (1987) 'Behavior modification in probation work: A review and evaluation', *Criminal Justice and Behavior*, **14**, pp. 156–74.

RENWICK, S. and EMLER, N. (1991) 'The relationship between social skills deficits and juvenile delinquency', *British Journal of Clinical Psychology*, **30**, pp. 61–71.

REPPETTO, T.A. (1976) 'Crime prevention and the displacement phenomenon', *Crime and Delinquency*, **22**, pp. 166–77.

REPPUCCI, N.D. (1973) 'Social psychology of institutional change: General principles for intervention', *American Journal of Community Psychology*, **1**, pp. 330–41.

RESCORLA, R.A. (1988) 'Pavlovian conditioning: It's not what you think it is', *American Psychologist*, **43**, pp. 151–60.

RESICK, P.A. and MARKAWAY, B.E.G. (1991) 'Clinical treatment of adult female victims of sexual assault', in C.R. HOLLIN and K. HOWELLS (Eds) *Clinical Approaches to Sex Offenders and Their Victims*, Chichester, Wiley.

ROBERTS, A.R. and CAMASSO, M.J. (1991) 'The effect of juvenile offender treatment programs on recidivism: A meta-analysis of 46 studies', *Notre Dame Journal of Law, Ethics and Public Policy*, **5**, pp. 421–41.

ROBERTSON, G. (1981) 'The extent and pattern of crime amongst mentally handicapped offenders', *Apex: Journal of the British Institute of Mental Handicap*, **9**, pp. 100–3.

ROBINS, L. (1966) *Deviant Children Grown Up*, Baltimore, MD, Williams and Wilkins.

ROBINS, L.N. and RUTTER, M. (Eds) (1990) *Straight and Devious Pathways from Childhood to Adulthood*, Cambridge, Cambridge University Press.

ROBINSON, S., VIVIAN-BYRNE, S., DISCOLL, R. and CORDESS, C. (1991) 'Family work with victims and offenders in a secure unit', *Journal of Family Therapy*, **13**, pp. 105–16.

ROSEN, L. and NEILSON, K. (1982) 'Broken homes', in L. SAVITZ and N. JOHNSTON (Eds) *Contemporary Criminology*, NY, Wiley.

ROSHIER, B. (1989) *Controlling Crime: The Classical Perspective in Criminology*, Milton Keynes, Open University Press.

ROSS, R.R. and FABIANO, E.A. (1985) *Time to Think: A Cognitive Model of Delinquency Prevention and Offender Rehabilitation*, Johnson City, TN, Institute of Social Sciences and Arts.

ROSS, R.R. and GENDREAU, P. (1980) *Effective Correctional Treatment*, Toronto, Butterworths.

ROSS, R.R., FABIANO, E.A. and EWLES, C.D. (1988) 'Reasoning and rehabilitation', *International Journal of Offender Therapy and Comparative Criminology*, **32**, pp. 29–35.

ROTENBERG, M. and NACHSHON, I. (1979) 'Impulsiveness and aggression among Israeli delinquents', *British Journal of Social and Clinical Psychology*, **18**, pp. 59–63.

ROTH, L.H. (1987) *Clinical Treatment of the Violent Person*, New York, Guildford Press.

ROTTON, J. and FREY, J. (1985) 'Air pollution, weather and violent crimes: Concomitant time-series analysis of archival data', *Journal of Personality and Social Psychology*, **49**, pp. 1207–20.

ROWE, D.C. (1990) 'Inherited dispositions toward learning delinquent and criminal behavior: New evidence', in L. ELLIS and H. HOFFMAN (Eds) *Crime in Biological, Social and Moral Contexts*, NY, Praeger.

ROWE, D.C. and OSGOOD, D.W. (1984) 'Heredity and sociological theories of delinquency: A reconsideration', *American Sociological Review*, **49**, pp. 526–40.

RUTTER, M. (1982) 'Syndromes attributed to "minimal brain dysfunction" in childhood', *American Journal of Psychiatry*, **139**, pp. 21–33.

RUTTER, M. and GILLER, H. (1983) *Juvenile Delinquency: Trends and Perspectives*, Harmondsworth, Middlesex, Penguin.

RUTTER, M., MAUGHN, B., MORTIMORE, P., OUSTON, J. and SMITH, A. (1979) *Fifteen Thousand Hours: Secondary Schools and their Effects on Children*, London, Open Books.

SADOFF, R.L. (1990) 'The role of the psychiatrist in capital punishment', *Journal of Forensic Psychiatry*, **1**, pp. 73–80.

SAVITZ, L.D., KUMAR, K.S. and ZAHN (1991) 'Quantifying Luckenbill', *Deviant Behavior*, **12**, pp. 19–29.

SCHAFER, S. (1976) *Introduction to Criminology*, NY, McGraw-Hill.

SCHMAUK, F.J. (1970) 'Punishment, arousal, and avoidance learning in sociopaths', *Journal of Abnormal Psychology*, **76**, pp. 325–35.

SCHNEIDER, A.L. and SCHNEIDER, P.R. (1985) 'The impact of restitution on recidivism of juvenile offenders: An experiment in Clayton County, Georgia', *Criminal Justice Review*, **10**, pp. 1–10.

SCULL, A. (1977) *Decarceration: Community Treatment and the Deviant — A Radical View*, Englewood Cliffs, NJ, Prentice-Hall.

SEGAL, Z.V. and MARSHALL, W.L. (1985) 'Heterosexual social skills in a population of rapists and child molesters', *Journal of Consulting and Clinical Psychology*, **53**, pp. 55–63.

SHAPIRO, A. (1969) 'Delinquent and disturbed behaviour within the field of mental deficiency', in A.V.S. DeRUECK and R. PORTER (Eds) *The Mentally Abnormal Offender*, London, J. and A. Churchill.

SHAPLAND, J., RUSHTON, J.P. and CAMPBELL, A. (1975) 'Crime and personality — further evidence', *Bulletin of the British Psychological Society*, **28**, pp. 66–8.

SHAW, C. and McKAY, H.D. (1932) 'Are broken homes a causative factor in juvenile delinquency?' *Social Forces*, **10**, pp. 514–24.

SHAW, C. and McKAY, H. (1932) *Juvenile Delinquency and Urban Areas*, Chicago, University of Chicago Press.

SIANN, G. (1985) *Accounting for Aggression: Perspectives on Aggression and Violence*, London, Allen and Unwin.

SIEGAL, L.J. (1986) *Criminology* (2nd ed.) St. Paul, MN, West Publishing.

SKINNER, B.F. (1974) *About Behaviourism*, London, Cape.

SKINNER, B.F. (1986) 'Is it behaviorism?', *Behavioral and Brain Sciences*, **9**, p. 716.

SLABY, R.G. and GUERRA, N.G. (1988) 'Cognitive mediators of aggression in adolescent offenders: 1. Assessment', *Developmental Psychology*, **24**, pp. 580–8.

SLAWSON, J. (1923) 'Marital relations of parents and juvenile delinquency', *Journal of Delinquency*, **8**, pp. 280–3.

SMART, C. (1976) *Women, Crime and Criminology: A Feminist Critique*, London, Routledge and Kegan Paul.

SNYDER, J. and PATTERSON, G.R. (1987) 'Family interaction and delinquent behavior', in H.C. QUAY (Ed.) *Handbook of Juvenile Delinquency*, NY, Wiley.

SNYDER, J.J. and WHITE, M.J. (1979) 'The use of cognitive self-instruction in the treatment of behaviourally disturbed adolescents', *Behavior Therapy*, **10**, pp. 227–35.

SORRELL, T. (1987) *Moral Theory and Capital Punishment*, Oxford, Blackwell.

SPARKS, R.F. (1981) 'Surveys of victimization—An optimistic assessment', in M. TONRY and N. MORRIS (Eds) *Crime and Justice: An Annual Review of Research*, **3**, Chicago, IL, University of Chicago Press.

SPARKS, R.F., GENN, H.G. and DODD, D.J. (1977) *Surveying Victims: A Study of the Measurement of Criminal Victimization, Perception of Crime, and Attitudes to Criminal Justice*, Chichester, Wiley.

SPENCE, S.J. (1981a) 'Difference in social skills performance between institutionalized juvenile male offenders and a comparable group of boys without offence records', *British Journal of Clinical Psychology*, **20**, pp. 163–71.

SPENCE, S.J. (1981b) 'Validation of social skills of adolescent males in an interview conversation with a previously unknown adult', *Journal of Applied Behavior Analysis*, **14**, pp. 159–68.

SPITZER, S. (1975) 'Toward a Marxian theory of deviance', *Social Problems*, **22**, pp. 638–51.

SPIVACK, G., PLATT, J.J. and SHURE, M.B. (1976) *The Problem-Solving Approach to Adjustment: A Guide to Research and Intervention*, San Francisco, Jossey-Bass.

SPRY, W.B. (1984) 'Schizophrenia and crime', in M. CRAFT and A. CRAFT (Eds) *Mentally Abnormal Offenders*, London, Baillière Tindall.

STANKO, E. (1988) 'Fear of crime and the myth of the safe home', in M. BORAD and K. YLLO (Eds) *Female Perspectives on Wife Abuse*, London, Sage.

STATTIN, H. and MAGNUSSON, D. (1989) 'The role of early aggressive behavior in the frequency, seriousness and type of later crime', *Journal of Consulting and Clinical Psychology*, **57**, pp. 710–18.

STEFANEK, M.E., OLLENDICK, T.H., BALDOCK, W.P., FRANCIS, G. and YAEGER, N.J. (1987)

'Self-statements in aggressive, withdrawn, and popular children', *Cognitive Research and Therapy*, **11**, pp. 229–39.

STERMAC, L.E. and QUINSEY, V.L. (1986) 'Social competence among rapists', *Behavioral Assessment*, **8**, pp. 171–85.

STRATTA, E. (1970) *The Education of Borstal Boys*, London, Routledge.

STUMPHAUZER, J.S. (1976) 'Elimination of stealing by self-reinforcement of alternative behavior and family contracting', *Journal of Behavior Therapy and Experimental Psychiatry*, **7**, pp. 265–8.

STURMAN, A. (1980) 'Damage on buses: The effects of supervision', in R.V.G. CLARKE and P. MAYHEW (Eds) *Designing Out Crime*, London, HMSO.

SUTHERLAND, E.H. (1939) *Principles of Criminology*, Philadelphia, PA, Lippincott.

SUTHERLAND, E.H. and CRESSEY, D.R. (1960) *Principles of Criminology* (4th ed.) Philadelphia, PA, Lippincott.

SUTHERLAND, E.H. and CRESSEY, D.R. (1974) *Principles of Criminology* (9th ed.) Philadelphia, PA, Lippincott.

SYNDULKO, K. (1978) 'Electrocortical investigations of sociopathy', in R.D. HARE and D. SCHALLING (Eds) *Psychopathic Behavior: Approaches to Research*, Chichester, Wiley.

TANNENBAUM, F. (1938) *Crime and the Community*, NY, Columbia University Press.

TARTER, R.E., HEGEDUS, A.M., ALTERMAN, A.I. and KATZ-GARRIS, L. (1983) 'Cognitive capacities of juvenile violent, nonviolent and sexual offenders', *Journal of Nervous and Mental Disease*, **171**, pp. 564–7.

TAYLOR, I., WALTON, P. and YOUNG, J. (1973) *The New Criminology: For a Social Theory of Deviance*, London, Routledge and Kegan Paul.

TAYLOR, L. (1984) *In the Underworld*, London, Guild Publishing.

TAYLOR, P.J. (1982) 'Schizophrenia and Violence', in J. GUNN and D.P. FARRINGTON (Eds) *Abnormal Offenders, Delinquency, and the Criminal Justice System*, Chichester, Wiley.

TAYLOR, P.J. (1985) 'Motives for offending among violent and psychotic men', *British Journal of Psychiatry*, **147**, pp. 491–8.

TAYLOR, P.J. (1986) 'Psychiatric disorder in London's life-sentenced offenders', *British Journal of Criminology*, **26**, pp. 63–78.

TAYLOR, P.J. and GUNN, J. (1984) 'Violence and psychosis II — Effect of psychiatric diagnosis on conviction and sentencing of offenders', *British Medical Journal*, **289**, pp. 9–12.

THIESSEN, D. (1990) 'Hormonal correlates of sexual aggression', in L. ELLIS and H. HOFFMAN (Eds) *Crime in Biological, Social and Moral Contexts*, New York, Praeger.

THOMAS, D.A. (1979) *Principles of Sentencing* (2nd ed.) London, Heinemann.

THORNTON, D.M. (1987a) 'Treatment effects on recidivism: A reappraisal of the "nothing works" doctrine', in B.J. McGURK, D.M. THORNTON and M. WILLIAMS (Eds) *Applying Psychology to Imprisonment: Theory and Practice*, London, HMSO.

THORNTON, D.M. (1987b) 'Correctional evaluation of custodial regimes', in B.J. McGURK, D.M. THORNTON and M. WILLIAMS (Eds) *Applying Psychology to Imprisonment: Theory and Practice*, London, HMSO.

THORNTON, D.M. and REID, R.L. (1982) 'Moral reasoning and type of criminal offence', *British Journal of Social Psychology*, **21**, pp. 231–8.

THORNTON, D.M., CURRAN, L., GRAYSON, D. and HOLLOWAY, V. (1984) *Tougher Regimes in Detention Centres: Report of an Evaluation by the Young Offender Psychology Unit*, London, HMSO.

TONRY, M., OHLIN, L.E. and FARRINGTON, D.P. (1991) *Human Development and Criminal Behavior: New Ways of Advancing Knowledge*, NY, Springer-Verlag.

TRASLER, G. (1986) 'Situational crime control and rational choice: A critique', in K.

HEAL and G. LAYCOCK (Eds) *Situational Crime Prevention: From Theory into Practice*, London, HMSO.

TRASLER, G. (1987) 'Biogenetic factors', in H.C. QUAY (Ed.) *Handbook of Juvenile Delinquency*, New York, Wiley.

TURK, A. (1969) *Criminality and the Legal Order*, Chicago, Rand McNally.

TUTT, N. (1971) 'The subnormal offender', *British Journal of Mental Subnormality*, **17**, pp. 42–7.

TYLER, R.R. (1990) *Why People Obey the Law*, New Haven, Yale University Press.

VAN DEN HAAG, E. (1982) 'Could successful rehabilitation reduce the crime rate?' *Journal of Criminal Law and Criminology*, **73**, pp. 1022–35.

VENABLES, P.H. (1987) 'Autonomic nervous system factors in criminal behaviour', in S.A. MEDNICK, T.E. MOFFITT and S.A. STACK (Eds) *The Causes of Crime: New Biological Approaches*, Cambridge, Cambridge University Press.

VENABLES, P.H. and RAINE, A. (1987) 'Biological theory', in B.J. McGURK, D.M. THORNTON and M. WILLIAMS (Eds) *Applying Psychology to Imprisonment: Theory and Practice*, London, HMSO.

VENEZIANO, C. and VENEZIANO, L. (1988) 'Knowledge of social skills among institutionalized juvenile delinquents: An assessment', *Criminal Justice and Behaviour*, **15**, pp. 152–71.

VIRKKUNEN, M., DEJONG, J., BARTKKO, J., GOODWIN, F.K. and LINNOILA, M. (1989) 'Relationship of psychobiological variables to recidivism in violent offenders and impulsive fire setters', *Archives of General Psychiatry*, **46**, pp. 600–3.

WALKER, N. (1965) *Crime and Punishment in Great Britain*, Edinburgh, Edinburgh University Press.

WALKER, N. (1968) *Crime and Insanity in England*, **1**, Edinburgh, Edinburgh University Press.

WALKER, N. (1985) *Sentencing: Theory, Law and Practice*, London, Butterworths.

WALKER, N. and McCABE, S. (1973) *Crime and Insanity in England*, **2**, Edinburgh, Edinburgh University Press.

WALTERS, G.D. and WHITE, T.W. (1989) 'Heredity and crime: Bad genes or bad research?', *Criminology*, **27**, pp. 455–85.

WARD, C.I. and McFALL, R.M. (1986) 'Further validation of the problem inventory for adolescent girls: Comparing Caucasian and black delinquents and nondelinquents', *Journal of Consulting and Clinical Psychology*, **54**, pp. 732–3.

WASHBROOK, R.A.H. (1981) 'Neuroticism and offenders', *International Journal of Offender Therapy and Comparative Criminology*, **24**, pp. 122–9.

WATSON, J.B. (1913) 'Psychology as the behaviorist views it', *Psychological Review*, **20**, pp. 158–77.

WEEKS, A.H. (1940) 'Male and female broken home ratios by types of delinquency', *American Sociological Review*, **5**, pp. 601–9.

WEINROTT, M.R., JONES, R.R. and HOWARD, J.R. (1982) 'Cost effectiveness of teaching family programs for delinquents: Results of a national evaluation', *Evaluation Review*, **6**, pp. 173–201.

WELCH, G.J. (1985) 'Contingency contracting with a delinquent and his family', *Journal of Behavior Therapy and Experimental Psychiatry*, **16**, pp. 253–9.

WELLS, L.E. and RANKIN, J.H. (1991) 'Families and delinquency: A meta-analysis of the impact of broken homes', *Social Problems*, **38**, pp. 71–93.

WEST, D.J. (1965) *Murder Followed by Suicide*, London, Heinemann.

WEST, D.J. (1967) *The Young Offender*, London, Pelican.

WEST, D.J. (1980) 'The clinical approach to criminology', *Psychological Medicine*, **10**, pp. 619–31.

WEST, D.J. (1982) *Delinquency: Its Roots, Careers and Prospects*, London, Heinemann.

WEST, D.J. and FARRINGTON, D. (1973) *Who Becomes Delinquent?* London, Heinemann.

WHITE, J.L., MOFFITT, T.E., EARLS, F., ROBINS, L. and SILVA, P.A. (1990) 'How early can we tell? Predictors of childhood conduct disorder and adolescent delinquency', *Criminology*, **28**, pp. 507–28.

WHITEHEAD, J.T. and LAB, S.P. (1989) 'A meta-analysis of juvenile correctional treatment', *Journal of Research in Crime and Delinquency*, **26**, pp. 276–95.

WHITEHEAD, T. (1983) *Mental Illness and the Law*, (2nd ed.) Oxford, Blackwell.

WIDOM, C.S. (1989) 'Does violence beget violence? A critical examination of the literature', *Psychological Bulletin*, **106**, pp. 3–28.

WIDOM, C.S. (1991) 'A tail on an untold tale: Response to "Biological and genetic contributors to violence—Widom's untold tale"', *Psychological Bulletin*, **109**, pp. 130–7.

WILLIAMSON, S., HARE, R.D. and WONG, S. (1987) 'Violence: Criminal psychopaths and their victims', *Canadian Journal of Behavioral Science*, **19**, pp. 454–62.

WILLIS, A. (1986) 'Help and control in probation: An empirical assessment of probation practice', in J. POINTING (Ed.) *Alternatives to Custody*, Oxford, Blackwell.

WILSON, J.Q. and HERRNSTEIN, R.J. (1985) *Crime and Human Nature*, New York, Simon and Schuster.

WOLFGANG, M.E., THORNBERRY, T.P. and FIGLIO, R.M. (1987) *From Boy to Man, from Delinquency to Crime*, Chicago, University of Chicago Press.

WOOD, G., GREEN, L. and BRY, B.H. (1982) 'The input of behavioral training upon the knowledge and effectiveness of juvenile probation officers and volunteers', *Journal of Community Psychology*, **10**, pp. 133–41.

WOOD, W., WONG, F.Y. and CHACHERE, J.G. (1991) 'Effects of media violence on viewers' aggression in unconstrained social interaction', *Psychological Bulletin*, **109**, pp. 371–83.

WORRELL, A. (1990) *Offending Women: Female Lawbreakers and the Criminal Justice System*, London, Routledge.

WRIGHT, M. (1991) *Justice for Victims and Offenders*, Milton Keynes, Open University Press.

YABLONSKY, L. (1963) *The Violent Gang*, NY, Macmillan.

YEUDALL, L.T., FROMM-AUCH, D. and DAVIES, P. (1982) 'Neuropsychological impairment of persistent delinquency', *Journal of Nervous and Mental Disease*, **170**, pp. 257–65.

YULE, W. and BROWN, B. (1987) 'Some behavioral applications with juvenile offenders outside North America', in E.K. MORRIS and C.J. BRAUKMANN (Eds) *Behavioral Approaches to Crime and Delinquency: A Handbook of Application, Research and Concepts*, New York, Plenum Press.

ZAGER, R., ARBIT, J., HUGHES, J.R., BUSELL, R.E. and BUSCH, K. (1989) 'Developmental and disruptive disorders among delinquents', *Journal of the American Academy of Child and Adolescent Psychiatry*, **28**, pp. 437–40.

ZURIFF, G.E. (1985) *Behaviorism: A Conceptual Reconstruction*, New York, Columbia University Press.

Note on the Author

Clive R. Hollin PhD is a Professor of Criminological Psychology at the University of Leicester. He is a Fellow of the British Psychological Society and a member of the British Society of Criminology. He teaches the psychology of criminal behaviour at both undergraduate and postgraduate levels and is involved in professional training for those who work with offenders. Formerly a Senior Psychologist in the Prison Department, he has published widely in the field of criminological psychology including the titles *Psychology and Crime* and *Cognitive Behavioural Interventions with Young Offenders*. A former chair of the Training Committee of the Division of Criminological and Legal Psychology of the British Psychological Society, he has also worked as advisor to the Home Office iniative on regime planning for sex offenders.

Index

Contemporary Psychology Series

Series Editor: Professor Raymond Cochrane
School of Psychology
The University of Birmingham
Birmingham
B15 2TT, UK

This series of books on contemporary psychological issues is aimed primarily at 'A' level students and those beginning their undergraduate degree. All of these volumes are introductory in the sense that they assume no, or very little, previous acquaintance with the subject, while aiming to take the reader through to the end of his or her course on the topic they cover. For this reason the series will also appeal to those who encounter psychology in the course of their professional work: nurses, social workers, police and probation officers, speech therapists and medical students. Written in a clear and jargon-free style, each book generally includes a full (and in some cases annotated) bibliography and points the way explicitly to further reading on the subject covered.

Titles in the Series:

Psychology and Social Issues:
A Tutorial Text
Edited by Raymond Cochrane,
University of Birmingham
and Douglas Carroll
University of Birmingham

Families:
A Context for Development
David White and Anne Woollett
University of East London

The Psychology of Childhood
Peter Mitchell
University of Birmingham

On Being Old:
The Psychology of Later Life
Graham Stokes
Gulson Hospital, Coventry

Health Psychology:
Stress, Behaviour, and Disease
Douglas Carroll
University of Birmingham

Food and Drink:
The Psychology of Nutrition
David Booth
University of Birmingham

Criminal Behaviour:
A Psychological Approach to
Explanation and Prevention
Clive Hollin
University of Leicester

Adult Psychological Problems:
An Introduction (2nd ed.)
Lorna Champion
Royal Edinburgh Hospital
and Mick Power
University of Edinburgh

Psychology of Sport
John Kremer
Queen's University of Belfast
and Deidre Scully
University of Ulster

Psychology of Addiction
Mary McMurran
Rampton Hospital, Retford

Gender, Sex and Sexuality
Gerda Siann
University of Dundee

Contemporary Psychology
Clive Hollin
University of Leicester

Environmental Psychology:
Behaviour and Experience in Context
Tony Cassidy
Nene College, Northampton